Baptists, Catholics, and the Whole Church

Baptists, Catholics, and the Whole Church

Partners in the Pilgrimage to Unity

Steven R. Harmon

New City Press
Hyde Park, New York

Published by New City Press
202 Comforter Blvd.,
Hyde Park, NY 12538
www.newcitypress.com

©2021 New City Press

Cover design and layout: Miguel Tejerina

Baptists, Catholics, and the Whole Church:
Partners in the Pilgrimage to Unity
Steven R. Harmon

Library of Congress Control Number: 2021943749

ISBN 978-1-56548-497-9 (paperback)
ISBN 978-1-56548-503-7 (e-book)
Printed in the United States of America

Contents

Acknowledgments 7

Foreword 11

Introduction 15

Chapter One
From Anti-Catholicism to Fellow Pilgrims 23

Chapter Two
What Do Baptists and Catholics
Have in Common? 46

Chapter Three
How Baptists Receive Gifts of Catholic
(and catholic) Christianity 69

Chapter Four
Ecumenical Healing of Ecclesial Memories 86

Chapter Five
The Cruciformity of Communion 107

Chapter Six
Unity as Christ's Victory and Our Task 126

Appendix One
Envisioning the Whole Church 136

Appendix Two
Moral Discernment with the Whole Church 162

Bibliography 176

Endnotes 203

Index of Names and Subjects 239

For the members of the Baptist-Catholic Joint Commissions for the Baptist World Alliance—Pontifical Council for Promoting Christian Unity International Dialogue, Phases II and III

Acknowledgments

Not unlike the report of an ecumenical dialogue, *Baptists, Catholics, and the Whole Church* owes its publication to the contributions of a community that extends far beyond the work of an individual author. Here I will do my best to credit the people who have shaped not only this book but also the theologian who wrote it.

The earliest expressions of the material in this book were invited lectures for academic institutions and presentations for various academic and ecclesiastical conferences, details of which appear in the Introduction that follows. I am grateful to my hosts and hearers of these lectures and presentations, in particular the faculties of the Department of Theological Studies at Lourdes College (now University) and the Department of Theology at Creighton University; the members of the Baptist-Catholic International Dialogue Joint Commission—Phase III who participated in our Year 3 meeting in Warsaw, Poland; the members of the College Theology Society and the National Association of Baptist Professors of Religion—Region at Large who attended our annual conventions in 2017 and 2018; the leadership of Eastern Area Community Ministries in Louisville, Kentucky, and the Kentucky Council of Churches who planned events associated with the 2012 Week of Prayer for Christian Unity as well as the participants in these events; the World Council of Churches Commission on Faith and Order, specifically the Plenary Commission that met in Crete in 2009 for work that shaped the convergence text *The Church: Towards a Common Vision* and also the working group tasked with the Commission's moral discernment project (thanks also to former Baptist World Alliance General Secretary Neville Callam for invitations to represent the BWA in the Plenary Commission and in the moral discernment project); and the BWA Commission on Baptist Doctrine and Christian Unity that tasked me with drafting the BWA response to *The Church: Towards a Common Vision* as a contribution to its process of reception by the global church. Feedback received in question-and-answer sessions and informal conversations connected with these events has helped to express my thoughts with greater clarity and extend them in new directions in ways that are reflected in the pages of this book.

Several of these lectures and presentations underwent a penultimate stage of revisions for publication as articles and book chapters before material from them was further revised and adapted for incorporation into portions of this book. I am grateful to the editors and publishers of these publications for granting me permission to include revisions and adaptations of them in the text of *Baptists, Catholics, and the Whole Church*: "From Anti-Catholicism to Fellow Pilgrims: Baptist Identity, *Unitatis Redintegratio*, and the Ecumenical Future," *The South African Baptist Journal of Theology* 26 (2017): 139-56; "Baptists and Catholics Together—Twitter Edition," *Baptist News Global* (February 13, 2014); "How Baptists Receive the Gifts of Catholics and Other Christians," *Ecumenical Trends* 39, no. 6 (June 2010): 1/81-5/85; "The Healing of Memories in Bilateral Dialogues with Anabaptist (and Baptist) Participation," *Journal of Baptist Theology in Context* no. 2 (Autumn 2020): 34-56; A Eucharistically-Malnourished Baptist's Desire for Intercommunion," *Horizons: The Journal of the College Theology Society* 45, no. 2 (December 2018): 399-402; and "Baptist Moral Discernment: Congregational Hearing and Weighing," in *Churches and Moral Discernment, Volume 1: Learning from Traditions*, ed. Myriam Wijlens and Vladimir Shmaliy (Faith and Order Paper no. 228; Geneva: WCC Publications, 2021), 99-114. In addition, Elisabeth Newman, Chair of the

Acknowledgments

BWA Commission on Baptist Doctrine and Christian Unity, granted permission to publish the text that I drafted as the BWA response to *The Church: Towards a Common Vision* on behalf of that Commission as Appendix 1 of this book; it was published previously as "Baptist World Alliance Commission on Baptist Doctrine and Christian Unity," a chapter in *Churches Respond to The Church: Towards a Common Vision*, ed. Ellen Wondra, Stephanie Dietrich, and Ani Ghazaryan Drissi (Faith and Order Paper No. 232; Geneva: World Council of Churches Publications, 2021), vol. 2, 279-95.

I am indebted to the administration and trustees of Gardner-Webb University and its School of Divinity for granting me a sabbatical leave for fall 2020 that provided me with the time free from teaching responsibilities that enabled me to propose and write this book. In particular, President William Downs, Provost Ben Leslie, School of Divinity Dean Robert Canoy, and School of Divinity Associate Dean Jim McConnell supported my application for a sabbatical leave and have encouraged and affirmed my work. I am grateful as well to the staff of New City Press for their interest in this project and assistance in transforming it into the present book and preparing for its promotion, especially Executive Director and Publisher Claude Blanc, Editorial Director Tom Masters, and Director of Sales Greg Metzger. Through them I have also come to have greater awareness of and appreciation for the remarkable ecumenical contributions of the Focolare Movement with which New City Press is associated.

The love and support of my wife Kheresa and son Timothy inform my theological work and inspire my writing in essential ways. I experience in my life with them the communion that is God's gift to a fractured world, and I cannot imagine my own contributions to the ecumenical movement's participation in God's community-making work apart from my life in community with my family. I have written this book in the context of a life lived more fully with them at home during the restrictions associated with the global COVID-19 pandemic. Our life together is the better for it, and I believe that the book is also better as a result.

Baptists, Catholics, and the Whole Church is dedicated to my colleagues who have been fellow members of the Baptist-Catholic Joint Commissions for the Baptist World Alliance—Pontifical Council for Promoting Christian Unity International Dialogue, Phases II and III, named here alphabetically (and including "observer" participants for particular dialogue meetings): Massimo Aprile, Nancy Elizabeth Bedford, Jeremy Bell, Brian C. Brewer, Sara Butler, Neville G. Callam, Peter Casarella, Fred Deegbe, Valerie Duval-Poujol, Gregory Fairbanks, Stephen Fernandes, Paul S. Fiddes, Curtis Freeman, Timothy George, Juan Usma Gómez, Avelino González, Derek C. Hatch, William Henn, Przemyslaw Kantyka, Glenroy Lalor, Lillian Lim, Denton Lotz, Nora O. Lozano, Tomás Mackey, Anna Maffei, Trisha Miller Manarin, Dennis McManus, Krysztof Mielcarek, Elizabeth Newman, Anthony Peck, John Radano, Frank Rees, Marie-Hélène Robert, Teresa Francesca Rossi, Jorge Scampini, Arthur Serratelli, Rachael Tan, Lina Toth, Fausto Aguiar de Vasconcelos, Mateusz Wichary, Susan Wood, and Tadeusz Zelinksi. May God bless the labors of these Baptists and Catholics, partners in the pilgrimage to unity, that the whole church and the whole world might receive God's gift of communion, the unity that comes from the Spirit, through Jesus Christ our Lord.

    Steven R. Harmon
    Boiling Springs, North Carolina, USA
    Feast of Saints Bridget of Sweden and John Cassian, 2021

Foreword

This concise, informative, and readable volume by an expert on Baptist-Catholic ecumenical dialogue offers an insightful overview of our relationship on the pilgrimage to unity. Steven Harmon's prayerful consideration of the numerous surprising convergences and the remaining issues noted by the representatives of the Baptist World Alliance and the Catholic Church points the way forward. In these days when the volume of ecumenical agreements and reflections makes it almost impossible to keep up, he offers a helpful overview that extends in the appendices to two recent important documents of the World Council of Churches.

Harmon reviews the troubled history of Baptist-Catholic relations and how since the Second Vatican Council (1962-1965) the Holy Spirit has brought us together to begin to resolve our difficulties. The Baptist World Alliance decided not to send official observers to the Council, though some individual Baptist leaders came to the Council as personal guests. However, by 1974 "Ecumenical Encounters" started to take place in the United States. The first international dialogue between the Alliance and the Vatican took place from 1984 to 1988 and the third phase of dialogue will conclude in 2022.

The book touches on and elaborates on many important contemporary ecumenical foundations. These include an emphasis on the Trinity and the church as communion; the guidance of the Holy Spirit; the church as oriented to the future—the reign of God is anticipated but not fully realized; a concern for the religious liberty of all and freedom of conscience; an emphasis on the fact that we are pilgrims and that our knowledge of the depths of the Gospel could always go deeper; and the commitment to spread the Gospel of Jesus Christ and thus to reduce or eliminate the cacophony of Christian voices that confuses/confounds/discourages outsiders.

Two current approaches to ecumenism—Differentiated Consensus and Receptive Ecumenism—are highlighted in this volume. The method of Differentiated Consensus—which is rooted in the Lutheran-Catholic *Joint Declaration on the Doctrine of Justification* (1999)—was used in the Second Phase of the Dialogue between the Baptist World Alliance and the Catholic Church (2006-2010).

The Receptive Ecumenism Movement emphasizes that God has given gifts to all the Christian churches and that Christian churches should adopt the gifts/good practices of others. Some refer to this as the "Ecumenical Gift Exchange." Harmon tells us that Baptists have been doing this for centuries up to the present moment. His discussion of sharing gifts in chapter 3 is highly informative, detailed, and helpful—it is a resource for other ecumenists. He concludes with some practical suggestions to encourage reception at the local level.

In chapter 4, Harmon discusses the need for healing. I believe that this is an important context for further progress. The Baptist communities are quite diverse; the Catholic community is noted for unity in doctrine and diversity in cultures. Healing involves examining together past conflicts in a very honest way; acknowledging past mistakes and sins by both parties; repenting and resolving to act differently moving forward; and having a ceremony of healing and reconciliation. This process not only provides a foundation for further progress in mutual understanding but also can lead to a deep healing of the emotional roots of our estrangement from one another in the past and in the present.

With spiritual depth, pastoral sensitivity, theological acuity and personal examples, chapter 5 examines the always controverted question of intercommunion between Catholics and other Christians—Baptists in this instance. His entitling the chapter "The Cruciformity of Communion" speaks volumes. His section "Toward One Eucharistic Fellowship" is worth both meditation and contemplation. Chapter 6 balances consideration of the cross with consideration of the resurrection. The reign of Christ is present but not fully realized in us. We need to pray daily for God's gift of unity and be willing to "be receptive to it and participate in it." A deeper conversion to Christ and an acceptance of the grace of the Holy Spirit are necessary.

In the course of this work Dr. Harmon proposes his "ecumenical dream." He hopes that Protestant Churches could be in full communion with the Catholic Church but without losing their distinctive Christian identity and distinctive gifts. He compares the Protestant Churches to religious orders, such as the Benedictines, with their distinctive identities and spirituality that are in full communion with the Catholic Church. Toward the close of chapter 6, he indicates that we may have to be patient for centuries—or even millennia—for full communion among the Christian churches to take place. Given that the Holy

Spirit can always surprise us, I would say that full communion could happen in a decade or two!

Father John Crossin, OSFS, is the former executive director of the Secretariat for Ecumenical and Interreligious Affairs of the United States Conference of Catholic Bishops. He is currently on sabbatical pursuing his interest in ecumenical ethics.

Introduction

Since the 2006 publication of my book *Towards Baptist Catholicity: Essays on Tradition in the Baptist Vision*,[1] a period that included writing and publishing my book *Baptist Identity and the Ecumenical Future: Story, Tradition, and the Recovery of Community* in 2016,[2] I have enjoyed opportunities to apply the ecumenical perspective on Baptist identity that I hammered out in those more academic constructions of Baptist ecumenical theology to various contexts of concrete ecumenical encounter. These have included two series of international ecumenical dialogues between the Baptist World Alliance and the Pontifical Council for Promoting Christian Unity, invited ecumenical lectures delivered at Catholic universities, participation in and responses to the work of the World Council of Churches Commission on Faith and Order, the scholarly ecumenical partnership of joint meetings of the (Catholic) College Theology Society and a group of theologians from the National Association of Baptist Professors of Religion, and an ecumenical workshop and worship service connected with the observance of the Week of Prayer for Christian Unity by a local council of churches. This book harvests and presents the fruit of these more concrete applications of my theoretical work as a Baptist ecumenical theologian, informed especially by various experiences of Baptist ecumenical encounter with the Catholic tradition.

Baptists and Catholics

Chapter 1, "From Anti-Catholicism to Fellow Pilgrims," had its origins in a keynote address delivered at Jesuit-founded Creighton University in Omaha, Nebraska, on February 7, 2015, as part of a symposium on the Vatican II Decree on Ecumenism *Unitatis Redintegratio* on the occasion of the fiftieth anniversary of its promulgation in 1964.[3] It acknowledges that the anti-Catholicism embedded in the early polemic against the Anglicanism from which the Baptist tradition emerged and persisted in its DNA in subsequent centuries initially kept many Baptists from appreciating the ecumenical revolution launched by *Unitatis Redintegratio*. But the chapter also tells the story of how Baptists were nonetheless drawn to participate in this ecumenical revolution, even entering into formal ecumenical dialogues with the Catholic Church made possible by the Decree on Ecumenism. It also envisions additional ways in which Baptists might live into the vision of this decree by joining Catholics as fellow pilgrims on the road that leads to the ecumenical future of one church under the rule of Christ.

The book then turns to two distinct but complementary forms of Baptist-Catholic ecumenical encounter: official bilateral dialogues between representatives of the two traditions and the less formal—but arguably much more influential—ecumenical paradigm of "receptive ecumenism" by which churches of one tradition may identify in other traditions the ecclesial gifts distinctively preserved by them that can help the receiving tradition form communities of more faithful followers of Jesus Christ. Chapter 2,

Introduction

"What Do Baptists and Catholics Have in Common?," summarizes the convergences between Baptists and Catholics identified during Phase II of the international ecumenical dialogue between the Baptist World Alliance and the Pontifical Council for Promoting Christian Unity (2006-2010), for which I had the privilege of serving as a member of the Baptist delegation to the joint commission. It began as the second of two lectures on "Baptists, Catholics, and the Ecumenical Future" that I delivered as the Mount Aloysius Fall Ecumenical Lectures at Mount Aloysius College (founded by the Sisters of Mercy) in Cresson, Pennsylvania on October 9, 2014.[4] Chapter 3, "How Baptists Receive Gifts of Catholic (and catholic) Christianity," identifies several ways in which Baptist churches and their members have been receiving into their patterns of Baptist faith and practice the gifts that have been preserved and stewarded beyond the Baptist tradition, in Catholicism and in lower-case "c" catholic Christianity. It is based on a lecture that I delivered as the Lourdes College Ecumenical Lecture at Lourdes College (sponsored by the Sisters of St. Francis) in Sylvania, Ohio, on March 21, 2010.[5] Chapter 4, "Ecumenical Healing of Ecclesial Memories," explores ecumenical dialogues between the Mennonite World Conference and the Pontifical Council for Promoting Christian Unity and the Lutheran World Federation, respectively, that gave attention to the healing of memories related to the persecution of the sixteenth-century Anabaptists by Catholics and Lutherans as a precondition for further ecumenical convergence today. I presented material in this chapter as a paper delivered to the third annual meeting of the Baptist-Catholic Joint International Commission for the dialogue between the Baptist World Alliance and the Pontifical Council for Promoting Christian Unity—Phase III in Warsaw, Poland, December 9-13, 2019, during which we gave attention to this earlier work on the healing of memories in dialogues with a communion similar in many ways to the Baptist tradition as precedents for the ecumenical healing that Baptists and Catholics need to experience in their mutual relations en route to engaging in "common witness," the theme of Phase III of our dialogue.[6]

Baptists, Catholics, and the Whole Church

The final two main chapters of this book are rooted homiletical applications of the perspective on Baptists, Catholics, and the whole church developed in the preceding portions of the book. Chapter 5, "The Cruciformity of Communion," begins with a homily I preached in an evening prayer service at the annual joint meeting of the College Theology Society—an organization of professors of religious and theological studies at Catholic colleges and universities—and the National Association of Baptist Professors of Religion Region-at-Large at Salve Regina University in Newport, Rhode Island, June 1-4, 2017. In that homily I addressed the pain felt by both Baptist and Catholic participants in the Eucharistic services during our joint annual meetings, at which Baptists are not able to receive communion along with their Catholic colleagues. The following year we held our joint annual meeting at Saint Catherine University in St. Paul, Minnesota, May 31-June 3, 2018. During that meeting one of the Baptist theologians presented a paper titled "Can Catholics and

Introduction

Baptists Share Communion Without Breaking the Rules?" in a panel session of the Evangelical Catholics and Catholic Evangelicals Consultation, with responses to his paper by Catholic and Baptist theologians. My contribution to that panel, which referred back to the previous year's homily, is also incorporated into chapter 5.[7] The final chapter, "Unity as Christ's Victory and Our Task," concludes the main portion of the book with a homily I preached for a Week of Prayer for Christian Unity service sponsored by Eastern Area Community Ministries, a local ecumenical partnership of churches in Louisville, Kentucky, on January 22, 2012, inviting readers to join Baptists, Catholics, and the whole church as fellow pilgrims in the quest for the unity for which Jesus prayed.

Engaging the Whole Church

This book also includes two appendices that offer Baptist perspectives on ecumenical engagement with the whole church that includes Baptists and Catholics, yet I envision somewhat different readerships than the book's main chapters. Nevertheless, I hope that many readers will find themselves interested in their subjects and read this final section as well. Appendix 1, "Envisioning the Whole Church," offers a Baptist response to *The Church: Towards a Common Vision* (*TCTCV*) issued by the World Council of Churches Commission on Faith and Order in 2013 as the WCC's second-ever "convergence text," a designation given previously to the landmark multilateral ecumenical breakthrough *Baptism, Eucharist and Ministry* (1982). I was commissioned by the Baptist World Alliance Commission on Baptist Doctrine and Christian Unity at its 2018 meeting in Zürich, Switzerland to draft a response to *TCTCV* on behalf of the BWA. I presented this response to the BWA commission at its next meeting in Nassau, The Bahamas, in 2019, and it was then forwarded to the WCC Commission on Faith and Order as one of the responses from Christian world communions solicited by the Introduction to *TCTCV*; Appendix 1 reproduces the text of this response.[8] Earlier I had been asked by Neville Callam, former General Secretary of the BWA, to present a paper outlining a Baptist perspective on ecclesial moral discernment on behalf of the BWA to the Moral Discernment Working Group of the WCC Commission on Faith and Order in Erfurt, Germany, July 24, 2016 (I did so remotely via Skype). Appendix 2, "Moral Discernment with the Whole Church," is an adaptation of that presentation and addresses the ethical issues that on the one hand appear to have occasioned further divisions in the church but on the other hand call for each of the churches to draw on the resources of the whole church in their work of moral discernment.[9]

Readers of this book will encounter some repetition in the expression of concepts that have informed my perspectives on my own Baptist tradition, its relation to the whole church, and the ecumenical task. For example, a "pilgrim church" ecclesiology, Alasdair MacIntyre's characterization of a "living tradition" as a constructively contested one, and the ecumenical paradigm of receptive ecumenism are mentioned and explained more than once, as is the WCC convergence text *TCTCV*, but the explanations are developed specifically in relation to the focus of particular chapters and appendices. I have chosen not to eliminate completely this repetition and overlap so that each chapter may stand on its own and as a way of highlighting the themes that weave these chapters into the thematic arc of the whole book as outlined above. If repetition is the mother of learning, as goes the old proverb, then hopefully a little of it in this book will advance the end of ecumenical learning.

Within the whole church, Baptists and Catholics might seem to be ecclesiological and liturgical polar opposites. Despite the commonalities and convergences highlighted in this book, these two traditions are arguably more dissimilar from one another than each is from almost any other Christian tradition. But this dissimilarity means that when Baptists and Catholics, through dialogue and other forms of ecumenical encounter, do succeed in drawing closer to one another, others in the whole church can envision their own patterns of faith and practice as included in these convergences. I offer this book in the hope that it will provide inspiration to Baptists, Catholics, and other Christians to travel further together as fellow travelers in the journey toward a visibly united church of Jesus Christ.

Chapter One

From Anti-Catholicism to Fellow Pilgrims

In 2015 I delivered a keynote address for a symposium on the Vatican II Decree on Ecumenism *Unitatis Redintegratio* held at Creighton University in Omaha, Nebraska (USA), during the 2014-2015 academic year in connection with the fiftieth anniversary of its promulgation on November 21, 1964. The fact that I, as an ordained Baptist minister and professor of theology in a Baptist-related school of divinity, was invited to deliver this address at Catholic-related Creighton University is one small piece of concrete evidence that the Vatican II Decree on Ecumenism accomplished something in the life of the one, holy, catholic, and apostolic church that left a lasting legacy both in the Catholic Church and in the Baptist tradition, for which anti-Catholicism had great historical influence in shaping its identity. This chapter tells the story of how some Baptists have been able to move beyond the anti-Catholicism that kept them from fully appreciating the significance and accomplishment of *Unitatis Redintegratio* at the time and identifies some ways in which both Baptists and Catholics can together live into the decree's promise as fellow pilgrims on the path to the ecumenical future.

Baptists and the Second Vatican Council

Back in 1964, the promulgation of *Unitatis Redintegratio* was an event experienced by Baptists incompletely and indirectly at best. Baptist Press staff writer W. Barry

Chapter One

Garrett, an accredited journalist for the second through fourth sessions of the Council, wrote this in his wrap-up reflections on the adjournment of the third session, published on November 25, 1964, by the news service of the Southern Baptist Convention (SBC):

> After twelve weeks of direct reporting on the council in action at the second and third sessions, this reporter finds it difficult to understand all he knows about what is going on. For those who have not been present it should be even harder to arrive at final conclusions of either approval or disapproval of what is happening.[10]

The difficulty many Baptists have had appreciating Vatican II in general and the Decree on Ecumenism in particular is not unlike Thomas the Apostle's difficulty with Jesus' resurrection—both difficulties are attributable not so much to a lack of perception as a lack of presence. Thomas was absent from the earliest post-resurrection appearance of Jesus to the gathered disciples, as were Baptists from the "Brotherhood of St. Longinus," the group of observers officially delegated by Christian world communions, who experienced the Council from the tribunal of St. Longinus in St. Peter's Basilica as well as through personal interactions with the Council Fathers and *periti* during their time in Rome.[11] On April 3, 1962, then-Monsignor Johannes Willebrands of the Secretariat for Promoting Christian Unity met in Geneva with the heads of the Christian world communions, including Josef Nordenhaug, the General Secretary of the Baptist World Alliance (BWA). Monsignor Willebrands communicated plans that delegated observers be included in the Council and asked the general secretaries to explore with their organizations the possibility of sending official observers. On April 25 General Secretary Nordenhaug received a letter from Monsignor Willebrands asking whether the BWA would send an observer if formally invited. Nordenhaug referred the letter to the BWA Executive Committee, which devoted a whole day of its meeting in Oslo, Norway, on August 22, 1962, to debate on the matter. The Executive Committee finally decided, "It is not agreed it would be desirable for the Baptist World Alliance to encourage a formal invitation to the forthcoming Second Vatican Council," and voted to exclude the record of the day's debate from the minutes. It is commonly understood that opposition from the SBC, the largest Baptist union and most significant financial contributor to the BWA, was a major factor in this decision, along with opposition from Latin American Baptist unions that had their origins in Southern Baptist missionary work and whose ecclesial identities were largely formed in contrast to the Catholic majority in their context. While anti-Catholicism was involved, opposition to this particular ecumenical opportunity was also part of a larger pattern of resistance to the modern ecumenical movement within part of the global Baptist community.[12]

Thus, the Baptist World Alliance became the only Christian world communion not to send observers, and the global Baptist community lost the opportunity to understand what was happening more fully and even to shape what was happening. According to Yves Congar, "The presence of…observers from the non-Roman Catholic Christian Communions [was] one of the most important elements in the conciliar situation";[13] throughout his *My Journal of the Council* Congar documented their many behind-the-scenes contributions.[14] Anglican bishop John Moorman recalled that Monsignor Willebrands told him, "The presence of observers here is very important. You have no idea how much they are influencing the Council."[15] A 2014 journal article by Donald Norwood on "The Impact of Non-Roman Catholic Observers at Vatican II" concludes that they "helped the council evolve from what could have been a purely domestic affair and a rubber-stamping exercise. . . into a genuinely ecumenical, deliberative, debating and decision-making council of the worldwide Church."[16] "On many disputed questions," Norwood argues, "the presence [of] and conversations with observers tipped the balance, [for example] in the case of what to say and not say about Mary or religious freedom."[17] The observers in turn played key roles in the post-conciliar reception of the Council by their own communions and beyond. Baptists missed out on the opportunity to have both kinds of influence, on what happened at the Council and on what happened in its aftermath.

Nevertheless, beyond W. Barry Garrett's journalistic representation, there was a Baptist presence among the *ad personam* guests of the Secretariat for Promoting Christian Unity. These included J. H. Jackson, president of the historically black National Baptist Convention, USA;[18] Stanley I. Stuber, a minister from the American Baptist Churches, USA, who was then serving as Executive Director of the Missouri Council of Churches; W. Morgan Patterson, professor of church history at The Southern Baptist Theological Seminary in Louisville, Kentucky; James Leo Garrett,

Jr., professor of theology at The Southern Baptist Theological Seminary, who was present for the promulgation of the Declaration on Religious Liberty in the Fourth Session (and who was later my own professor at Southwestern Baptist Theological Seminary in Fort Worth, Texas). Another Baptist guest was Claude Broach, then pastor of St. John's Baptist Church in Charlotte, North Carolina. Broach was dismayed that Baptists had declined to send an observer, and as an act of grassroots ecumenical engagement he was able to secure an invitation from a local bishop to visit the final session of the council as his personal guest.[19] But none of these Baptist guests had the status and vantage point of the delegated observers, and consequently Baptist reception of Vatican II was dependent largely on second-hand reports and third-hand interpretations of the Council's actions. In spite of this, ecumenical relationships between Baptists and the Catholic Church have made great strides since the non-participation of Baptists in the "Brotherhood of St. Longinus."

Baptist Reception of Unitatis Redintegratio

The Decree on Ecumenism has been variously interpreted by Baptists in terms of its relation to prior and subsequent developments and the perceived intentions behind it. From my perspective, there are four major sorts of impressions and interpretations that Baptists have tended to have of the decree and its significance for how they understand the Catholic Church and its ecumenical commitments.

First, Baptists have sometimes seen the ecumenical openings articulated in *Unitatis Redintegratio* as radically discontinuous with a decidedly un-ecumenical pre-Vatican II Catholic Church. While the initial Latin words that give the Decree its title do name "the restoration of unity" as "one of the principal concerns of the Second Vatican Council,"[20] it was hardly a new Catholic concern. To regard Vatican II as the beginning of Catholic ecumenical engagement is to ignore the very long history of concern for "the repair of unity" that stretches back to the church that preceded the division between Catholicism and Orthodoxy. The early ecumenical councils were "ecumenical" not only because they involved representatives from the *oikoumene*, from the church spread throughout the inhabited world; they were also ecumenical in that their aim was not to divide the church into heretics and non-heretics but to contest important differences in Christian doctrine that all might be persuaded toward a unity in the truth. After the schism of 1054, the churches of neither Rome nor Constantinople wanted their division to continue indefinitely and made earnest attempts to restore the unity they had lost, as—despite their undone outcomes—the reunion councils of Lyons and Florence attest. In the sixteenth century the Catholic Church kept lines of communication open with Protestant leaders, engaged in theological disputations with them, and invited Protestants to participate in the Council of Trent in ways that went well beyond the official role of the observers at Vatican II— though political and ecclesiastical complications ultimately prevented their attempted participation.[21] Likewise Pius IX invited Orthodox and Protestant observers to attend

From Anti-Catholicism to Fellow Pilgrims

the First Vatican Council, but on terms that those invited decided they could not accept.[22]

Although the institutional beginnings of the modern ecumenical movement with the Edinburgh World Missionary Conference in 1910, the Stockholm Conference on Life and Work in 1925, and the Lausanne Conference on Faith and Order in 1927 were essentially Protestant ventures (with Orthodox participation in the latter two), there was much Catholic ecumenical energy manifested during those years. The Week of Prayer for Christian Unity birthed by then-Episcopalian Paul Wattson in 1908 received the blessing of Pope Pius X in 1909, and his successor Benedict XV commended its observance throughout the Catholic Church.[23] With intentional significance, Pope John XXIII announced his plans to convene the Second Vatican Council on January 25, 1959, in a service at St. Paul's Outside the Walls on the concluding day of the Week of Prayer for Christian Unity. While the Faith and Order and Life and Work movements were getting underway in the 1920s, Catholic theologians, with the blessing of Pope Pius XI, were engaging in the Malines Conversations with Anglican counterparts.[24] And among the Catholic theologians whose influence may be discerned in the documents of Vatican II, Congar had already in 1937 published his book *Divided Christendom*, the original French subtitle of which translates as "Principles of a Catholic Ecumenism."[25] That more ecumenically-oriented stream of Catholic academic theology had tributaries much further upstream in the thought of Johann Adam Möhler and John Henry Newman.[26] Even if its course seemed diverted from time to time—for example, through the sanctions imposed on Congar in the 1940s and

29

1950s[27]—at Vatican II it becomes the stream from which the magisterium drinks. All this is to say: while it is true that, in the words of Walter Cardinal Kasper, the Catholic Church "joined the ecumenical movement officially only with the Decree on Ecumenism,"[28] and therefore it does represent something new in the ongoing development of a Catholic ecumenism, Baptists cannot dismiss *Unitatis Redintegratio* as discontinuous with what preceded it.[29]

Second, some Baptists have also seen the Decree on Ecumenism as discontinuous with more recent developments. When the Congregation for the Doctrine of the Faith issued the "Declaration '*Dominus Iesus*' On the Unicity and Salvific Universality of Jesus Christ and the Church" in 2000 and the "Responses to Some Questions Regarding Certain Aspects of the Doctrine of the Church" in 2007,[30] many Baptists and many others thought the ecumenical openings of Vatican II were now being narrowed. Not everyone recognized that these documents in fact reiterated what *Unitatis Redintegratio* and Pope John Paul II's encyclical "*Ut Unum Sint* (On Commitment to Ecumenism)" had clearly affirmed regarding the presence of Christ and the work of the Spirit in other churches and ecclesial communities that are separated from the Catholic Church yet nevertheless "are in communion with the Catholic Church even though this communion is imperfect." Furthermore, this take on the relation of Vatican II to more recent developments is influenced by a widespread reading of the Council only in terms of its emphasis on *aggiornamento*, an Italian word meaning "updating," which does not acknowledge its dependence on *ressourcement*, a French terms that refers to the critical retrieval of and reengagement with the tradition that supplies the resources for church-renewing *aggiornamento*.[31] When Vatican II is interpreted only in light of *aggiornamento*, reassertions of *ressourcement* or efforts to clarify tenets of Catholic ecclesiology for the Catholic faithful come off looking like a conservative rollback of a liberalizing council.

And speaking of clarifying tenets of Catholic ecclesiology for the Catholic faithful: for many Baptists and many others besides, the neuralgic point of these documents from the CDF was the insistence of *Dominus Iesus* that "the ecclesial communities which have not preserved the valid Episcopate and the genuine and integral substance of the Eucharistic mystery, are not Churches in the proper sense [*in sensu proprio*]"; also troublesome was the repetition of this language in the final sentence of "Responses to Some Questions."[32] The literal translation of the Latin *sensu proprio* into English as "in the proper sense" unfortunately did not help matters.[33] A better but more cumbersome translation would be "in the sense that is not in common with others" or "in the sense that is our own."[34] In context, the meaning is this: "the ecclesial communities...are not Churches in the sense that is our own understanding of Church." It is an internal word of ecclesiological clarification rather than an external assessment of the ecclesiality of non-Catholic communities. Furthermore, the distinction between the sense of "Church" that is the Catholic Church's own understanding of Church and the "ecclesial communities" so denominated in the Vatican II Decree on Ecumenism must be understood in terms of the conceptual and chronological connection of *Unitatis Redintegratio* to *Lumen Gentium*, the Dogmatic Constitution on the Church.³⁵ The order of promulgation on November 21, 1964 was this: first, the Dogmatic Constitution on the Church, which sets forth in detail what it means to be Church in the sense of the Catholic understanding of Church; second, the Decree on the Catholic Churches of the Eastern Rite *Orientalium Ecclesiarum*,³⁶ which explains the full participation that these Churches have in the Catholic understanding of what it means to be Church; and finally the Decree on Ecumenism, which notes that the Council "has already declared its teaching on the Church"³⁷ and then recognizes as a warrant for Catholic participation in the modern ecumenical movement the ecclesiality present in other embodied understandings of what it means to be church. This ecclesiality may not be identical with the Catholic understanding of Church as set forth in *Lumen Gentium*, but in it "very many of the significant elements and endowments which go together to build up and give life to the Church itself, can exist outside the visible boundaries of the Catholic Church," including "liturgical actions" that "can truly engender a life of grace" and "must be regarded as capable of giving access to the community of salvation."³⁸ Thus to be designated "ecclesial communities" does not have to be taken as a negation of churchly status. Indeed, it is strong affirmation thereof: to describe a community as "ecclesial" is to attribute to it ecclesiality, that which shares in the essence of *ekklēsia*. Baptists therefore can embrace their status as "ecclesial communities" along with their differences from the full Catholic understanding of what it means to be church, for most Baptists—maybe even all Baptists—would agree that the Baptists' own understanding of what it means to be church and the Catholics' understanding of what it means to be church differ in very significant ways. But in both understandings and their embodiments there is ecclesial essence. The Decree on Ecumenism recognizes that, as does subsequent Catholic ecclesiology and its clarifications in the first decade of the twenty-first century.

Third, some Baptists have suspected that all the talk about ecumenical openness in the Decree on Ecumenism and the Council in general was merely camouflage for the real Catholic ecumenical agenda of unity achieved through everyone "coming home to Rome" as the one true church of Christ. This suspicion is not entirely groundless. After all, in section 4 of *Unitatis Redintegratio* the "unity which Christ bestowed on His Church"—"the one and only Church"—"from the beginning" is said to "[subsist] in the Catholic Church as something she can never lose."[39] This language of something that "subsists in the Catholic Church" parallels the teaching of *Lumen Gentium* 8 that the one Church established by Christ "subsists in the Catholic Church, which is governed by the successor of Peter and by the Bishops in communion with him."[40] There has of course been a fifty-year-long debate within and without the Catholic Church as to whether the use of *subsistit in* instead of *est* in that construction[41] implies a distinction between the one Church of Christ and the Catholic Church as a distinctive concrete historical manifestation of this Church but not the only possible such manifestation. As a Baptist theologian I do not wish to render judgment in the case. But I do think the language of the subsistence of the Church of Christ and its unity "in" the Catholic Church, combined with the final deci-

Chapter One

sion against explicitly equating the mystical body of Christ and the Catholic Church, opened up enough ecumenical space to exclude "home to Rome" as the ecumenical vision of *Unitatis Redintegratio* and the Council itself. Some of the Council Fathers did seem to envision visible unity in terms of a return to the Catholic Church,[42] but their perspective did not carry the day. Some individual Catholics may continue to see the Catholic Church itself as the only acceptable form of visible unity, even as some Baptists and other Protestants may find it impossible to conceive of a visible unity that would include the Church of Rome among other churches. But the Catholic Church of the Second Vatican Council does not teach "return to mother church" as its ecumenical program.

Some Baptists may view the Vatican II Decree on Ecumenism as discontinuous with what preceded the Council, discontinuous with what has followed the Council, or disingenuous in its ecumenical affirmations, but **many Baptists have a fourth perspective on the Decree: that the approval of *Unitatis Redintegratio* is a significant moment in the ongoing development of Catholic relations with non-Catholic Christians that influentially participates in God's gift of the Spirit's work of unifying the body of Christ.** This latter perspective celebrates the Catholic Church's commitment to the modern ecumenical movement in the Decree and responds to its recognition of the presence of Christ, the work of the Spirit, the life of grace, and the communion of salvation among the individuals, communities, and churches that are not currently in full communion with the Catholic Church by recognizing these same things in the Catholic Church. It knows that

From Anti-Catholicism to Fellow Pilgrims

the Catholic Church graciously initiated new possibilities for reconciled ecclesial relationships in the act of issuing this Decree, and over the next five decades the fruit of that gracious initiative has included the willingness of Baptists to enter into formal dialogue with the Catholic Church.

Post-Vatican II Baptist-Catholic Ecumenical Encounters

An early instance of the Baptist-Catholic ecumenical encounters that Vatican II and its Decree on Ecumenism made possible was the Ecumenical Institute founded in 1968 by Baptist-related Wake Forest University in Winston-Salem, North Carolina, which in 1974 became a jointly sponsored venture with Belmont Abbey College, an institution founded and led by the Benedictines in Belmont, North Carolina. The Wake Forest University/Belmont Abbey College Ecumenical Institute was active for nearly five decades, during which it sponsored conferences and a lecture series, facilitated various forms of regional and national Baptist-Catholic dialogues, and with an annual award recognized individuals who have contributed to ecumenical progress.[43] Earlier this chapter mentioned Claude Broach, pastor from 1944 through 1974 of St. John's Baptist Church in Charlotte, North Carolina, in connection with his voluntary presence in the final session of the Second Vatican Council. Upon his retirement Broach became the first executive director of the Ecumenical Institute, installed at a worship service in Belmont Abbey Cathedral commemorating the tenth anniversary of the promulgation of *Unitatis Redintegratio*. Broach is honored as the namesake of the Claude Broach Ecumenical Lectures sponsored by what was most recently known as the Ecumenical Institute of the Carolinas, with Mepkin Abbey and Baptist-related Furman University in South Carolina joining Belmont Abbey and Wake Forest as sponsoring institutions.[44] Also following Vatican II, The American Baptist Churches USA engaged in a series of dialogues with the United States Conference of Catholic Bishops from 1967 through 1973, as did the Southern Baptist Convention from 1978 through 1999.[45] Ongoing dialogues in France between Baptists and Catholics have produced notable reports, including a 1992 commentary on the report of the first series of international dialogues between the Baptist World Alliance and the Catholic Church and reports of subsequent thematic dialogues on baptism, the Eucharist, and the church in 2006 and on Mary in 2009.[46] Also in 2009, Italian Baptists and Catholics issued "A Common Document for a Pastoral Approach to Marriages between Catholics and Baptists in Italy."[47]

At the international level, the Baptist World Alliance and the Catholic Church have held three series of dialogues: Phase I, 1984-1988; Phase II, 2006-2010; and Phase III, 2017-2022. The very fact that these conversations happened is remarkable. The one Christian world communion that found itself unable to accept an invitation to send observers to the Second Vatican Council approved the proposal to enter official bilateral dialogue with the Catholic Church less than twenty years later, despite the persistence of some of the same misgivings among part of the global Baptist family that precluded a Baptist presence among the observers at Vatican II. The outcomes of the Council, and the Decree on Ecumenism in particular, had changed something about Baptist perceptions of the Catholic Church that opened up new possibilities for convergence toward unity. When the BWA and the Catholic Church engaged in the first series of conversations to explore the unity they had and the impediments to more visible expressions of it, the two communions were able to say a great deal about their agreement on "God's saving revelation in Jesus Christ, the necessity of personal commitment to God in Christ, the ongoing work of the Holy Spirit, and the missionary imperative that emerges from God's redemptive activity on behalf of humankind." This is reflected in paragraph 2 of the seventeen-page report "Summons to Witness to Christ in Today's World," which summarizes the matters on which Baptists and Catholics were able to say something together about their common commitment to the good news of their testimony that "Jesus Christ is Lord."[48] That report also identified deep differences evident in those conversations that warranted continued exploration: theological authority and method; the shape of ecclesial *koinonia*; the relationship between faith, baptism, and Christian witness; and the place of Mary in faith and practice.[49]

When I served as a member of the Baptist delegation to Phase II of the conversations between the BWA and the Catholic Church from 2006 through 2010, we confronted those ongoing differences. Taking as our overarching theme "The Word of God in the Life of the Church," working within the theological framework of the Trinitarian *koinonia* (or "fellowship") as the source of the church's *koinonia*, and employing the paradigm of "differentiated consensus," we arrived at and articulated surprisingly substantial convergences concerning ongoing differences identified in the first series of conversations.⁵⁰ These included mutual affirmations such as: the liturgical location of the normativity of Scripture;⁵¹ the coinherence of Scripture and Tradition;⁵² initiation into Christ and his church as a process wider than the act of baptism itself that takes place as a "journey of Christian beginnings";⁵³ Mary as a model for discipleship and as one from whom the church learns to pray and with whom the church prays in the communion of saints;⁵⁴ and the recognition that differing patterns of ecclesial *episkopē* (or "oversight") are exercised in personal, collegial, and communal ways in the church and have as one principal purpose the promotion of Christian unity, which is the vocation of all Christians.⁵⁵ (Chapter 3 in this book, "What Do Baptists Have in Common with Catholics?" will explore the common affirmations discovered in Phase II more fully.) Phase III of the Baptist-Catholic dialogue, for which I serve as co-secretary, commenced in 2017. This new phase of the dialogue re-engages the prospect of a common Baptist-Catholic witness borne to Jesus Christ first articulated three decades earlier in Phase I, this time guided by the theme "The Dynamic of the Gospel and the Witness of the Church." These dialogues, the convergences they yield, and their ongoing reception have been made possible by Vatican II and its Decree on Ecumenism.

The Ongoing Relevance of *Unitatis Redintegratio* for Baptists, Catholics, and the Whole Church

Unitatis Redintegratio still provides relevant theological paradigms for ecumenical recognition and convergence that Baptists and other non-Catholic Christians can embrace. In some ways it was ahead of the rest of the modern ecumenical movement in the way it roots the unity of the church in the unity of the Triune God. The end of section 2 declares:

> This is the sacred mystery of the unity of the Church, in Christ and through Christ, the Holy Spirit energizing its various functions. It is a mystery that finds its highest exemplar and source in the unity of the Persons of the Trinity: the Father and the Son in the Holy Spirit, one God.[56]

Faith and Order ecumenism has now embraced the potential of this Trinitarian rationale and framework for the conceiving of the church and its unity. The 2013 Faith and Order paper *The Church: Towards a Common Vision* (*TCTCV*) has the potential to serve as this generation's *Baptism, Eucharist and Ministry* (*BEM*), the landmark convergence text from 1982.[57] If we compare the two documents, one feature of *The Church: Towards a Common Vision* that seems most obviously an advance beyond *BEM* is its invocation of this Trinitarian motif, not only in the chapter on "The Church of the Triune God"[58] but elsewhere in the document. Two other emphases that are more prominent in *TCTCV* compared with *BEM* are likewise anticipated by *Unitatis Redintegratio*. In chapter 1, titled "God's Mission and the Unity of the Church,"[59] *TCTCV* recovers the roots of the modern ecumenical movement in the modern missions movement by framing the quest for Christian unity as a participation in God's mission in the world. The next chapter, "The Church of the Triune God," affirms that the church "is by its very nature missionary, called and sent to witness in its own life to that communion which God intends for all humanity and for all creation in the kingdom."[60] The Decree on Ecumenism anticipates this linkage of missiology and ecumenism. Section 2 of the decree, in the chapter on "Catholic Principles on Ecumenism" begins with this sentence: "What has revealed the love of God among us is that the Father has sent into the world His only-begotten Son, so that, being made man, He might by His redemption give life to the entire human race and unify it."[61] In addition, more strongly than *BEM*, *TCTCV* develops the church's ecumenical imperative eschatologically, portraying the church as "an eschatological reality, already anticipating the kingdom, but not yet its full realization," and therefore also "[a]s a pilgrim community" on a "journey towards the full realization of God's gift of communion."[62] The thoroughly eschatological motif of a pilgrim church likewise was already expressed in *Unitatis Redintegratio* section 2, where it is said that the church "makes its pilgrim way in hope toward the goal of the fatherland above," with that goal defined in the next sentence as "the sacred mystery of the unity of the Church."[63] In some ways large sections of *TCTCV* are fuller developments of important aspects of the ecumenical theology already outlined in the Decree on Ecumenism. (Appendix 1 of this book, "Envisioning the Whole Church," will engage *TCTCV* more fully from a Baptist perspective.)

Beyond these, two other dimensions of *Unitatis Redintegratio* converge with concepts near and dear to Baptists: religious liberty and the responsibility of all Christians for the ministry of the church. In the formative period of their tradition, Baptists were religious minorities and frequently experienced persecution at the hands of larger communities of majority, state-established Christian churches—a common experience that both Baptists and Catholics shared during certain periods of English history. With the Second Vatican Council, Catholics joined Baptists as on-record defenders of religious liberty. Though the Decree on Ecumenism does not directly mention religious liberty, and while the Declaration on Religious Liberty *Dignitatis Humanae* was still undergoing its own contentions process of development in 1964 and was not promulgated until the following year during the final session of the Council, in post-conciliar perspective it is clear that religious liberty, as a safeguard against the coercion of conscience, is conceived as the precondition of genuine ecumenical encounter. John Paul II's encyclical on ecumenism *Ut Unum Sint* insisted that *Unitatis Redintegratio* "takes into account everything affirmed in the Council's Declaration on Religious Freedom *Dignitatis Humanae*."[64] It is significant that in the schemas of the Council documents, a statement on religious liberty was earlier conceived not as a separate declaration but as a chapter of the decree on ecumenism. This commitment to religious liberty and its connection with ecumenism Baptists can enthusiastically affirm and humbly acknowledge as an example of "receptive ecumenism" in the sense of the exchange of ecclesial gifts by the churches.[65]

Baptists have also understood themselves to be committed to the principle of "the priesthood of all believers" in a distinctive way. Although it did not originate among Baptists—it is, after all, a biblical concept (1 Peter 2:9) and was emphasized by the Protestant Reformers in the century preceding Baptist origins—it is an ecumenically shared concept (expressed by Catholics especially in terms of "the apostolate of the laity"). But Baptists have given much attention to understanding the church as a community in which all its members are responsible for doing its ministry. *Unitatis Redintegratio* applies the priestly ministry of all believers to the church's work of ecumenical engagement. It insists that every Catholic, and by implication every Christian, has the obligation to embrace personally the quest for Christian unity. It says in section 4, "The Sacred Council exhorts all the Catholic faithful to recognize the signs of the times and to take an active and intelligent part in the work of ecumenism," and again in section 5, "The attainment of union is the concern of the whole Church, faithful and shepherds alike."[66] We might call this the "ecumenist-hood of all believers." Baptists and all Christians would do well to take note and likewise encourage this ecumenist-hood of all believers, for every Christian is baptized simultaneously into the one church of Jesus Christ and into its divisions. Seeing to their reconciliation belongs to the priestly ministry to which all are commissioned in their baptism.

The Decree on Ecumenism still serves as a challenge to the whole church to go further in its pilgrim journey toward being fully under the rule of Christ, a rule that can be regarded as complete only when the one body of Christ is visibly united with all its members as well as its head. Significantly, the Decree on Ecumenism challenges the whole church by serving as the manifesto through which, in the words of John Paul II's *Ut Unum Sint*,

"At the Second Vatican Council, the Catholic Church committed herself irrevocably to following the path of the ecumenical venture."[67] The Catholic embrace of the modern ecumenical movement declared in the Decree on Ecumenism has helped ensure that the quest for visible unity in faith and order must be "thick." Had the ecumenical movement remained a primarily Protestant affair, it might have proceeded along the lines of a "thin" ecumenism that relativizes existing differences in doctrine and church order and seeks to attain the ecumenical goal of one Eucharistic fellowship by means of the lowest common ecclesiastical denominator. That might seem to be the ecumenical path of least resistance, but in ways that cannot be fully foreseen there are multiple bridges out along that road. Catholic engagement with the ecumenical movement keeps ecumenism "thick" by insisting that the visibly united Church we seek be marked by a catholicity that is not merely quantitative in the sense of belonging to the whole Church, but also qualitative in the sense of a catholic pattern of faith and practice.[68] Qualitative catholicity does subsist in the Catholic and Orthodox churches, and their presence in the ecumenical movement requires that the rest of us cultivate it as well, attending to our own communions' deficiencies in catholicity so that the catholicity that is among us be mutually recognized. What *Unitatis Redintegratio* seems to suggest as Catholic perceptions of others' deficiencies in qualitative catholicity should be received not as an affront to or diminishment of our churchly status, but as a challenge toward self-examination—are there indeed deficiencies in catholicity that we need to recognize and rectify in our pilgrim journey toward visible unity?

The Baptist tradition has emphasized the renewal of the church through the restoration of ancient Christian patterns of faith and practice that are often thought to have been lost or corrupted in later periods of the church in its historical pilgrimage.[69] But this retrieval of the Christian past should be done in dialogue with the churches that have more intentionally maintained historically-extended, socially-embodied continuity with the Christian past.[70] We must be open to the possibility that the churches of the historic episcopate have faithfully conserved gifts from the Christian past that need to be received in the present by the traditions now separated in various ways from this more intentional historical continuity. Having the Catholic Church as a fully engaged dialogue partner helps us guard against distortions of the Christian past, including distortions of the New Testament norm of the Christian tradition, to which we are vulnerable when we make our Bibles and our brains our sole resources for renewing the Church in our age—even while the presence of the Baptists in the ecumenical movement can help others guard against overly-realized eschatologies of the Church through the gift of the pilgrim church vision that is at the heart of the Baptist vision,[71] but which also belongs to *Unitatis Redintegratio* as a profound recognition of our common status as fellow pilgrims in this journey.

An Ecumenical Dream

My own ecumenical dream is that to be Baptist—or to be Lutheran, Presbyterian, or Methodist—might come to be regarded as a distinctive way of being Catholic, in full communion with the Catholic Church but without ceasing to be Baptist in ecclesial identity, comparable to the manner in which being a Benedictine is a distinctive way of living together as an ecclesial community that is in communion with Rome but has a particular historically-extended, socially-embodied pilgrim journey that enables this community to be the bearer of distinctive gifts the whole church needs to become fully catholic qualitatively as well as quantitatively. God alone knows how or when that dream will be realized. But I am convinced that we are headed in the right direction when we are "moving forward from the footsteps" of the Decree on Ecumenism in our Baptist identity as a community on pilgrimage to the church fully under the rule of Christ in an ecumenical future that includes our sisters and brothers in the Catholic Church and all Christian churches.[72] The next chapter of this book turns to some concrete steps that Baptists and Catholics have taken together in that pilgrimage through the work of formal ecumenical dialogue.

Chapter Two

What Do Baptists and Catholics Have in Common?

The title of this chapter may seem like the set-up for a joke of some sort—or at least for a very brief response. Whether we are talking about how we worship (liturgy), or what we believe (theology), or how the church is structured (ecclesiology), it would seem to many that Baptists and Catholics are at opposite ends of the ecclesiastical spectrum. But as we have come to know each other better over the past five decades of various forms of formal Baptist-Catholic dialogue introduced briefly in the previous chapter, we have realized that we have much more in common than our polar-opposite stereotypes might suggest. As the previous chapter detailed, this realization was made possible by the ecumenical commitments made by the Catholic Church at the Second Vatican Council, in particular in its Decree on Ecumenism *Unitatis Redintegratio*. In that decree the Catholic Church committed itself to participation in the modern ecumenical movement. It recognized the presence of Christ, the work of the Spirit, the life of grace, and the communion of salvation among the individuals, communities, and churches that are not currently in full communion with the Catholic Church. It recognized us as separated brothers and sisters, who though separated do have a certain though imperfect communion with the Catholic Church. Thus, it was the Catholic Church that graciously initiated new possibilities for reconciled ecclesial relationships, and over the next five decades the fruit of that gracious initiative has included the international bilateral dialogues between the Catholic Church and other churches and ecclesiastical communities.[73]

On the Way to Common Affirmations

Baptists are among those who embraced this new opportunity for dialogue. When the Baptist World Alliance (BWA) and the Catholic Church engaged in a first series of international conversations from 1984 through 1988 to see what they might be able to say together, the two communions were actually able to say a great deal about their agreement. The second paragraph of the report, "Summons to Witness to Christ in Today's World," summarizes the matters on which Baptists and Catholics were able to say something together about our common commitment to the good news of our testimony that "Jesus Christ is Lord": "God's saving revelation in Jesus Christ, the necessity of personal commitment to God in Christ, the ongoing work of the Holy Spirit, and the missionary imperative that emerges from God's redemptive activity on behalf of humankind."[74]

That report from Phase I of the Baptist-Catholic dialogue also identified deep differences evident in those conversations that warranted continued exploration: theological authority and method; the shape of ecclesial *koinonia*; the relationship between faith, baptism, and Christian witness; and the place of Mary in faith and practice (§§ 45-57). When I served as a member of the Baptist delegation to a second series of conversations between the BWA and the Catholic Church from 2006 through 2010, we

Chapter Two

directly addressed those ongoing differences. A planning session for Phase II of the dialogue in March 2006 in Rome had established the goals and agenda for the conversations:

> The goal of these conversations is to respond to the prayer of our Lord Jesus Christ to his Father for his disciples 'that they may all be one... that the world may believe' (John 17:21). Facing the challenges of our world today, we believe this means that we should continue to explore our common ground in biblical teaching, apostolic faith and practical Christian living, as well as areas that still divide us, in order to:
>
> 1. Increase our mutual understanding, appreciation of each other and Christian charity towards each other;
>
> 2. Foster a shared life of discipleship within the communion of the Triune God;
>
> 3. Develop and extend a common witness to Jesus Christ as the Saviour of the world and the Lord of all life; and
>
> 4. Encourage further action together on ethical issues, including justice, peace and the sanctity of life, in accord with God's purpose and to the praise of God's glory.[75]

Toward that end, the planning commission proposed the theme, "The Word of God in the Life of the Church: Scripture, Tradition and *Koinonia*."

We met for a week each December for the next five years. In 2006 we met at Samford University's Beeson Divinity School in Birmingham, Alabama, where in addition to our dialogue work sessions we visited together the local provenance of Martin Luther King, Jr.'s "Letter from Birmingham Jail" and toured the 16th Street Baptist Church, site of the 1963 bombing that killed four young girls. We worshipped together each day in morning and evening prayer services in Beeson Divinity School's Hodges Chapel, where among the sixteen representatives of the communion of saints whose frescoes encircle the chapel's dome are Thomas Aquinas and Martin Luther, depicted side-by-side facing worshippers. In Birmingham we addressed two themes: "The *Koinonia* of the Triune God and the Church" and "The Authority of Christ in Scripture and Tradition." In 2007 we met in Rome, where we continued to reflect on our developing consensus on Scripture and Tradition and took up the theme "Baptism and the Lord's Supper or Eucharist: The Visible Word of God in the *Koinonia* of the Church." There we were privileged to have a private audience with Pope Benedict XVI. After bringing greetings to our delegations, wishing us well in our work, and offering prayer for us, Pope Benedict sat back in his chair as the heads of our delegations delivered to him our greetings. Baptist co-chair Paul Fiddes of Oxford University mentioned that as we had discussed the relationship of Scripture and Tradition that week, we had found help in a commentary on the Vatican II Dogmatic Constitution on Divine Revelation *Dei Verbum* written by the young theologian Joseph Ratzinger shortly after the Council.[76] At that moment his eyes brightened and he leaned forward; he was not only the pope, but a career academic theologian delighted to learn we were reading something he had written and eager to follow where our interaction with it might take us. Another highlight of that week was our lunch with Walter Cardinal Kasper, who was soon to retire as Secretary of the Pontifical Council for Promoting Christian Unity. He had been an energetic encourager of plans for this series of conversations and had been instrumental behind the scenes in clarifying for Baptists, especially in Latin America, what the Congregation for the Doctrine of the Faith's *Dominus Iesus* and "Responses to Some Questions Regarding Certain Aspects of the Doctrine of the Church" meant and did not mean with reference to the separated brothers and sisters.[77]

In 2008 we met at Duke University Divinity School in Durham, North Carolina, hosted by the school's Baptist House of Studies. There we took up the theme "Mary as a Model of Discipleship in the Communion of the Church." In 2009 we returned to Rome, where we tackled "The Ministry of Oversight (or *Episkope*) and Unity in the Life of the Church." During this meeting in Rome we were again graced by a visit from Cardinal Kasper, by now retired; he shared with us his own perspectives on the progress of the ecumenical movement and his own dreams of what sorts of unity might be possible in a visibly united church.

Finally, in 2010 we convened at Oxford University, which provided a setting suggestive of just how far ecumenical relations have progressed in some ecclesial locales. In the neighborhood of multiple markers commemorating the martyrdoms Protestants and Catholics inflicted on one another during the sixteenth century, the joint commission had lodging, meals, morning and evening prayer, and working sessions at Regent's Park College. Regent's Park is

What Do Baptists and Catholics Have in Common?

a Baptist-founded "Permanent Private Hall" of the University of Oxford that owes its beginnings to the fact that until the 1870s students who were not members of the Church of England were excluded from admission to the major British universities (an experience shared by Baptists and Catholics in England, it is worth noting). Nestled along St. Giles' between St. Benet's Hall and Blackfriars Hall, Regent's Park enjoys warm collegial relations with these Catholic neighbors among the Oxford colleges. When Greyfriars Hall, another Catholic private hall at Oxford, was closed in 2007, Regent's Park accepted the remaining Greyfriars students and began hosting Mass in its chapel to provide for their spiritual needs. The faculty and student makeup of Regent's Park College is ecumenical, and members of the teaching staff are full members of the thoroughly ecumenical Oxford University faculty.

In Oxford we devoted ourselves to consolidating the fruit of our conversations from the preceding four years and beginning the work of drafting the report from our dialogue. The result was a report of nearly 100 pages, "*The Word of God in the Life of the Church*," published as a special issue of the *American Baptist Quarterly* and available online on the Vatican website, linked from the page for the Pontifical Council for Promoting Christian Unity.[78] The document is not merely a description of our differences. It's rather a statement of our surprisingly substantial consensus on the church's participation in the *koinonia*, the "fellowship" of the Triune God; the authority of Christ in Scripture and tradition; baptism and the Eucharist or Lord's Supper; Mary as a model of discipleship; and the ministry of oversight (or *episkope*) and unity in the life of the church.

We presented these agreements as a "differentiated consensus." This is an ecumenical paradigm that we took from the *Joint Declaration on the Doctrine of Justification* issued by the Catholic Church and Lutheran World Federation in 1999 (subsequently joined by the Methodist World Council in 2006, and in 2017 by the World Communion of Reformed Churches and the Anglican Communion).[79] Paragraphs set in bold type expressed our basic consensus, followed by paragraphs set in regular type that offered commentary on the nature of that consensus and/or identified the ways in which there are remaining differences in how each communion understands and embodies what Baptists and Catholics have been able to say together.

Having said these things together, Baptists and Catholics now have the responsibility of the "reception" of the report. In a "Glossary of Key Ecumenical Terms" in my book *Ecumenism Means You, Too: Ordinary Christians and the Quest for Christian Unity*, I offer the following definition of that task: *Reception* is "The process by which worldwide communions, national churches and denominations, local parishes and congregations, and individual Christians become informed about, consider, and act upon the proposals and agreements that result from bilateral and multilateral ecumenical dialogue."[80]

When the "*The Word of God in the Life of the Church*" went online in October 2013, I launched an experiment in utilizing social media to encourage reception of the report. Beginning on October 11 that year, I began posting a semi-daily tweet from my Twitter account summarizing in 140 characters or less a statement of agreement from the bold-type consensus paragraphs of the report. (Each of these tweets was actually a good bit less than 140 characters, as the inclusion of the hashtag #BaptistsCatholics and the condensed URL link to the report left only 89 characters for summary and paragraph number reference, and unfortunately this was prior to Twitter's doubling of the tweet character limit to 280 characters in 2017 and the launch that year of its "threads" feature.) Since Facebook status updates did not have the 140-character restriction then in effect on Twitter, I posted a parallel series of Facebook updates with the full consensus statements from which the tweets were abridged.

I posted the final #BaptistsCatholics tweet on January 3, 2013. The following is the tweet-by-tweet "Twitter edition" of the bold-type consensus paragraphs from "*The Word of God in the Life of the Church*," prefaced by paragraph numbers but sans hashtags and URLs, and my own commentary on significant convergences in each section of the report interspersed.

The *Koinonia* of the Triune God and the Church

7. The one God exists from eternity in a life of relationship--a koinonia of persons

7. Jesus Christ, God's self-revelation, draws us into communion with God & each other

7. The Word of God in the Church in the fullest sense is Christ himself

11. The Church is a koinonia (fellowship) grounded in the koinonia of the Triune God

Chapter Two

11. Believers are joined in koinonia through participation in communion of Triune God

11. Believers also in koinonia through participation in community gathered by Christ

11. "Communion ecclesiology" expresses the heart of the nature of the Church

12. Principle of koinonia applies both to local church & to gatherings of congregations

12. Local church does not derive from universal Church, nor is universal a mere sum of local forms

12. There is mutual existence & coinherence between local and universal Church of Christ

16. The koinonia of the Church may also be understood as a 'covenant community'

16. Covenant is God's initiating relationship with us & our commitment to each other & God

16. Church is gift in being gathered by Christ, & gathers in response to call of Christ

16. Koinonia of Church is both gift & calling, as unity of church is both gift and task

20. Communion with Triune God & whole Church is continually actualized in Eucharist/Supper

20. In Euch we share communion not only w/ congregation but whole Church in time & space

20. Because we hear word of God in Eucharist, it is a sharing in both word and sacrament

23. Local churches must be in visible communion w/ each other, or communion lacks fullness

26. Local churches have communion w/ each other to hear Word of God & find mind of Christ

These short-form expressions of convergences between Baptists and Catholics are rooted in our shared Trinitarian faith and our common indebtedness to two interrelated recent trends in ecumenically-shared systematic/constructive theology: the renewal of Trinitarian theology through the exploration of its implications for human relational existence, and the application of this revitalized Trinitarianism to ecclesiology (theological reflection on the church) that has come to be called "communion ecclesiology."[81] A key term for communion ecclesiology and our common embrace of it is the New Testament Greek word *koinōnia*, translated "sharing" or "participation" or "communion," found in 1 Corinthians 10:16-17: "The cup of blessing that we bless, is it not a sharing (*koinonia*) in the blood of Christ? The bread that we break, is it not a sharing (*koinonia*) in the body of Christ? Because there is one bread, we who are many are one body, for we all partake of the one bread." Communion ecclesiology holds that all the members of the church, and all local church communities, are one body by virtue of their participation in Christ that is actualized in the Eucharist. This common sharing in Christ is the basis for envisioning the communion that all expressions of church community have with one another, which is a Trinitarian communion: just as the persons of the Triune God have a full participation (*koinōnia*) in the being and work of one another, so the members of the church and the churches to which they belong should have this participation both in the life and work of the Triune God and in the lives and work of

Chapter Two

one another. Our shared Baptist and Catholic convictions about the church as a community of Trinitarian participation, inclusive of the whole church extended through time and space and made visible in Eucharistic sharing, served as a theological framework that led to other convergences regarding the themes we addressed in the dialogue.

The Authority of Christ in Scripture and Tradition

37. The Bible is the divinely-authorized written norm for faith and practice

37. The normativity of Scripture is principally located in the worship of the Church

37. The Bible was canonized by and for the worshipping community

37. Bible supplies narrative content of acts of worship that recall/represent acts of God

37. Scripture is the source of story of the Triune God in which worshippers participate

41/42. God is the author of Sacred Scripture...through human instrumentality

46. OT and NT together form coherent story that requires a Christ-centered interpretation

56. Bible is written embodiment of living tradition handed down through work of H. Spirit

56. The source of this process of transmission is the living Word of God, Jesus Christ

58. Scripture & tradition coinherent--mutual indwelling & interweaving of 1 in the other

58. Scripture and tradition should not be considered as separate and unrelated sources

58. Scripture & tradition = 2 streams flowing together from same source: God's revelation

63. Apostolic tradition distinguished from merely ecclesiastical trad; apostolic normative

Baptists and Catholics have long been distinguished from each other by their respective attitudes toward the authority of Scripture and its relation to the later traditional teaching of the church. Baptists have often been characterized as "biblicists" because they hold that the Bible is the only sufficient norm for faith and practices, while Catholics have been associated with a more authoritative expression of ecclesial tradition. A mutual examination both of formal expressions of Baptist and Catholic theology and of the role of Scripture and tradition in the practices of Baptist and Catholic ecclesial life led us to surprising discoveries about one another beyond the stereotypes. The Baptist theologians were able to appreciate a Catholic commitment to the normativity of Scripture in relation to the subsequent tradition of the church, thanks especially to a close mutual reading of *Dei Verbum* from Vatican II.[82] At the same time, the Catholic theologians discerned in the Baptist theological tradition a growing recognition that the Scriptures and their canonization are the fruit of the living tradition of Hebrew and Christian communities of faith and that when the church today seeks to configure their faith and practice on the basis of the Scriptures, it relies on the church's efforts in previous ages to do so. Together we affirmed that the principal location of Christian formation by the Scriptures and by the church's tradition that transmits their normativity—both flowing from divine revelation—is the worship of the church.[83]

Baptism and Lord's Supper, or Eucharist: The Visible Word of God in the *Koinonia* of the Church

> 73. Sacraments/ordinances = signs through which God acts, visible signs of invisible grace
>
> 77. Sacrament and ordinance express both God's gift of love & faith-filled human response
>
> 77. Sacrament/ordinance becomes intersection between divine commitment & human commitment
>
> 79. Christ central to meaning of sacraments/ordinances & their relationship to the Church
>
> 81. There is a coinherence between sacraments/ordinances and preaching of the Word of God
>
> 83. Baptism and the Eucharist/Lord's Supper are central to the life of the Church
>
> 85. Sacraments/ordinances are encounters w/ Christ that transform worshipers by the Spirit
>
> 85. No experience of salvation is fully whole without entrance of the believer into Church
>
> 85. There can be no experience of grace apart from faith
>
> 91. Rel. of faith & sacrament/ordinance involves faith of individual believer & community
>
> 93. We baptize in obedience to Christ's command "Go therefore...baptizing them" Mt 28:19-20

93. Baptism has its foundation & meaning in the doctrines of the Trinity and Christology

93. Through baptism we are brought more deeply into the communion of the Triune God

93. Through baptism...we [also] share in the life, death, and resurrection of Christ

97. Faith is always necessary for baptism

101. Initiation into Christ & his Church is a process wider than the act of baptism itself

101. Can recognize different forms of initiation as an entire journey of faith and grace

107. Baptism is with water, in name of Father & Son & Holy Spirit, & a once-for-all event

109. In baptism we are united with other believers in the Church of Christ (1 Cor 12:13)

113. Baptism signifies forgiveness of sins and new birth

116. Eucharist/Lord's Supper is essential to the Church & celebrated in obedience to Jesus

119. The Bible must play a formative role in the liturgy of the Eucharist/Lord's Supper

121. There is a Trinitarian pattern in the order of worship of the Eucharist/Lord's Supper

125. Christ is really present to his disciples in celebration of Eucharist/Lord's Supper

130. There is a strongly ethical & eschatological dimension to the Eucharist/Lord's Supper

Our discussion of the sacraments required that we attend to our terminology, which has differed not only between Baptists and Catholics but also within the Baptist communion. While early Baptists referred to Baptism and the Supper as "sacraments," later reactions against what some Baptists regarded as a problematic "sacramentalism" led some Baptists to eschew the language of "sacraments" in favor of "ordinances," the latter term employed in the sense of acts that Jesus instructed his followers to observe—though other Baptists have continued to call these "sacraments" in the sense of acts in which people encounter the gracious and transformative action of God. Our report therefore consistently employed the convention "sacraments/ordinances." Likewise, while some Baptists join Catholics in referring to the Supper as the Eucharist, other Baptists have resisted that term as associated with what they regard as a problematic "sacramentalism," preferring instead to call it the "Lord's Supper." We accordingly referenced this central meal of Christian worship as the "Eucharist/Lord's Supper" in our report.

Together we were able to affirm that whether they are called ordinances or sacraments, they are both symbolic (a typical Baptist affirmation that Catholics also affirm) and signs through which God acts graciously (a Catholic emphasis that Baptists are also able to embrace). Baptists have insisted on the necessity of personal faith as essential to baptism and the whole experience of salvation, but the Baptist delegation appreciated a Catholic insistence that God's gracious work in salvation must always be joined with faith. Our most noteworthy convergence was recognizing that for Baptists and Catholics alike, the same essential elements are intertwined: the believing faith and the sanctifying grace of God that belong to the whole journey of beginnings in the Christian life. Although these elements may occur in different chronologies in our respective practices, both include baptism, the flowering of personal faith, and full incorporation into the life of the church. It was also significant that even if we might not advance the same explanatory theories as to how Christ is present in the Eucharist/Lord's Supper, we do agree that in its celebration we experience the real and transformative presence of the Lord.

Mary as Model of Discipleship in the Communion of the Church

133. Mary has significant place in NT—witness to Christ, mother of Savior, called blessed

133. Beliefs about Mary should be rooted in, warranted by, & not contradicted by Scripture

135. Mary belongs to the Jewish people....Mary may be called "Daughter of Israel"

137. A number of Old Testament passages may be interpreted as referring to Mary

139. The Gospels present Mary as "hearer of the Word"—a disciple who heard, obeyed Word

140. Jesus conceived by Spirit, born of Virgin Mary—sign of divine origin & true humanity

143. Mary is properly named the Theotokos or "God-bearer"—safeguards identity of Christ

146. Mary has a special calling in plan of salvation, but also redeemed by Christ by grace

150. Mary is a model of discipleship in faithful listening and obedience to God's Word

154. Mary is not only a member, but also representative figure, of the Church of Christ

156. The Church prays with Mary and learns to pray like Mary in the communion of saints

159. The representations of Mary in particular cultures are subject to the gospel as norm

One might reasonably suppose that the place of Mary in the life of the Church is a matter of much disagreement between Baptists and Catholics. Our dialogue did surface significant disagreements, but it also led to convergences that may surprise many Baptists and Catholics. While Baptists have preferred to speak of Mary primarily in the biblical terms highlighted in our report, the Baptist delegation was able to draw on the Baptist theological tradition in affirming the appropriateness of the definition of Mary as *theotokos*, "the one who gives birth to God," by the Council of Ephesus in AD 431. To speak of Mary in these terms is to insist on the uniqueness of Jesus Christ as the human being in whom "all the fullness of God was pleased to dwell" (Colossians 1:19). We agreed that there is a uniqueness to Mary's own role in God's redeeming work through Christ, with Mary included among the redeemed. Together we commended Mary as a model disciple, not only for women but also for men as an example of the Christian way of life. We were not able to find agreement about the place of Mary in the intercession of the saints, though the Baptists were able to appreciate the Catholic rationale for Marian devotion in the life of prayer beyond the stereotypes many Baptists have had regarding these practices. But while the Baptists were not able to envision joining Catholics in addressing their petitions to Mary in asking for her intercession, we found that we could appeal together for a greater consciousness among Baptists as well as Catholics that whenever we pray, we are praying along with Mary in the communion of the saints.

The Ministry of Oversight (*Episkopē*) and Unity in the Life of the Church

> 162. Christ is the head of the Church, her founder, creator and cornerstone
>
> 162. The Church owes her whole existence to Christ, who is her "episkopos" (1 Pet 2:25)
>
> 162. Christ nourishes/sustains Church with Gospel & celebration of sacraments/ordinances
>
> 165. Episkope (oversight) is Christ's gift to Church to enable ministry of people of God
>
> 165. Christ calls whole people of God to share in his ministry as prophet, priest & king
>
> 165. The episkope of some is a gift of Christ to enable & equip body of Christ as a whole
>
> 168. Our differing patterns of episkope seek to be faithful to Scripture & apostolic trad
>
> 173. Episkope is exercised in personal, collegial and communal ways in the Church
>
> 176. Episkope primarily exercised in local church, but always in communion w/ wider Church

Chapter Two

> 179. Personal episkope is established by Christ for the good of the Church
>
> 182. One principal purpose of the ministry of episkope is the promotion of Christian unity
>
> 184. Jesus' prayer for unity (= both spiritual & visible) sets out vocation of all Christians
>
> 186. The unity of the Church reflects its apostolicity, expressed both by faith & ministry
>
> 186. Ministry is apostolic if it hands on apostolic faith & fulfills missionary mandate
>
> 200. Past failures of both Baptists & Catholics must be addressed with due repentance & appropriate action

Baptists and Catholics have certainly differed in their understandings of how God's provision of *episkopē*—the early Christian Greek term for the ministry of "oversight"—for the church should function in the structures of the Church and its leadership. Yet we did find agreement that our respective configurations of this ministry of oversight, for which both Baptists and Catholics appeal to the New Testament and the apostolic tradition for authoritative precedents, are rooted in the conviction that Christ is the ultimate overseer of the Church and that all members of the Church have a share in the exercise of Christ's ministry of oversight. We insisted together than one of the key tasks of the ministry of oversight is the promotion of Christian unity—not only spiritual unity, but a unity that must become ever more visible. Since all Christians share in this ministry of oversight, they also are responsible for seeking the unity that Christ himself prayed his followers would manifest in John 17. (In chapter 1, I called this responsibility the "ecumenist-hood of all believers.") We acknowledged together that if we are to make further progress toward a more visible form of unity, we must address the ways members of our communions have wronged one another in furthering our divisions and repent of them in concrete ways. (Chapter 4 of this book takes up the question of how Baptists and Catholics might engage in mutual efforts to heal the memories of the past wrongs against one another that have contributed to our present divisions.)

Receiving Baptist-Catholic Convergences

That Catholics and Baptists have been able to say these things about what they share in common is a truly remarkable ecumenical development. The report itself says those things much more fully than my Twitter summary of its agreements and the commentary on them I have provided in this chapter, with all the necessary qualifications and distinctions. I hope this radical abridgement of the Baptist-Catholic consensus expressed in *The Word of God in the Life of the Church* will pique the interest of readers of this book enough to encourage further reception of the report, starting with its reading. Reception is not necessarily agreement with the report's proposals about Baptist-Catholic consensus, but rather "the process by which worldwide communions, national churches and denominations, local parishes and congregations, and individual Christians become informed about, consider, and act upon the proposals and agreements that result from bilateral and multilateral ecumenical dialogue."[84]

While the Catholic Church has more formal structures for reception that include review and approval of ecumenical dialogue reports by the Congregation for the Doctrine of the Faith, which may include the identification of reservations about their convergences as well as commendation of them, the Baptist insistence on the freedom of local churches to follow the leadership of the Spirit in discerning what it means for them to be faithful communities of followers of Christ in their context means that Baptist reception of ecumenical convergences depends on the persuasion of Baptists of their importance to faithful Christian discipleship. But as the reception of ecumenical convergences by Catholic parishioners at the grassroots similarly depends on their persuasion that they should make a difference in how they relate to non-Catholic Christians in their communities, I suggest that the following Baptist perspective on how ecumenical reception might be persuasively encouraged has applicability to the ecumenical formation both of Catholic priests and of the laypersons for whose formation they are responsible.[85]

For Baptists, there are two principal locations for Baptist attention to ecumenical reception: institutions of theological education and local churches. Baptist theological educators, especially theologians and church historians, can introduce seminarians to the documents of multilateral dialogue and bilateral dialogues with Baptist participation. When reports or agreed statements from such dialogues are issued, Baptist-related seminaries, divinity schools, and universities can sponsor symposia on the documents and invite members of the communions that have been in conversation with Baptists as program personalities and guests.

Unless the institutions of theological education responsible for the educational preparation of Baptist ministers and their post-graduate continuing education take the lead in encouraging ecumenical reception, it is unlikely to happen in the local churches.

In local churches, pastors can study reports of ecumenical dialogues with Baptist participation as part of their ongoing ecumenical formation—in particular, this report from Phase II of the Baptist-Catholic dialogue. They can share them with their fellow Baptist pastors and with Catholic priests in their communities, and perhaps form local clergy discussion groups to work through the texts together. Pastors and priests can share these dialogue texts also with their church members, who have day-to-day relationships with members of other churches in which they live out visible Christian unity—and who may already be doing so in the context of their marriages and other family relationships. A Baptist-Catholic ecumenical dialogue report can easily serve as the basis of local church formation study groups, which ideally might also involve members of neighboring Baptist and Catholic churches. Reception of ecumenical convergences may involve recognition that a concretely altered relationship is possible between neighboring Baptist and Catholic churches, and perhaps with churches from other traditions in the community. On the basis of that recognition, it may be possible to formalize a local ecumenical covenant between neighboring churches, with members and ministers pledging to abide by it in their local relations.[86] All of these are opportunities for making persuasive cases for why ecumenical convergence should matter to the life of the church and the Christian life of its members.

Reading, discussing, and acting at the grassroots on the convergences of ecumenical dialogues such as those detailed in *The Word of God in the Life of the Church* are important expressions of ecumenical reception that contribute to making our unity more visible. But whether or not they ever have any awareness of such ecumenical developments, both Baptists and Catholics have already been engaging in an even more influential expression of ecumenical reception through the many ways both traditions have received gifts from other Christian traditions, including from one another's traditions, in ways that have enriched their own Baptist and Catholic patterns of faith and practice. The next chapter of this book turns to these practices of ecumenical gift reception.

Chapter Three

How Baptists Receive Gifts of Catholic (and catholic) Christianity

One might well expect a chapter on this topic to be painfully brief. Baptists have a reputation as the "problem children" of the modern ecumenical movement, and the stereotype is not without foundation. Baptists have been quick to declare other traditions to be false churches. John Smyth, co-founder of the earliest Baptist congregation in Amsterdam in 1609, not only rejected his baptism in the Church of England as a false baptism; Smyth concluded that no communion in Amsterdam was qualified as a true church to administer a true baptism—not even the believer-baptizing Mennonites with whom his group of English Separatist exiles had connections—so he baptized himself before baptizing the other members of his community.[87] Smyth soon regretted this action, for he decided that the Mennonites were a true church after all and sought to lead his congregation to be received into the Mennonite fellowship. Yet Smyth's se-baptism (the technical term for baptizing oneself) foreshadowed the refusal of many recent Baptists to embrace the biblical and theological rationale for mutual recognition of baptism commended by *Baptism, Eucharist and Ministry* (*BEM*).[88] Some Baptists have received *BEM* gladly. The Myanmar Baptist Convention, for example, publicly affirmed *BEM*'s call to refrain from re-baptizing those previously baptized as infants and commended the document to the Convention's churches as a study guide to help Baptists appreciate the significance of infant baptism in other communions.[89] Nevertheless, many Baptist congregations insist that candidates for church membership previously baptized as infants be re-baptized, and some Baptist churches with "open membership" policies do not explicitly recognize the validity of these infant baptisms, tending to receive such candidates on the basis of their profession of Christian faith instead.

Baptists also have been quick to divide among themselves whenever some Baptists become convinced that other Baptists have developed unbiblical patterns of faith and practice. This happened in the earliest community of Baptists in Amsterdam when a small group of its members led by Thomas Helwys insisted on the validity of their baptisms as administered by Smyth and in 1611 or 1612 returned to England to establish Baptist ecclesial life in their homeland.[90] Baptists ever since have tended to follow this fissiparous precedent in their local congregations, associations, national denominational organizations, and international Baptist bodies. Formal relations even with other Baptist denominational groups would be a considerable ecumenical stretch for some Baptists. It is true that a Baptist missionary to India named William Carey anticipated the modern ecumenical movement with his proposal in 1806 that "a general association of all denominations of Christians from the four quarters of the earth" meet each decade at the Cape of Good Hope,[91] and some Baptist denominations such as the Baptist Union of Great Britain and the American Baptist Churches, USA have been member bodies of the World Council of Churches since its inception. Nevertheless, Baptists in the main have not been the most enthusiastic supporters of Faith and Order ecumenism and its goal of "visible unity in one faith and one Eucharistic fellowship."[92]

When William Estep published a book on *Baptists and Christian Unity* in 1966, he cited rationales for Baptist wariness about conciliar ecumenism that included fears that visible unity would come at the cost of sacrificing what many Baptists would consider non-negotiables: the Baptist witness to believers' baptism as a disciple-making practice, the Baptist commitment to congregational ecclesiology as the local embodiment of a fully committed fellowship, Baptist objections to sacramental theologies of baptism and the Eucharist, the Baptist aversion to the use of creeds as coercive tests of fellowship or as substitutes for the authority of the Scriptures themselves, and Baptist advocacy for religious liberty safeguarded through the separation of church and state.[93] Such fears ultimately proved to be unfounded, and there are more nuanced Baptist expressions of each of these concerns that represent openings for greater degrees of Baptist convergence toward other traditions. But some older approaches to ecumenism did unfortunately give the strong impression that the cost of unity would be the surrender of some of the things held most dear by each church.

A newer paradigm called "receptive ecumenism" is gaining traction in the institutional expressions of the modern ecumenical movement. Receptive ecumenism is an approach to ecumenical dialogue according to which the communions in conversation with one another seek to identify the distinctive gifts that each tradition has to offer the other and which each could receive from the other with integrity.[94] Pope John Paul II gave expression to this paradigm for ecumenical engagement in *Ut Unum Sint*: "Dialogue is not simply an exchange of ideas. In some ways it is always an 'exchange of gifts'."[95] Some bilateral dialogues, such as the eighth series of dialogues between the Catholic Church and the World Methodist Council that issued its report in 2006, have worked toward concrete proposals for the exchange of ecclesial gifts.[96]

The exchange of ecclesial gifts in receptive ecumenism is mutual—each tradition has something to offer the others, and each has something it needs to receive. Yet as an international conference on receptive ecumenism held in 2006 defined the enterprise, "the primary emphasis is on learning rather than teaching.... [E]ach tradition takes responsibility for its own potential learning from others and is, in turn, willing to facilitate the learning of others as requested but without dictating terms and without making others' learning a precondition to attending to one's own."[97]

In many respects, receptive ecumenism is friendlier to Baptist participation in ecumenical engagement than some earlier models may have been. It assumes that because Baptists have been entrusted with a unique journey as a people of God, they possess distinctive gifts to be offered to the rest of the body of Christ. It also suggests the possibility that Baptists can incorporate the gifts of others into their own faith and practice without abandoning or distorting the gifts that already define the Baptist identity. Receptive ecumenism may also reveal Baptists as being much more receptive ecumenically than one might assume. Throughout their history and in their ecclesial life today, Baptists have received from the Catholic Church (upper-case "C") and from other expressions of the church catholic (lower-case "c") much that forms the core of Baptists' identity as Christians while also enriching their distinctive identity as Baptists.

Creedal and Confessional Gifts

The earliest Baptists received gifts from the English Separatists and Continental Anabaptists that helped distinguish these Free Churches or Believers' Churches from other Christian communities. Yet together with the Separatists and the Anabaptists, the early Baptists received from the pre-Reformation church the canon of Scripture and the core doctrines of orthodox Christianity in light of which they read this canon. These gifts combined with their unique historical experiences as a socially embodied community to form a quintessentially Baptist pattern of faith and practice, at the core of which is ancient catholicity. Early Baptist confessions of faith underscored Baptist indebtedness to these gifts with language and concepts drawn directly from the ecumenical creeds, Anabaptist confessions, the Anglican *Thirty-Nine Articles*, and the *Reformed Westminster Confession*.

Two important seventeenth-century Baptist confessions of faith illustrate this Baptist reception of the creedal and confessional gifts of the rest of the church. The *Second London Confession* was adopted by English Particular (Calvinistic) Baptists in 1677; the *Orthodox Creed* was issued by English General (Arminian) Baptists in 1678. In keeping with Baptist confessions that preceded them, these two confessions are replete with echoes of Nicaeno-Constantinopolitan Trinitarianism and Chalcedonian Christology. In addition,

Chapter Three

the *Second London Confession* calls the church "Catholick or universal," and the *Orthodox Creed* confesses faith in "one holy catholick church," the language of three of the four marks of the church in the Nicene Creed.[98] The most explicit reception of the ancient catholic tradition among Baptist confessions of faith takes place in the *Orthodox Creed*, which reproduces the text of the Apostles', Nicene, and Athanasian Creeds and encourages Baptists to receive and believe them. Much language of that article on the creeds is lifted almost verbatim from article 8 of the Anglican *Thirty-Nine Articles*.[99] Likewise, when the *Second London Confession* and the *Orthodox Creed* call the Church "catholic," they are indebted to chapter 25 of the *Westminster Confession*, which served as the model for the articles on the Church in both confessions.[100] Also derived from the *Westminster Confession* are the echoes of the Nicene Creed and the Chalcedonian definition in the Trinitarian and Christological portions of the *Second London Confession* and the *Orthodox Creed*.[101]

Liturgical Gifts

Baptists have also received patterns and practices of worship from other Christians. With other Christians, Baptists have received the overarching pattern of gathering for worship described by Justin Martyr in the middle of the second century: the act of gathering on Sunday, the reading of Scripture, a sermon, prayers, corporate responses, communion (when celebrated), and an offering.[102] Baptist worship in all its variety and the *ordo* of the Roman Mass alike reflect common reception of the essential elements of this ancient pattern of worship—as do other traditions from the Orthodox divine liturgy to Pentecostal and charismatic worship.

By the middle of the twentieth century, the singing of hymns had become such a typical feature of Baptist worship that British Baptist Ernest Payne could describe Baptist worship as "Scripture, prayer and sermon, interspersed with hymns."[103] With some adjustment for the advent of songs and choruses in "contemporary" worship, that description continues to describe the worship of many Baptist churches throughout the world. That was not always the case. The early General Baptists opposed congregational singing of all types on the grounds that such "set forms" hindered Spirit-led spontaneity. The early Particular Baptists followed the practice of other Calvinistic Dissenters in permitting congregational singing only in the form of metrical Psalms. The Baptist practice of hymn-singing seems to have been introduced by Benjamin Keach, a former General Baptist who became pastor of a Particular Baptist congregation in Southwark, England, in the 1670s. By 1700 many British Baptist congregations had adopted the practice, which spread rapidly over the next half-century. Baptist hymn-singing soon crossed the Atlantic, and in 1742 the Philadelphia Baptist Association issued a confession that added to the Second London Confession an article commending congregational hymn singing as a "divine institution."

Baptist hymnals are arguably the most significant ecumenical documents produced by Baptists. They implicitly recognize hymn writers from a wide variety of traditions throughout the history of the church as sisters and brothers in Christ by including their hymns alongside hymns by Baptists. Since many Baptist hymnals are produced by denominational commissions and published by denominational presses, this recognition carries some degree of official Baptist imprimatur. Baptist hymnals functioned as ecumenical documents in this sense from the inception of their use in Baptist churches. As Baptist liturgical theologian Christopher Ellis observes, "Despite the existence of Baptist hymn writers, there has never been a corpus of 'Baptist hymns' which has expressed or nourished an identity for the denomination in the way that the Wesleys' hymns have done for Methodists."[104] The most widely used hymnal among Baptists in Great Britain and North America by the late eighteenth and early nineteenth centuries was John Rippon's *Selection of Hymns*. Most hymns in the collection were not by Baptists, and in the preface Rippon wrote:

> It has given me no small pleasure, to unite, as far as I could, different Denominations of Ministers, and Christians on Earth, in the same noble Work, which shall for ever employ them above. . . . [H]ence it will be seen, that Churchmen and Dissenters, Watts and Tate, Wesley and Toplady, England and America sing Side by Side, and very often join in the same Triumph, using the same Words.[105]

Baptist hymnals have functioned as key facilitators of receptive ecumenism. They have helped Baptists to sing and receive the theologies of patristic and medieval Christianity, the Protestant Reformation, and a wide denominational variety of more recent hymn writers including post-Reformation Catholics as well as Protestants of all stripes. One significant counterintuitive feature of recent Baptist hymnals is their receptive retrieval of patristic hymnody. *The Baptist Hymnal* published in 1991 by the Southern

Baptist Convention (SBC), for example, is the hymnal used for the better part of the past two decades not only by most Southern Baptist congregations but also by those that now identify more closely with the Cooperative Baptist Fellowship (CBF). This hymnal included seven hymns with texts of patristic composition: *Let All Mortal Flesh Keep Silence* from the fifth-century *Liturgy of St. James*; *All Glory, Laud, and Honor* by Theodulph of Orleans; *The Day of Resurrection* by John of Damascus; *Of the Father's Love Begotten* by Prudentius; the fourth-century *Gloria Patri*; and the anonymous Latin hymns *Christ Is Made the Sure Foundation* and *O Christ, Our Hope, Our Heart's Desire*.[106] All but two were the gifts of John Mason Neale, an Anglo-Catholic priest and scholar of the nineteenth century whose translations of Greek and Latin patristic and medieval hymns greatly enriched the hymnody of the Church of England en route to their reception by Baptists and other communions. A new *Baptist Hymnal* published in 2008 by the SBC retained four of those seven patristic hymns.[107] The *Celebrating Grace Hymnal* closely associated with the CBF, published in 2010, includes six of the seven patristic hymns in the 1991 *Baptist Hymnal* and adds three others: the fifth-century Latin hymn *That Easter Day with Joy Was Bright*; *Come, Ye Faithful, Raise the Strain* by John of Damascus; and *Christ Be Near at Either Hand* from the *Breastplate* attributed to St. Patrick.[108] Beyond these patristic hymns, Baptists receive through their hymnals the gifts of Francis of Assisi and Teresa of Jesus, Martin Luther, the post-Reformation Roman Catholic author of *Fairest Lord Jesus* from the *Münster Gesangbuch*, the Methodist Charles Wesley, and more recently the Pentecostal pastor Jack Hayford, to name a few hymn writers whose ecclesial gifts Baptists have gladly received with their voices and hearts—even if not always aware of the hymns' denominational origins.

Baptists have benefited from the trans-denominational liturgical renewal of the late twentieth century, and today a growing number of Baptist congregations have incorporated other liturgical gifts from beyond the Baptist tradition into their worship: the full Christian year and the liturgical colors that accompany its seasons, the lectionary, the imposition of ashes on Ash Wednesday and processions with palm fronds at the start of Holy Week, and even incense and icons here and there. As examples of liturgical reception that defy Baptist stereotypes, I point to two communities in rather different contexts—one in the Southwestern United States, and one in the Republic of Georgia.

DaySpring Baptist Church in Waco, Texas, describes itself as "a Baptist Church in the contemplative tradition."[109] In elaborating this description, the church's website explains:

> DaySpring has an ecumenical spirit. Drawing on the rich heritage of the Great Tradition of 2000 years of Christian history, DaySpring stands on the shoulders of those who have come before. Our forefathers and foremothers are our teachers and our brothers and sisters. Enduring through centuries, the Apostles' Creed and Nicene Creeds articulate core Christian beliefs and witness to Christian hope as brief summaries of biblical teaching. We "pray" the Creeds together as part of our baptism services and on other occasions through the year.[110]

DaySpring's worship features the celebration of communion each Sunday and follows the seasons of the liturgical year: "The spiritual rhythm of the year traces the life of Christ and the life of the church through the liturgical seasons. Each has its own gifts to offer us." A section of its website is devoted to detailed explanations of the gifts offered by each of these seasons: Advent, Christmastide, Epiphany, Lent, Holy Week, Easter and the Great 50 Days, Pentecost, Ordinary Time, and Christ the King Sunday.[111] The order of service from Trinity Sunday in 2020 begins with an adaptation of the ancient Eucharistic dialogue between minister and congregation. The text that guides a time of silent congregational meditation is a prayer to the Eternal Trinity by Catherine of Siena, preceding the readings of the lectionary texts for the day, and the service concludes with the corporate recitation of the Apostles' Creed.[112] The church regularly incorporates the discipline of silence in its services of worship, with an explanation of this practice introduced with a quotation from Thomas Merton.[113]

The congregations of the Evangelical Baptist Church of Georgia represent a fascinating case study in Baptist receptive ecumenism that includes striking forms of liturgical as well as ecclesiological reception. In a culture that is historically Eastern Orthodox, the Evangelical Baptist Church of Georgia has maintained "belief in believer's baptism, autonomy of the local church, freedom of conscience and religious liberty,"[114] while adopting an ecclesial structure that is a hybrid of congregational and episcopal governance with a threefold ministry of bishops, presbyters,

79

and deacons. In this structure the local congregations are autonomous in relation to one another and to the structure of the Evangelical Baptist Church of Georgia, but they are presided over by a bishop, whose office is a "symbol of unity" with the "responsibility . . . to provide spiritual guidance to the whole church as prophet, preacher, and teacher of the Gospel."[115] The ministers of the Evangelical Baptist Church wear Orthodox vestments and employ the Orthodox use of the sign of the cross, incense, and icons in their worship services.[116] The Church sponsors monastic orders for men and women and a school of iconography. As their former archbishop puts it, they "technically should be considered a Reformed Orthodox Church. On the one hand," he says, "we are committed to the principles of the European Radical Reformation, and on the other hand we hold to our own Orthodox legacy."[117] In other words, they have received the gifts of the Orthodox tradition and incorporated them into their Baptist pattern of faith and practice.

Gifts of Theological Scholarship

Much Baptist receptive ecumenism is mediated by Baptist educational institutions. Baptist theological educators have long taught Baptist seminarians that the resources they need for the work of the ministry are not exclusively Baptist in origin. Baptist ministers thus routinely glean the riches of non-Baptist biblical scholarship in their sermon preparation. They learn in church history courses that the four-century-long Baptist tradition can be appreciated only as part of the whole history of the whole church. Significantly, a remarkable number of younger Baptist historians and historical theologians are now making patristics their specialization. Baptist ministers are enriched by the contemplation of systematic theologies written by theologians of other churches. They learn to incorporate practices of pastoral care forged in other traditions into their own approach to the care of souls. They are shown how to plan worship and craft programs of Christian education that weave the gifts of other Christians into the fabric of Baptist congregational life.

Gifts of Spiritual Practices

There is also a Baptist receptive ecumenism that belongs to the sphere of personal piety. Many younger Baptists have a keen interest in spirituality and are drawn to the practice of spiritual disciplines that originated in other communions. These same younger Baptists are taking up the practice of meditating on Scripture according to the pattern of *lectio divina*, walking labyrinths, and even using the sign of the cross as an embodied act of personal devotion and experimenting with praying the Rosary and using Orthodox chotkis to pray the Jesus Prayer.

Baptists have received the gifts of Catholics and other Christians through an ecumenism of the confession of faith, an ecumenism of the sanctuary and especially of the hymnal taken in hand therein, an ecumenism of the seminary classroom and pastor's study, and an ecumenism of personal devotion. They have received these gifts from the Church in its catholicity *along with* Catholics and other Christians and more directly *from* Catholics and other Christians in a contemporary convergence toward our common catholicity.

Chapter Three

Toward a More Intentional Baptist Receptive Ecumenism

One of the distinctive gifts of the Baptist tradition may be its unique capacity for receptive ecumenism. Lacking a foundational theologian like Martin Luther or John Calvin, a mandated liturgy, or a binding confession, Baptists and their churches are free to incorporate the gifts of others into their own faith and practice without ceasing to be Baptist—but this ought to be done more intentionally.

At a conference on receptive ecumenism in 2007, British Baptist theologian Paul Fiddes—co-chair of the Baptist delegation to Phase II and a member of the Baptist delegation to Phase III of the international Baptist-Catholic dialogue—identified four specific areas in which Baptists might more intentionally learn something from the wider church: tradition, episcopacy, infant baptism, and the visibility of the church.[118] Beyond the new Baptist appreciation for the coinherence of Scripture and tradition that surfaced in the current series of conversations between the Baptist World Alliance and the Pontifical Council for Promoting Christian Unity, Fiddes suggests that Baptists might intentionally extend the communal interpretation of Scripture that takes place within the local church to the church in its historic and contemporary catholicity. Furthermore, Baptists might incorporate the broad contours of the catholic tradition into their worship through "the more regular use of the creeds" as acts of worship that "celebrate God's drama" and "present the Trinity as the supreme meta-narrative." Regarding episcopacy, Fiddes sees potential for convergence between Anglican conceptions of the episcopate as a sign of apostolic succession and the Baptist practice of appointing trans-local or regional ministers, who may similarly serve as "a focus of unity and continuity" in the church. Concerning infant baptism, Fiddes proposes that Baptists might learn from this practice the recognition that God's grace is at work in the lives of very young children, that the faith of the church plays an important role in the formation of Christians, and that infant baptism may be regarded as a legitimate practice within a "whole process of initiation" or "journey of beginnings" (even if Baptists continue to baptize only believing disciples within their own communities). And in dialogue with the Eastern Orthodox tradition, Fiddes suggests that Baptists, who already affirm the visibility of the local church but typically regard the catholic or universal Church as the invisible community of all the redeemed of all the ages, might work toward thinking "in terms of a constant *becoming* visible of the whole catholic church." I heartily affirm these proposals for a more intentional receptive ecumenism among Baptists and add two of my own—which can apply to other Christian communions as well.

First, Baptists might take the reports and agreed statements from bilateral ecumenical dialogues in which Baptists have been involved as the basis of congregational study and grassroots ecumenical encounter with neighboring churches from the traditions with which we've been in dialogue. The Baptist World Alliance has held such dialogues with the World Alliance (now Communion) of Reformed Churches, the Catholic Church, the Lutheran World Federation, the Mennonite World Conference, the Anglican

Consultative Council, the World Methodist Council, and partially with the Ecumenical Patriarchate of the Orthodox Churches. The reports of these conversations recount the stories of the two communions in relation to one another, explain the things the two traditions can affirm together, and name the ongoing matters of disagreement that merit further conversation. Sometimes they propose practical steps that can be taken at the local level to enhance unity between the two communions. The bilateral dialogues accomplish little if they are not received at the local level, and local reception must begin with reading and discussing the reports within Baptist congregations and together with our local ecclesial neighbors. Such discussions can foster receptive ecumenism at the grassroots.

Second, Baptists might intentionally engage the more communal forms of theological and ethical deliberation exemplified by Catholic magisterial teaching, including the *Catechism of the Catholic Church*, the documents of Vatican II, papal encyclicals, and bishops' letters. The place to begin encouraging the consideration of these sources of Christian teaching is graduate/professional theological education. Baptist ministers have much to learn from Catholic processes of conciliar theological and ethical deliberation, even if they may not always agree with what these resources propose as Christian teaching. The communal consultation that funds these proposals has the capacity for transcending the subjectivity of the theological constructions and moral judgments of individual theologians and ethicists, and ought to be weighed accordingly—even if such weighing may result in heavily qualified reception among Baptists.

I do believe that my own Baptist tradition has been entrusted with gifts that the rest of the church needs in order to become fully catholic. These gifts include the Baptist zeal for guarding conscience from coercion by civil or ecclesiastical powers, the insistence that each person must embrace the faith personally and that baptism should normally be accompanied by such a commitment, and the emphasis on the mutuality of covenant responsibilities for doing the work of ministry among the members of the church and its leaders. We are able to offer these as ecclesial gifts only because of their relation to the gifts of catholic Christian identity we have received from the churches that preceded our 1609 origins. We have received the gifts of Catholics and other catholic Christians, and we must continue to do so if we are to help the church make progress toward its "visible unity in one faith and one Eucharistic fellowship." The next chapter of this book will address another task which Catholics and Baptists must undertake together if they are to progress further toward this ecumenical goal: the healing of memories of the ways our traditions have inflicted wounds upon one another that have deepened our divisions.

Chapter Four

Ecumenical Healing of Ecclesial Memories

The previous two phases of international Baptist-Catholic dialogue have touched upon memories of wounds suffered by Baptists and Catholics in relation to one another. The report from Phase I, *Summons to Witness to Christ in Today's World*, notes this among the "challenges to common witness":

> In certain traditionally Roman Catholic countries civil constitutions and laws enacted prior to the Second Vatican Council have not been changed to reflect the teaching of the Council. In some settings with a dominant Baptist majority the traditional Baptist stress on separation of church and state as a means to assure religious freedom has been weakened. Both groups need to exercise greater vigilance to ensure respect for religious liberty (§ 43).[119]

The implication is that in contexts in which one communion has existed as a religious minority where the other communion is politically or culturally established—in Catholic-dominated Latin American countries or in the Baptist-dominated American South, for example—members of each communion have suffered some infringement of religious liberty, though this recognition is not expressed in terms of an explicit confession of wrongdoing or a call to repentance. The report from Phase II, *The Word of God in the Life of the Church*, however, directly calls for repentance and concrete actions that embody repentance in two paragraphs of the penultimate section of the report on "The Ministry of Oversight (*Episkopè*) and Unity in the Life of the Church":

200. The historical failures of the past among both Baptists and Catholics must be addressed, with due repentance and appropriate action in the present.

201. The new situation created by the spirit of ecumenism invites all brothers and sisters in Christ to re-examine the past and, if appropriate, to revise some of the earlier stances taken by members of our communities. Many within both Christian communions wish to distance themselves from the negative judgments made of each other in the past. Historical failures have been acknowledged from the Catholic side, for instance by John Paul II in his encyclical on ecumenism *Ut unum sint* ('That they may be one') and on occasions such as the liturgy of reconciliation on the First Sunday of Lent during the Jubilee Year 2000. For their part, most contemporary Baptists wish to disassociate themselves from harsh names applied to the papacy by their ancestors in very different circumstances.[120]

Other international bilateral dialogues have addressed such historical failures revealed by a re-examination of the past as occasions for working toward the "healing of memories." When the joint commission for Phase III of the Baptist-Catholic dialogue during its second annual meeting in Rome in 2018 began planning in its final session for its 2019 focus on the challenges of common witness, the discussion surfaced the need to discuss possibilities for Baptists and Catholics to work toward the healing of memories. Members of the joint commission mentioned the precedent offered by the 2005-2008 dialogue between the Lutheran World Federation and Mennonite World Conference, the report from which is titled *Healing of Memories: Reconciling in Christ*.[121] It was decided that a brief paper on the Lutheran and Mennonite approach to the healing of memories could serve as a basis for discussion of how Baptists and Catholics might address the challenges to offering a common witness posed by historical failures in their relationships with one another. This chapter, which is based on the paper I presented to the Baptist-Catholic joint dialogue commission during its 2019 meeting, summarizes the background, findings, and proposals of the Lutheran-Mennonite *Healing of Memories* report, along with the efforts taken by both communions to act on its recommendations, and then suggests how Baptists and Catholics might approach the healing of memories in their own mutual relations.

The Healing of Memories in Catholic-Mennonite Dialogue

While the healing of memories was a central focus of the Lutheran-Mennonite dialogue and actions taken on its basis were widely reported, this was not the first time an international bilateral dialogue with Mennonite participation had addressed the need for the healing of memories. Nor was an explicit concern for the healing of memories original to ecumenical dialogue. Attention to the healing of memories had emerged as a religious accompaniment to the truth and reconciliation process that followed the end of the apartheid regime in South Africa; Healing of Memories Workshops held in South Africa beginning in 1995 were in 1998 extended to Rwanda, Ireland, and other international contexts.[122] Two years before the Lutherans and Mennonites began their formal dialogue in 2005, the Catholic Church and the Mennonite World Conference had wrapped up a six-year dialogue and published its report, *Called Together to Be Peacemakers*, which culminated in Part III, "Toward a Healing of Memories."[123] While the focus of the present paper is the paradigm for the ecumenical healing of memories offered by the Lutheran-Mennonite dialogue, a brief overview of the role of the healing of memories in the Catholic-Mennonite dialogue is warranted both by the participation of the Catholic Church in that dialogue and by the historical and theological connections between Mennonites and Baptists.

The expressed purpose of the Catholic-Mennonite dialogue "was to assist Mennonites and Catholics to overcome the consequences of almost five centuries of mutual isolation and hostility" and "to explore whether it is now possible to create a new atmosphere in which to meet each other," for "despite all that may still divide us, the ultimate identity of both is rooted in Jesus Christ" (§ 2). Part I, "Considering History Together" (§§ 23-68) recounts the attempt of the joint commission to re-read together three historical eras important to their ecclesial memories. First, they took a fresh look at the sixteenth-century rupture between Catholics and Anabaptists (§§ 38-52). They were able to recognize that theological difference over the practice of infant baptism and the rejection thereof in the practice of "believer's baptism" were greatly exacerbated by a relationship between church and state that no longer prevails (§ 40) and by inaccurate associations of all Anabaptists with the Peasants' War and the Münster Anabaptist revolt

(§ 39). Furthermore, they pointed out that while "Catholics never suffered any persecution at the hands of Mennonites," there were contexts in which Catholics too had for a time been persecuted religious minorities, particularly in England, Scandinavia, and the Netherlands, so that the ecclesial identity forged in persecution that has been an important feature of Mennonite ecclesiology could be appreciated in both Catholic and Mennonite rememberings of their stories. Second, a reconsideration of the Constantinian era that began in the fourth century (§§ 53-62), which the Anabaptist tradition had long conceived of as the "Constantinian Fall" of the church while Catholics had tended to interpret this era in terms of ecclesial continuity with what preceded it and a salutary Christianization of culture, led both traditions to "regret certain aspects of the Constantinian era" but to "recognize that some developments of the fourth and fifth centuries had roots in the early history of the church, and were in legitimate continuity with it" (§ 57). At the same time, they acknowledged that Mennonites were now becoming integrated with their societies, and that the Catholic Church since the Second Vatican Council and its Decree on Religious Liberty *Dignitatis Humanae* had moved beyond the Constantinian symbiosis and now "1) affirmed freedom of religion and conscience for all, 2) opposed coercion in matters of religion, and 3) sought from the state for itself and all communities of believers only freedom for individuals and communities in matters of religion" and "thus renounced any desire to have a predominant position in society and to be recognized as a state church" (§ 56). Third, "reviewing our respective images of the Middle Ages" led Catholics to see in the Middle Ages not only the positives of the Christian civilization of that era but also "the elements of violence, of conversion by force, of the links between the church and secular power, and of the dire effects of feudalism in medieval Christendom" (§ 64). This led Mennonites to recognize that the Middle Ages were not characterized only by aspects of spiritual decline, but also by movements of renewal in spirituality and discipleship that served as "the spiritual roots of the Anabaptist-Mennonite tradition" (§§ 65 and 67).

Part II, "Considering Theology Together" (§§ 69-189), reports on the engagement in theological dialogue in the present made possible by the foregoing reconsideration of the past. This most extensive section of the report parallels in many respects the entirety of the report from Phase II of the Baptist-Catholic bilateral, *The Word of God in the Life of the Church*. Besides their much-controverted respective perspectives on baptism and the Eucharist, Catholics and Mennonites engaged in substantial dialogue that revealed convergences as well as divergences regarding various aspects of ecclesiology, especially two: the unity of the church that belongs to the essence of the church in Catholic understanding, and the church's commitment to peace that belongs to the essence of the church in Mennonite understanding.

Two paragraphs in Part III emphasize the contribution of this mutual consideration of theology to the healing of memories:

> 207. Theological dialogue can contribute to healing of memories by assisting the dialogue partners to ascertain the degree to which they have continued to share

Chapter Four

the Christian faith despite centuries of separation. Mennonites and Catholics in this dialogue explained their own traditions to one another. This contributed to a deeper mutual understanding and to the discovery that we hold in common many basic aspects of the Christian faith and heritage. These shared elements, along with unresolved questions and disagreements, are outlined in Chapter II.

210. While recognizing that we hold basic convictions of faith in common, we have also identified significant differences that continue to divide us and thus require further dialogue. Nonetheless, and although we are not in full unity with one another, the substantial amount of the Apostolic faith which we realize today that we share, allows us as members of the Catholic and Mennonite delegations to see one another as brothers and sisters in Christ. We hope that others may have similar experiences, and that these may contribute to a healing of memories.

The healing of ecclesial memories was a principal aim of this dialogue from its inception (§ 190). The joint commission identified four requirements for the healing of memories. First, there must be a purification of memories through the mutual reconsideration of respective ecclesial histories (§§ 192-97), to which Part I was devoted. This reconsideration enabled them to discern not only in the Anabaptist tradition but also in the heritage of the Catholic Church in medieval ecclesiastical peace movements a common "Christian witness to peace and non-violence based on the Gospel" (§ 195). Second, there must be a "penitential spirit" (§§ 198-206), which the joint commission sought to embody by adopting the following common statement:

> 206. Together we acknowledge and regret that indifference, tension, and hostility between Catholics and Mennonites exist in some places today, and this for a variety of historical or contemporary reasons. Together we reject the use of any physical coercion or verbal abuse in situations of disagreement and we call on all Christians to do likewise. We commit ourselves to self-examination, dialogue, and interaction that manifest Jesus Christ's reconciling love, and we encourage our brothers and sisters everywhere to join us in this commitment.

Third, there must be a recognition of a shared Christian faith (§§ 207-10). This is the contribution of theological dialogue to the healing of memories. The joint commission concluded through this dialogue, as we saw previously, that "the substantial amount of the Apostolic faith which we realize today that we share, allows us as members of the Catholic and Mennonite delegations to see one another as brothers and sisters in Christ" (§ 210). And fourth, there must be an effort to foster new and improved relationships (§§ 211-14). The joint commission identified and commended already-existing examples of Catholic-Mennonite cooperation in various parts of the world (§ 213) and suggested possibilities for living more intentionally into a new pattern of Catholic-Mennonite relationships: "[A] review of history text books on each side, participation in the week of prayer

Chapter Four

for Christian unity, mutual engagement in missiological reflection, peace and justice initiatives, some programs of faith formation among our respective members, and 'get acquainted' visits between Catholic and Mennonite communities, locally and more widely" (§ 214).

The Healing of Memories in Lutheran-Mennonite Dialogue

The roots of the 2005-2008 dialogue between the Lutheran World Federation and Mennonite World Conference lie in the celebration by Lutherans of the 450th anniversary of the Augsburg Confession in 1980. Mennonite representatives were invited to participate in the Lutheran observances of this anniversary. But as the introduction to the report from that dialogue noted,

> The Mennonites, however, aware that the Augsburg Confession explicitly condemned the Anabaptists and their teachings, wondered whether or how they could celebrate their own condemnation, since they regarded the Anabaptists of the sixteenth century as their spiritual forebears. Most Lutherans, on the other hand, had little awareness of the condemnations of Anabaptists, their persecution and marginalization, or of the ongoing memories of this painful history still alive among Mennonites today.[124]

Since the condemnations of the Anabaptists in the Augsburg Confession are not quoted in full in the report, here are the condemnations both explicitly (regular type) and implicitly (italics) directed against the Anabaptists:

V. Condemned are the Anabaptists and others who teach that we obtain the Holy Spirit without the external word of the gospel through our own preparation, thoughts, and works.[125]

VIII. Likewise, although the Christian church is, properly speaking, nothing else than the assembly of all believers and saints, yet because in this life many false Christians, hypocrites and even public sinners remain among the righteous, the sacraments—even though administered by unrighteous priests—are efficacious all the same. . . . Condemned, therefore, are the Donatists and all others who hold a different view.[126]

IX. Rejected, therefore, are the Anabaptists who teach that the baptism of children is not right.[127]

XII. Rejected here are those who teach that whoever has once become righteous cannot fall again.[128]

XVI. Concerning civic affairs they teach that lawful civil ordinances are good works of God and that Christians are permitted to hold civil office, to work in law courts, to decide matters by imperial and other existing laws, to impose just punishments, to wage just war, to serve as soldiers, to make legal contracts, to hold property, to take an oath when required by magistrates, to take a wife, to be given in marriage. They condemn the Anabaptists who prohibit Christians from assuming such civil responsibilities.[129]

XVII. Rejected, therefore, are the Anabaptists who teach that the devils and condemned human beings will not suffer eternal torture and torment.[130]

Chapter Four

> *XXVII. Still others think that revenge is not right for Christians at all, even on the part of political authority.*[131]

Their qualms about these condemnations notwithstanding, the Mennonites graciously accepted the invitation to participate in the celebration, and the Lutheran World Federation issued a statement expressing regret for the history of suffering inflicted by the Augsburg Confession's condemnation of the Anabaptists. Soon national dialogues between Lutherans and Mennonites sprang up to address these wounds, first in France (1981-84), then in Germany (1989-92), and finally the United States (2001-04). The shared theological scholarship of these national dialogues paved the way for the international dialogue, for which plans began in earnest following a joint recommendation adopted by the Mennonite World Council Executive Committee and the Lutheran World Federation Standing Committee for Ecumenical Affairs at their meetings in July and September 2002. Their recommendation was to:

> Approve the establishment of an international study commission with the following mandate: Drawing upon the results of previous national dialogues in Germany, France, and the United States, the commission shall: a) Consider whether condemnations of Anabaptists articulated by the Augsburg Confession (1530) apply to Mennonite World Conference member churches and related churches, and b) Submit a report of the commission's conclusions to the governing bodies of the Mennonite World Conference and

the Lutheran World Federation for further action and with a view toward a possible official statement.[132]

After meeting annually from 2005 through 2008, the joint commission published in 2010 a hefty report—110 pages exclusive of appendices. The largest portion of it—52 pages—is devoted to "Telling the Sixteenth-Century Story Together: Lutheran Reformers and the Condemnation of Anabaptists."[133] It is an accessible summary of the historical scholarship in Reformation and Anabaptist studies that recontextualizes this story. It gives attention to the emergence in the 1520s of various groups that came to be associated with Anabaptism, including the Swiss Brethren, the Hutterites, and the Mennonites. It engages at length the early Lutheran responses to the Anabaptists, including the treatises written against them by Martin Luther and Philip Melanchthon as well as Johannes Brenz's legal contention that the application to the Anabaptists of Roman law prescribing capital punishment for heresy and sedition was misguided, and places these responses in the context of the political realities of the day. This substantial section also details the condemnations of the Anabaptists in the Augsburg Confession and explains their implications for the subsequent treatment of Anabaptists, along with a narration of the consequences experienced from the 1530s onward.

In this reframing of the Anabaptist condemnations, the report notes that "these statements were not intended primarily to reflect or refute the theological positions held by specific Anabaptist leaders" but "were meant to distance the reformers theologically and politically from a group with which their Roman opponents had falsely identified

Chapter Four

them and whose behavior could ... be construed as worthy of capital punishment" and that "some were even designed, indirectly, to accuse their Roman opponents of supporting Anabaptist positions."[134] Furthermore, the Reformers lacked firsthand knowledge of Anabaptist convictions, for there were few Anabaptists then present in Saxony, and the Anabaptists did not have wide access to the printing press as a means of disseminating their views.[135] In concluding the "Telling the Sixteenth-Century Story Together" section, the report observes that "although the condemnations themselves may seem to reflect theological differences and not political consequences, it is quite clear that from the very beginning the condemnations of Anabaptists were framed in the midst of political struggle and, from their very inception, entailed severe consequences for those labeled Anabaptists."[136] It insisted:

> In the common telling of the history of Lutherans and Mennonites, these results must be acknowledged and dealt with in the present. For Mennonites, the history of persecution has always remained an integral part of their identity; for Lutherans it is essential to rediscover the history of their complicity in such persecution in order to face it honestly today.[137]

Part 3 of the report, "Considering the Condemnations Today," first identifies the condemnations that no longer apply in light of what are now to be regarded as Lutheran misunderstandings or mischaracterizations of the Anabaptists: those in articles V, VIII, XII, XVII, and XXVII.[138] The remaining condemnations in IX and XVI, however, regard matters about which the dialogue revealed ongoing disagreements between Lutherans and Mennonites that may be addressed through ongoing theological dialogue today: baptism (article IX)[139] and the relation of the church to the political order (article XVI).[140] One result of this attention to baptism as a disagreement warranting further dialogue is the launch of a Catholic-Lutheran-Mennonite trilateral dialogue on baptism (2011-2017) that connected the conversations about baptism in the Lutheran-Mennonite bilateral with parallel discussions of baptismal theology in the Catholic-Mennonite dialogue; the report will be titled "Baptism and Incorporation into the Body of Christ, the Church."[141]

Part 4 turns to "Remembering the Past, Reconciling in Christ: Moving beyond Condemnations."[142] This concluding section insists that Mennonites and Catholics now recognize one another as Christians and in many contexts of the world have already engaged in "forms of bearing witness and being open to the witness of others" that include "common service projects, shared worship and even eucharistic fellowship."[143] It proposes that a process be envisioned by which the Lutheran World Federation might implement at the level of that Christian world communion what the Lutheran members of the joint commission had already done in asking forgiveness "for the harm that their forebears in the sixteenth century committed to Anabaptists, for forgetting or ignoring this persecution in the intervening centuries, and for all inappropriate, misleading and hurtful portraits of Anabaptists and Mennonites made by Lutheran authors, in both popular and academic publications, to the present day," and by which the Mennonite World Conference might plan to respond to such an act of confession and repentance, "with the goal of a mutual granting of forgiveness in a spirit of reconciliation and humility."[144] The Lutheran World Federation publicly issued an apology and asked forgiveness from representatives of the Mennonite World Conference at the assembly of the LWF in Stuttgart, Germany, on July 22, 2010. The representatives of the MWC publicly accepted the apology and offered forgiveness. Immediately after these actions, the leaders of the LWF and MWC led assembly participants in a procession to another location for a worship service devoted to repentance and healing, featuring the sharing of stories, music, and prayers from both Lutheran and Mennonite traditions.[145]

Implications for a Baptist-Catholic Healing of Memories

Baptists are not Anabaptists, strictly speaking, though the two denominational traditions do have an ecclesial family kinship, the precise nature of which has sometimes been the subject of debate among Baptist historians. Baptists originated in the early seventeenth century in the context of the later English Reformation as a development of Puritan Separatism; the first identifiably Baptist church was founded by a community of English Separatist expatriates in Amsterdam when in 1609 John Smyth baptized himself and then the other adult members of his congregation. They met in a bakery owned by a Mennonite, and when in the following year Smyth became convinced that the Mennonite community there was a true church, he sought to lead his congregation to unite with it. This led to the first Baptist church schism, with a portion of the church dissenting from Smyth's effort; this group ultimately returned to England under the leadership of Thomas Helwys and in 1611 or 1612 formed the first Baptist church on English soil in Spitalfields on the outskirts of London.[146] My point in this brief recounting of Baptist origins is to highlight the early connection with Mennonites, with whom Baptists ever since have had much in common, including the practice of "believer's baptism" and congregational church governance rooted in covenantal relationships. Both Baptists and Mennonites are expressions of what has been called the free church tradition,[147] the believer's church tradition,[148] and the lower-case "b" baptist tradition.[149] Thus, as Baptist theologian Tarmo Toom (an Estonian Baptist now teaching in the United States) mentions in a journal article on whether Baptists might be able to join the *Joint Declaration on the Doctrine of Justification* that was originally presented as a paper for the preliminary conversations that preceded Phase II of the Baptist-Catholic dialogue, Baptists have felt themselves included in the condemnations originally directed against Anabaptists, and this became an issue addressed in the international dialogue between the Baptist World Alliance and the Lutheran World Federation.[150] Therefore, attention to the healing of memories in the Lutheran-Mennonite dialogue does have important implications for Baptists as well in relationship to some of their ecumenical dialogue partners.

While the Lutheran-Mennonite dialogue report was not structured in precisely the same way as the Catholic-Mennonite report, it is evident that the former has attended to the four requirements for the healing of memories identified by the latter: (1) a purification of memories through the mutual reconsideration of respective ecclesial histories; (2) a penitential spirit; (3) a recognition of a shared Christian faith; and (4) an effort to foster new and improved relationships. The three phases of the Baptist-Catholic international dialogue have also devoted attention to these four requirements. While the Baptist-Catholic dialogue has not engaged in the same kind of sustained mutual historical reconsiderations that have featured prominently in the Catholic-Mennonite and Lutheran-Mennonite dialogues, aspects of Phase I and Phase II did explore dimensions of our communions' respective histories in relationship to one another, as did Phase III's attention to more recent histories of Baptist-Catholic relationships in particular contexts in the focus of the 2018 meeting in Rome on the "Contexts of Common Witness." All three phases have been approached with a penitential spirit, reflected in the sections of the reports *Summons to Witness to Christ in Today's World* and *The Word of God in the Life of the Church* quoted in the opening of this chapter[151] and in our attention during the 2019 meeting in Warsaw to "Challenges to Common Witness" that may call for the healing of ecclesial memories. Phase I recognized among Baptists and Catholics a shared Christological faith, and Phase II extensively documented a rich and sometimes surprising degree of convergence in a shared faith, articulated in the bold print common affirmations of the report from that phase of dialogue. Efforts to foster new and improved relationships may well be envisioned as a result of the discussion during Phase III—Year 3 of attention to the healing of memories in specific contexts; the focus of Phase III—Year 4 on "Forms of Common Witness" may propose concrete actions of common witness that can embody new and improved relationships.

It may be that the expressed intention of the joint commission for Phase III of the Baptist-Catholic dialogue to craft a report in such a way as to facilitate broad reception and to accompany the report with a study guide and other multimedia materials can offer opportunities for ensuring that this phase of dialogue explicitly highlights the four aforementioned requirements for the healing of memories. With regard to the purification of memories through the mutual reconsideration of respective ecclesial histories, the report could have a section that presents an honest narration of a past that in various contexts has been sullied by mutual hostility, but it could also note, as did the Catholic-Mennonite joint commission, that in the history of their respective ecclesial journeys in England both Baptists and Catholics share the experience of having been persecuted religious minorities at the hands of an Anglican alliance of church and state. In this connection, the report could also emphasize that having had such experiences in our histories strengthens the current mutual Baptist and Catholic commitments to safeguarding religious liberty for all persons.

With regard to cultivating a penitential spirit, the report could acknowledge that members of both communions have sometimes failed to safeguard the religious liberty of all persons in contexts in which one tradition is in the majority and the other tradition is in the minority, and not only where there is a state establishment of a particular expression of Christian religion, for the cultural establishment of religion can be a powerful and even dangerous form of establishment that sometimes does not foster the liberty of religious minorities. Particular examples of failures in safeguarding the religious liberty of all persons can be named. While the experiences of Baptists in Latin American countries would immediately come to mind for some readers of the report, Baptist failures may be named as well. For example, in Nagaland in India, where Baptists comprise an overwhelming majority of the population, the Anatanger Village Council in 1991 prohibited the foundation of churches that were not Baptist, and in 2010 villagers tore down a Catholic church in an incident that was widely reported by the media.[152]

Not unrelated to a penitential spirit as a requirement for the healing of memories is the need for an explicit recognition of a shared Christian faith. It is undeniable that earlier in their respective histories, there were members of both communions who did not regard the members of the other communion as Christians. But the report from Phase I clearly reflected a recognition of one another as Christians, and the report from Phase II provided thorough documentation of the shared faith of Baptists and Catholics. Baptists and Catholics should say clearly, once again, that they regard one another as sisters and brothers in Christ. There has been a long history of Baptist missions in predominantly Catholic countries that were sometimes motivated by the belief that Catholics were not really Christians; and some Baptists have been led to think that Catholics were going back on Vatican II and regarding them as non-Christians because of certain ways of interpreting the "Declaration *'Dominus Iesus'* On the Unicity and Salvific Universality of Jesus Christ and the Church," issued in 2000 by the Congregation for the Doctrine of the

Faith, as well as the 2007 document "Responses to Some Questions Regarding Certain Aspects of the Doctrine of the Church."[153] After such mutual disapprovals, Baptists and Catholics need to affirm unambiguously their regard for one another as fellow Christians who have a shared faith. (It should be noted that those documents may be understood in less exclusionary ways as internal guidance about how Catholics should think about the nature of the church in Catholic understanding.)

Finally, Phase III—Year 4 will offer an opportunity for exploring more directly how Baptists and Catholics might foster new and improved relationships in embodying the healing of memories by imagining the forms that bearing witness to Christ together might assume—especially at the local level, where members of Baptist congregations and Catholic parishes may have very specific memories that need healing on the way to forging new ecumenical relationships that seek the good of the cities they inhabit. In doing so, the joint commission and the local communities that receive their work will be making good the hopes that their predecessors in Phase I of the dialogue expressed in the concluding paragraph of the report they issued in 1988:

> 58. Conversations between Baptists and Roman Catholics will not lead in the near future to full communion between our two bodies. This fact, however, should not prevent the framing of concrete ways to witness together at the present time. It will be helpful to think of several different levels—international, national, regional, and local—in which Catholics and Baptists could speak or act in concert. Such coopera-

tion is already taking place in a variety of ways: translation of the Scriptures into indigenous languages, theological education, common concern and shared help in confronting famine and other natural disasters, health care for the underprivileged, advocacy of human rights and religious liberty, working for peace and justice, and strengthening of the family. Baptists and Catholics could enhance their common witness by speaking and acting together more in these and other areas. A whole row of issues vital to the survival of humankind lies before us. The prayer of Jesus, "that they may all be one; even as thou, Father, are in me and I in thee, that they also may be in us, so that the world may believe that thou hast sent me" (Jn 17:21), has given a sense of urgency to our conversations. We testify that in all sessions during the past five years there has been a spirit of mutual respect and growing understanding. We have sought the guidance of the Lord of the church and give honor and glory to him for the presence and guidance of the Holy Spirit. We pray that God, who has begun this good work in us, may bring it to completion (cf. Phil 1:6).[154]

The next chapter of this book turns from how Baptists and Catholics might address painful aspects of their shared past to a painful dimension of their mutual relations in the present: the visible manifestation of their divisions in their current inability to share the Eucharistic table with one another.

Chapter Five

The Cruciformity of Communion

Since 1996, a small group of Baptist theologians in the United States from the membership of the National Association of Baptist Professors of Religion known as its "Region-at-Large" has been meeting jointly with the annual convention of the College Theology Society, an organization of predominantly Catholic college and university professors of theological and religious studies.[155] During each year's meeting we share in two common worship services: a Friday evening prayer service jointly led by Baptist and Catholic participants, and a Saturday evening Catholic Mass celebrated by a local priest. Because as Baptists we are not in communion with the bishop of Rome and because we have what Catholicism regards as an insufficiently orthodox understanding of what happens in the Eucharist, the Baptist theologians are not permitted to receive the Eucharist during the Mass. Instead we proceed to the altar with arms crossed in front of our chests to indicate that we wish to receive a blessing from the priest at the altar in place of bread and wine. Conversely, if our Catholic colleagues were to attend a Baptist worship service that celebrated the Lord's Supper, Catholic canon law would not permit them to receive communion with us, for in Catholic understanding our celebrations of the Supper are not truly the Eucharist. All of us gathered for worship at these meetings, Catholics as well as Baptists, grieve the divisions manifested publicly in our separation at the Lord's Table, sometimes with visible tears, even while rejoicing that we are able to participate together in other acts of worship during the Mass. In these experiences of the brokenness of the body of Christ, we are reminded that the quest for Christian unity is a cruciform practice in which Christ suffers the brokenness of his body and the divided members of his body enter into Christ's own sufferings for the sake of our oneness.

This is the background for a homily that I preached during the Friday evening prayer service of the 2017 joint meeting of the College Theology Society and the National Association of Baptist Professors of Religion Region-at-Large at Salve Regina University in Newport, Rhode Island. The Gospel Lesson for the Divine Office of Evening Prayer on June 2, 2017 was John 21:15-19; in the sanctoral cycle, June 2 was the Feast of Saints Marcellinus and Peter, Martyrs. The following is the text of the homily I preached on that occasion.

Feeding Christ's Lambs as Catholic and Baptist Theologians

In the name of the Father, and of the Son, and of the Holy Spirit, Amen.

Our lesson from John's gospel is significant—significant in more ways than one. But its significance isn't necessarily in the exegetical details. Some interpreters find significance in the different Greek verbs for loving in the dialogue between Jesus and Peter, and in the varied language for feeding and tending and lambs and sheep, but that's not what seems most significant here. I'm convinced by the commentators who contend that these words function synonymously, and the message of these words is this: the one who loves Jesus will take good care of the people who belong to Jesus.

It's significant in light of the nature of our gathering that Peter in particular is the one who's told this, that Peter in particular must express his love for Jesus by taking good care of the people who belong to Jesus. We are Catholic theologians and Baptist theologians, and it goes without saying that we have differing perspectives on the question of Petrine primacy (and some of those differences may be with each other *within* our respective communions!). But it's not a uniquely Catholic position that here and elsewhere in the New Testament Jesus is commissioning Peter to a distinctive role of leadership in the church. Many Protestants, Baptists among them, have been glad to take up Pope John Paul II's invitation to engage in a "patient and fraternal dialogue" about how the Petrine office might serve the whole church.[156] But the patristic interpreters of this text didn't relate Jesus' charge to Peter to feed and tend sheep and lambs to the question of primacy. For them, this text was about the bishop's responsibility to serve the church through pastoral care, which included not only the ministerial practices of presence and comfort and counsel, but also catechesis—teaching. Not all of us are clergy, but as Catholic and Baptist theologians we do have a certain function as *doctores ecclesiae*, teachers of the church, in our varied institutional contexts.

In that connection, in relation to our shared work as teachers of theology, doing our own work of feeding Christ's sheep, there's something significant about where

Jesus says the task of feeding his sheep will take Peter. And that brings us to the literally significant language in our text. Jesus says to Peter, "'When you were younger, you used to dress yourself and go where you wanted; but when you grow old, you will stretch out your hands, and someone else will dress you and lead you where you do not want to go.' He said this *signifying* by what kind of death he would glorify God" (John 21:19, emphasis added). In this Gospel full of signs, surely this is the oldest reference in Christian literature to that which symbolizes the cross—in this case, hands outstretched in cruciform posture signifying a death like Christ's death. There's no sign more symbolic of the essence of the Christian life than the sign of the cross. I began this meditation with the ancient practice of the sign of the cross, first attested by Tertullian but no doubt practiced long before. Many of the earliest symbols in Christian art signified the cross—Christ as the Good Shepherd who gives his life for the sheep, carrying a sheep across the shoulders as if the beam of a cross; the anchor; the chi-rho symbol. Perhaps the earliest was the orant. The orant was originally a figure of a pagan priest with arms outstretched in prayer, but Christians repurposed it as a figure whose very posture in prayer is cruciform, imagining the life of prayer as one of the ways we take up our cross and follow Jesus.

The New Testament offers us two overarching paradigms of the Christian life—the cross and the resurrection. We're almost through our seventh week of celebrating resurrection. But at the end of the final week of Eastertide, it's appropriate that we be reminded that the dominant paradigm for the Christian life, this side of our own resurrection, is the cross. Today the sanctoral reminds us of that. June 2 is a feast day commemorating two early fourth-century martyrs, Saint Marcellinus, a priest, and Saint Peter the Exorcist. We know little about them, besides their beheading in Rome during the persecution under Diocletian and the traditional location of their tomb in the Roman catacombs that bear their name. But they're familiar to many because they're named among the martyrs invoked in Eucharistic Prayer I in the Missal, just before Felicity and Perpetua.

What might it mean for our vocations as theologians to be cruciform? How might the martyrdoms of St. Peter the Apostle and Saints Marcellinus and Peter the Exorcist serve as examples for the way we take good care of the people who belong to Jesus? How might we deny ourselves and take up our cross and follow Jesus in our teaching, in our research and writing, in our various forms of service to both academy and church? Are we willing for our theological vocation to lead us where we do not want to go, stretching out our arms in following our crucified Lord for the sake of the other, in a world that seems more and more averse to welcoming the other?

With very specific application: what might it mean for us to take up our cross and follow Jesus, to be led where we may not want to go, in taking on the brokenness that Jesus continues to suffer over the brokenness of his body—the brokenness that *we* have inflicted on Jesus through the divisions that we've inflicted on one another, the body of Christ? Tomorrow we'll experience that brokenness at the Eucharistic table that we will not share. And so will Jesus. As my Baptist theologian friend Curtis Freeman, who's here with us, said to me earlier this week, if anything's going to change about that, it will have to be the church's theologians who insist on raising the question and challenging our failures in working toward one Eucharistic fellowship. Might that be one way we can take up our cross and follow Jesus in our teaching vocations, so that Jesus' lambs might be fed? If we are reconciled to God in one body through the cross, as the writer of Ephesians suggests (Eph 2:16), taking up the cross ourselves is how we participate in the reconciling, one-body-making work of God. The cruciformity of the Christian life is an ecumenically shared conviction, and it's an ecumenically shared set of practices. If we love Jesus, we will take good care of the people who belong to Jesus by teaching these things and practicing these things, that together we might join God in God's reconciling, one-body-making work in the world. May it be so, O God, through Jesus Christ our Lord, who lives and reigns with you in the unity of the Holy Spirit, one God, for ever and ever. Amen.

Can Catholics and Baptists Share Communion?

The following year, we gathered again for the 2018 joint meeting of the College Theology Society and the National Association of Baptist Professors of Religion Region-at-Large at Saint Catherine University, St. Paul, Minnesota. At that meeting one of the College Theology Society's program units, the Evangelical Catholics and Catholic Evangelicals Consultation, devoted a panel session to the question "Can Catholics and Baptists Share Communion Without Breaking the Rules?"[157] Baptist theologian Curtis Freeman (Duke Divinity School) presented a lead paper proposing an answer to that question in light of the thought of the late Baptist theologian James Wm. McClendon, Jr.—one of the driving forces behind the launching of the collaboration between the two organizations—and Freeman's reading of Catholic texts allowing for intercommunion in certain exceptional circumstances. Freeman began by telling this story about McClendon and the Mass at the first joint CTS/NABPR meeting at the University of Dayton in 1996:

> On Saturday evening of that CTS convention in Dayton, we found ourselves attending Mass. As we Baptists made our way forward to the altar, one by one we crossed our arms signaling that we wished to receive a blessing rather than asking to be communed. Though we lacked any knowledge of canon law, we understood (or at least we thought we understood) enough to know that Protestants and Catholics do not intercommune. But when McClendon came forward, instead of crossing his arms, he held out his hands, and received the elements. Afterward, I said, "Jim, you know the rules." He nodded, and then said with a playful tone, "Some rules were meant to be broken."[158]

Freeman went on first to explain McClendon's understanding of the "rules" that govern the Christian practice of communion, which reflected the influence of philosopher Ludwig Wittgenstein's concept of language-games and the rules that govern them:[159] some rules constitute a practice, so that to break them is to engage in some other practice, while other rules have the status of adaptable general principles. In some expressions of the Baptist tradition, baptism according to the "biblical pattern" of baptism by immersion following an experience of personal faith in Christ is a constitutive rule for the practice of the Lord's Supper, which is therefore restricted to church members who have been baptized according to this biblical pattern. These are "closed communion" Baptists. Other Baptists regard faith in Christ, rather than a particular mode of baptism or chronological relationship of baptism to personal faith, as a constitutive rule along with other essentials such as Jesus' words of institution. These are "open communion" Baptists, with McClendon among their number. "So," Freeman said, "from the standpoint of the Baptist rules of open communion, McClendon's intercommunion at a Catholic Eucharist did not break the rules, nor would it break the rules of Baptist communion practice for other Baptists to share in the breaking of bread with Catholics at the Lord's table."[160]

But what about the Catholic rules? Freeman pointed to possible openings for an intercommunion of Baptists with Catholics in the Vatican II Decree on Ecumenism *Unitatis Redintegratio* (1964) § 8 and the *Ecumenical Directory* issued by the Pontifical Council for Promoting Christian Unity in two parts in 1967 and 1970. The *Ecumenical Directory* set forth four conditions for the admission of Protestants to a Catholic Eucharistic table: (1) a lack of access to a minister in their own tradition, (2) a voluntary request for the sacrament, (3) a Eucharistic faith consistent with that of the Catholic Church, and (4) a "right disposition," with other exceptional cases referred to the judgment of local bishops. Freeman noted also the clarifications offered by a 1972 "Instruction" and a 1973 "Note" on the interpretation and applications of these conditions, as well as in the update of the *Ecumenical Directory* issued in 1993 as the *Directory for the Application of Principles and Norms on Ecumenism*. These subsequent clarifications slightly "tighten the rules and restrict the possibilities of exceptional communion of non-Catholic Christians."[161] After surveying the interpretations of several Catholic theologians with varying degrees of openness toward widening these openings for intercommunion under certain circumstances, Freeman argued that Baptist theologians attending Mass during CTS conventions might meet the conditions for intercommunion according to the Catholic rules (including the condition of "serious spiritual need" specified in the 1972 "Instruction") and suggested that requests for the admission of Baptists to the Eucharist might be made to bishops of dioceses where the annual conventions are held in advance of the meetings. He also proposed that the Baptists might include a celebration of communion during the Friday evening prayer services and invite Catholics to commune while noting that this would not be a valid Eucharist according to Catholic understanding.

A panel of Catholic and Baptist theologians then offered responses to Freeman's paper and added their own perspectives on the prospect of Baptist-Catholic intercommunion. Catholic theologian Timothy Brunk (Villanova University) said of Freeman's rationale for an exceptional intercommunion of Baptists attending CTS meetings, "I agree with this line of thinking in general, but I am not sure that the 'serious spiritual need' of 1972 [in the "Instruction"] will be of assistance."[162] Brunk mentioned the 2018 decision of German bishops to authorize communion in certain circumstances for Lutherans who are married to Catholics, but noted that "[t]he German bishops are addressing situations where a Catholic and a Lutheran are joined in the bond of sacramental marriage, not joint attendees at theological conferences"[163] before concluding with the suggestion that further attention to what constitutes "spiritual need" may be the way forward for now. Baptist theologian Philip E. Thompson (Sioux Falls Seminary) expressed reservations about inviting Catholic colleagues to commune at a Baptist celebration of the Eucharist, for "[r]ather than inviting Baptists to share what Catholics believe is the full sacramental sharing with the Lord, it would ask Catholics to share in what is according to Catholic teaching a deficient, defective one."[164] Furthermore, while an ordained Baptist theologian celebrating the Eucharist in a service at a CTS convention might hold an understanding of the sacramentality of the Supper more in keeping with a Catholic account of it, the same could not be said about Baptist churches in which Catholics might contemplate communing. Thompson invited us to continue thinking about the rules of Eucharistic sharing not merely as what leaves us with the interim option of Avery Cardinal Dulles's "penitential abstention" mentioned in Freeman's paper, but as "creating metaphorical space within which virtue is formed"—namely, the Christian virtue of patience that has particular relevance for ecumenical endeavors.[165]

Catholic theologian Sandra Yocum (University of Dayton), like Freeman and Thompson a participant in the joint CTS/NABPR gatherings for over two decades, likewise voiced the hope that there might be a path leading to Catholic-Baptist intercommunion along with the lament that the rules have not yet made this possible. She pointed to the connection between the very concept of rules and the monastic tradition of a "Rule" that provides guidance for a community of followers of Christ who commit themselves to Christ and one another to follow together his Way, such as the *Rule of St. Benedict* that has provided guidance for communities that aspire to "share in the sufferings of Christ," and asked:

> So, is there any way in which our participation in intercommunion might bear some semblance to Benedict's monks following the Rule to which they are committed and yet do not fully embody? Is there any way in which a deeply intentional practice of intercommunion in particular settings such as the annual gathering of members of the College Theology Society and those of the NABPR might be a witness to the rules around intercommunion, in particular of that profound spiritual need for a foretaste, however fleeting, of the fullness of life by communion, which is Christ's Body?[166]

Baptist theologian Derek Hatch (then at Howard Payne University, now at Georgetown College) articulated a series of questions as contributions to our ongoing discussion of the possibilities of and obstacles to this limited form of shared Eucharistic communion between

Baptists and Catholics: Do we hope to obtain permission for a singular observance of shared communion, or do we wish to establish it as an ongoing practice? Would such a request create conflict between local bishops and the College Theology Society that serves the Catholic Church through the work of religious education in college and university settings? If we were successful in securing intercommunion in Masses at CTS conventions as an ongoing practice, would it still be considered an "extraordinary" communion? In the meantime, does Baptist reception of a blessing instead of the Eucharist have its own ecumenical contribution to make? Might one of these contributions be a witness by these Baptists to a recognition that the church of Jesus Christ is present in the Catholic Church in which they cannot currently commune? Would the realization of intercommunion in this setting have any implications for the life of the Baptist churches to which these Baptist theologians belong?[167]

A Eucharistically-Malnourished Baptist's Desire for Intercommunion

My contribution to the panel, which was published along with the other contributions as a theological roundtable on "Shared Communion" in *Horizons*, the journal of the College Theology Society, is adapted below in the next section of this chapter on the cruciformity of the quest for the full communion of Baptists and Catholics at the Eucharistic table.[168]

In a homily based on a Gospel lesson from John 21 that I delivered during our Friday joint evening prayer service for the 2017 annual convention at Salve Regina University I asked this by way of very specific application:

> What might it mean for us to take up our cross and follow Jesus, to be led where we may not want to go, in taking on the brokenness that Jesus continues to suffer over the brokenness of his body—the brokenness that *we* have inflicted on Jesus through the divisions that we've inflicted on one another, the body of Christ? Tomorrow we'll experience that brokenness at the Eucharistic table that we will not share. And so will Jesus. As my Baptist theologian friend Curtis Freeman said to me earlier this week, if anything's going to change about that, it will have to be the church's theologians who insist on raising the question and challenging our failures in working toward one Eucharistic fellowship. Might that be one way we can take up our cross and follow Jesus in our teaching vocations, so that Jesus' lambs might be fed?

While I'm not claiming credit for this year's panel session devoted to the question of intercommunion in the context of College Theology Society conventions with Baptist participation, I'm deeply gratified that we as the church's theologians, Baptist and Catholic, are now raising the question in this manner, and that Curtis has made clear for us what the ground rules seem to be for playing the hypothetical game of Baptist-Catholic intercommunion at a CTS meeting. I have nothing to add to his spot-on summary of the Baptist "rules" for open communion and the Catholic "rules" for currently exceptional intercommunion articulated in the documents he's cited.

Chapter Five

In my years attending CTS, I've been content to follow Dulles's commendation of penitent abstention noted by Freeman,[169] understanding it as a painful motivation to work toward a unity we don't currently have. I've found deeply meaningful other acts of worship during the Mass in which we are able to embody our unity—our common confession of the apostolic faith in creedal recitation, something I don't always get to do in Baptist worship;[170] the singing of hymnody that often turns out to be shared between our traditions;[171] the passing of the peace; our hearing together of the Word of God that comes through Scripture, which has a sacramentality to it in which we mutually participate; the sign of the cross, which in this context I'm able to make without the slightest bit of self-consciousness or worry about being scorned as a Papist by my Baptist co-religionists.[172] But Curtis Freeman's paper has made me considerably less content for us to maintain the *status quo ante*.

I've previously experienced a Catholic-Baptist intercommunion individually—when I was doing a year of graduate studies in patristics at The Catholic University of America during the 1994-95 academic year. A couple of my fellow students were preparing for the priesthood as Eastern Rite Maronites, and they invited me to join them for Mass on the Feast of the Holy Cross at Our Lady of Lebanon Maronite Church in Northwest Washington, DC across the street from the original campus of Walter Reed Hospital, where the Maronite bishop was to be the celebrant. At this stage in my acquaintance with proper decorum for participating in Catholic worship as a non-

Catholic, I didn't yet know about the practice of crossing my arms to receive a blessing, though I did know that according to the rules I was not supposed to receive communion, so when the time came for the Eucharist I simply stepped into the aisle to let my friends walk forward and return to my seat. But though they knew I was Baptist, they motioned me toward the altar and said, "No, you should go." I told them that I shouldn't, since I wasn't Catholic, but by this time the bishop noticed what was happening and started gesturing for me to come forward. So I did, and I received communion from him—possibly against the rules. But I was separated from my usual Eucharistic community for an academic year, and while I did attend regularly two Baptist churches in Washington and my church in Texas on trips home during that year, the infrequency of typical Baptist observance of the Lord's Supper—for some churches, as seldom as four times a year, and not necessarily on the same quarterly schedule—meant that I never managed to be in the right Baptist church at the right time to commune. Thus, I arguably met that condition, and the bishop did invite me—though he didn't know anything about my faith or intention.

As someone who now as an ordained minister working in theological education occasionally preaches and teaches in other churches than my own congregation on Sunday, this sometimes means that now I go long stretches without receiving the Eucharist. I'm chronically Eucharistically malnourished. But I can count on spiritual food on which I might feed being available in the Saturday Mass at our CTS conventions—available, and yet held just beyond the reach of me and my fellow Baptists, whom I suspect are likewise malnourished. We desire this food, with what I believe is a right faith and right intention, in a circumstance in which it's unlikely that we can easily find a Baptist church that can feed us the Supper during our Sunday morning schedule. (I point out that when we met in Newport, Rhode Island in 2017, some of us departed our convention early on Sunday morning to worship at the First Baptist Church in America in Providence—and there was no communion that day). Will this food always remain just beyond our reach? I believe it's time for us to ask to be fed. Asking first is our first step toward communing according to the rules.

In the meantime, I wonder if there's another baby step that could be taken toward intercommunion, but it requires a clarification of the Catholic rules regarding concelebration. Is it possible for us to have two Eucharists simultaneously, in the same space, but separately at the Saturday Mass—with one of the ordained Baptists consecrating and administering communion to the Baptists? Is this possible, according to the rules? I suggest this in part not because it would make it easier for us to have communion, but because it would make our division at the table even more starkly obvious than proceeding toward the priest, blending in line with our Catholic sisters and brothers, but with arms crossed for a blessing instead of the bread and wine.

* * *

Regarding the suggestion with which I concluded my panel response, in a conversation following the panel a Catholic member of CTS shared with me an experience of a Eucharistic service in which there were two altars from which two Eucharists were offered to worshippers, a Catholic Eucharist and a Protestant Eucharist, with the resulting implication that they represented options from which the worshippers might choose as if they were consumers in a marketplace. This is not an implication any of us involved in the CTS intercommunion conversation, whether Baptist or Catholic, would want to convey with an alternative interim Eucharistic practice. Our desire for Eucharistic fellowship with our fellow theologians continues, as does our willingness to make whatever contributions we can through our theological exploration of this desire to the larger quest for the visible unity of the one body of Christ.

Toward One Eucharistic Fellowship

Whatever might be the outcome in the near future of this exploration by Baptist and Catholic academic theologians of the possibility of sharing Eucharistic communion in the context of our annual joint meetings, reflection on these continuing discussions has helped me articulate three convictions about their relation to the larger ecumenical tasks of Baptists, Catholics, and the whole church. First, what we seek together is not merely shared communion at our academic conferences, but the full communion of all Baptists and all Catholics at the table as members of one Eucharistic fellowship. We pray that our efforts toward an exceptional practice of shared communion may make some contribution to the larger pilgrim journey toward full communion. Second, there are gifts to be received ecumenically from one another in our respective Baptist and Catholic perspectives on the possibility of sharing communion. Both the Catholic exclusion of Baptists from Catholic Eucharists and the "closed communion" stream of the Baptist tradition are important objections to a "lowest common denominator" ecumenism as the means of achieving full communion. At the same time, the "open communion" stream of the Baptist tradition gestures toward a Eucharistic hospitality that seeks a unity among the churches that is visibly manifested—which Catholic ecumenical engagement also seeks. Third, the pain that Baptist and Catholic theologians—who arguably share more consciously in common with one another in terms of examined Christian convictions and theological commitments than may be true of our relations with many members of our own local churches and parishes with whom we do enjoy Eucharistic fellowship—experience at not being able to share a central sacrament of Christian worship with one another should be borne as a particular form of cross-bearing. Naming our division at the table as a scandal while resisting easy fixes that do not reckon seriously with our disagreements about important matters of faith and order is part of what it means for us to take up our cross and follow Jesus, to be led where we may not want to go, in taking on the brokenness that Jesus continues to suffer over the brokenness of his body—the brokenness that *we* have inflicted on Jesus through the divisions that we've inflicted on one another, the body of Christ. The final main chapter of this book will frame this call to the cruciformity of communion in terms of an invitation to enter not only the fellowship of the sufferings of the crucified Christ whose body is torn asunder but also the reconciling triumph of Christ over division, a victory already won that becomes our ongoing task.

Chapter Six

Unity as Christ's Victory and Our Task

Each year from January 18 through 25, many Christians throughout the whole church participate in the Week of Prayer for Christian Unity. This observance began in 1908 outside the Catholic Church as the initiative of two American Episcopalians, Fr. Paul Wattson and Sr. Lurana White, who were co-founders of the Franciscan Friars and Sisters of the Atonement. This was initially an Episcopalian religious order that took on the pursuit of Christian unity as its vocation and sought especially the reunion of Anglican and Catholic Christianity. Eventually Wattson, White, and their order were received into the Catholic Church, and in 1916 Pope Benedict XV granted the observance official Catholic recognition. Today it is sponsored by the World Council of Churches Commission on Faith and Order and the Catholic Church's Pontifical Council for Promoting Christian Unity, and now many Baptists join Catholics and others in the whole church in observing the Week of Prayer for Christian Unity.[173]

In connection with the Week of Prayer for Christian Unity in 2012, I was invited by the Kentucky Council of Churches and the Ecumenical Relations Committee of Eastern Area Community Ministries, an ecumenical ministry partnership of churches in East Louisville, Kentucky, to lead a workshop on grassroots ecumenical engagement based on my book *Ecumenism Means You, Too: Ordinary Christians and the Quest for Christian Unity*[174] and to deliver the homily for the Week of Prayer for Christian Unity service held by the churches of Eastern Area Community Ministries at Lyndon Baptist Church in Louisville, where I had also preached in the Sunday worship service earlier in the day before the workshop and ecumenical prayer service. The homily I delivered during that Week of Prayer for Christian Unity service has been adapted as the final main chapter in this book, inviting Baptist, Catholic, and other readers in the whole church to heed the book's summons to walk further together on the pilgrimage of unity.

Christian Unity: Christ's Victory, Our Task (1 Corinthians 15:51-58)

May the one Spirit who gives us the many gifts entrusted to our churches lead us to share those gifts more fully with one another, that we might become more truly one body of Christ. Through Jesus Christ our Lord, who lives and reigns with the Father in the unity of the Holy Spirit, one God, forever and ever. Amen.

I think I'm fairly safe in assuming that if you're attending a Week of Prayer for Christian Unity service (or reading this book), you think that Christian unity is a good thing and that it's a good thing to pray for it. And it goes without saying that if we're gathering to pray for Christian unity, then we're agreed that we don't yet have Christian unity, at least not in its fullest, most visible sense.

The theme for the 2012 Week of Prayer for Christian Unity expresses a truth that we who are grieved by our divisions and pray earnestly that we might yet be visibly one desperately need to hear: "We Will All Be Changed

Chapter Six

by the Victory of Our Lord Jesus Christ."[175] This hopeful word from 1 Corinthians 15 gives us the encouragement we need to persist in the quest for the visible unity of the church at a time when its divisions seem to be going from bad to worse and apathy regarding these divisions is widespread. As Presbyterian ecumenist and Louisville resident Joseph Small put it so well during a consultation in which we both participated at the Graymoor Spiritual Life Center near Garrison, New York—the birthplace of the Week of Prayer for Christian Unity—our progress toward visible unity is paralyzed by "the scandal of a division that ceases to offend." We seem resigned to Christian division as the normal Christian way of life. It's a difficult moment for summoning the energy to do something to move people to make things different. But tonight, we hear this word that things will be different: "We Will All Be Changed by the Victory of Our Lord Jesus Christ."

In context, Paul's hopeful word has to do with what academic theologians call "individual eschatology"—the "last things" that have to do with God's goals for every single person. Paul is writing about the transformation of our bodies through the resurrection—God's transformation of our whole selves into the fullness of everything God intended humanity to be from the beginning. Resurrection is all about change: what perishes is changed into what lasts; what is dishonorable is changed into what is glorious; what is merely physical is changed into what is also fully spiritual; what lives is changed into what also gives life; what comes from the earth is changed into what also comes from heaven; what dies is changed into what lives forever. Paul is confident that God wants this change for everyone: "we will all be changed." Which is to say, "we will all be converted."

And who in particular was it that Paul was so confident would be changed, converted, by the resurrecting power of God? The Corinthian Christians—those quarrelsome, cliquish, divisive, schismatic Corinthian Christians to whom Paul announced his reason for writing this letter: "I appeal to you, brothers and sisters, by the name of our Lord Jesus Christ, that all of you be in agreement and that there be no divisions among you, but that you be united in the same mind and the same purpose" (1 Cor 1:10). We're therefore not doing violence to Paul's hopeful word in chapter 15 if we hear it tonight as a word about the eschatology of Christian unity. "Listen, I will tell you a mystery: we will all be changed. We will all be one in a way the world can see. Division will be changed into unity; discord will be changed into agreement; separation will be changed into communion. Where, O division, is your victory? Where, O division, is your sting? Thanks be to God, who gives us the victory through our Lord Jesus Christ."

We can receive that hopeful word only in light of the eschatology that belongs to the core of the Christian vision. The basic premise of the hope for the realization of God's creative purposes in the victory of Christ is this: the reign of God that has come near in Christ is already a present reality, but it isn't yet fully realized. That's the biblical framework for the quest to realize the unity Christ prayed for his church in John 17. We already have unity, for we belong to the one body of Christ, and we're indwelt by one Spirit. But as the current divisions of the church attest, this unity is not yet fully realized, for its fullness is not visible. Visible unity requires change, our conversion.

How do we know when our unity is visible? In our workshop on grassroots ecumenical engagement this afternoon we discussed one particular definition of the unity sought by the modern ecumenical movement, approved by the World Council of Churches at their 1961 assembly in New Delhi, India. It's stood the test of time as the clearest statement of the goal of the ecumenical movement:

> We believe that the unity which is both God's will and his gift to his Church is being made visible as all in each place who are baptized into Jesus Christ and confess him as Lord and Savior are brought by the Holy Spirit into one fully-committed fellowship, holding the one apostolic faith, preaching the one Gospel, breaking the one bread, joining in common prayer, and having a corporate life reaching out in witness and service to all and who at the same time are united with the whole Christian fellowship in all places and all ages, in such wise that ministry and members are accepted by all, and that all can act and speak together as occasion requires for the tasks to which God calls his people.[176]

According to the New Delhi definition, if all churches don't recognize baptisms performed by other churches as expressions of the one baptism that belongs to the one body of Christ, we don't have a unity the world can see. If all Christians can't celebrate the Eucharist together in one another's churches, we don't have a unity the world can see. If all churches can't confess together the essence of the apostolic faith, we don't have a unity the world can see. If our churches don't accept the ministers and members of one another's churches as their own, we don't have a unity the world can see. If we can't share the Gospel and serve the needy and work to liberate the oppressed together, we don't have a unity the world can see. If we can't speak prophetic words to the world with a unified voice whenever God calls us to do so, we don't have a unity the world can see. We don't yet have that kind of unity. We all need to be changed, converted, by the victory of our Lord Jesus Christ. The unity we seek is not yet.

It's true that our unity is already a present reality. There is—present tense—one body, one Spirit, one hope, one Lord, one faith, one baptism, one God. That's already true of the church, even in all its divisions. These are the fundamental unifying realities that undergird what we call "spiritual ecumenism." It's a present reality. But if we conceive of this unity primarily as an already-realized spiritual reality, we may see little reason to devote our energies to the hard work of contesting earnestly the issues of faith and order that continue to divide us.

Likewise, if visible unity is only fully realized in the age to come, we may decide that there's little or no reason to seek it in the present age. Many of my fellow Protestants have insisted that the four "marks of the church" in the Nicene Creed that we will confess later in this service, including its affirmation that the church is "one" as well as "holy, catholic, and apostolic," are eschatological marks of the church—fully realized only in the final victory of Christ. That's true enough. But one legacy of this insistence is an aversion to efforts to realize these marks in the present, especially the mark of visible oneness. Even if the oneness, holiness, catholicity, and apostolicity of the church will fully be realized only in the end, that doesn't mean that the church shouldn't seek to attain those marks here and now.

It's helpful to think of the eschatology of the quest for Christian unity in light of our quest for holiness of life. Even now in this earthly life, the saints already are just that—"saints," "holy ones," who are "seated with Christ in the heavenly places," in the language of the letter to the Ephesians (Eph 1:3). But in this earthly life the saints are not yet fully holy. We're on a lifelong journey of conversion, a lifelong journey of becoming more and more fully the holy ones that we already are. The full completion of sanctification comes only at the end, when we will be changed, converted, into the holiness that belongs to God.

Just as our already-present holiness in Christ doesn't warrant our refusal of the sanctifying work of the Spirit in the present, and just as the deferral of our glorification until the resurrection shouldn't de-motivate the present pursuit of the sanctification that will be completed in the life of the age to come, so it is with the already-but-not-yet nature of Christian unity. Because we've already been entrusted with the lasting reality of oneness in Christ and in the Spirit, we must seek to make this oneness visible to the world in advance of the age to come. Our conversion to visible unity is Christ's victory, but it's also our task.

Because visible unity is a vision of the last things disclosed by Jesus himself in his prayer that we might be one, we can be confident that when we take action to seek the visible unity of the church, we're joining God in what God intends to do in and through the church in the culmination of God's goals for all things in the victory of Christ. Tonight, we make Christian unity our task by praying together that Christ's victory may change us all by making us more visibly one in him.

The task of praying for unity gives us a proper perspective on our other forms of human participation in the quest for visible Christian unity. Praying for unity reminds us that unity is ultimately God's gracious gift. It comes about as the divided churches are converted to Christ by the work of the Holy Spirit in our midst. Such conversion is the work of the Triune God, but we must be receptive to it and participate in it. Praying for unity teaches us the ecumenical virtue of patience. One day we will be one, but we're not there yet. Getting there may require centuries of patient commitment to the quest for Christian unity—maybe even millennia. Praying for unity keeps the church from losing heart in what increasingly seems to be a losing struggle from a human point of view.

In January 2006 I participated in a consultation convened to examine the factors behind the failure of plans for a Second Conference on Faith and Order in North America that was to commemorate the fiftieth anniversary of the 1957 Oberlin Conference on Faith and Order. We met at the Graymoor Spiritual Life Center, the birthplace of the Week of Prayer for Christian Unity that I mentioned earlier. That gathering seemed like a funeral for the death of an ecumenical dream. And yet when we joined in common worship each morning and evening, singing Taizé chants and praying together for the unity of the church, we

Chapter Six

experienced the rekindling of a hope that didn't seem warranted by the circumstances. At the end of that same year, I served as a member of the Baptist World Alliance delegation to a five-year series of conversations with the Pontifical Council for Promoting Christian Unity. The mood of these conversations was far from somber, yet we were acutely aware of the inevitable impasses that lay ahead. But when we gathered for morning and evening prayer each day, even though we weren't yet able to be united at the Lord's table, we shared a powerful experience of unity in praying together that we might be one through the victory of our Lord Jesus Christ.

As we continue to pray for unity, as we confess the apostolic faith we share in common, as we engage in other acts of worship that embody our unity, may we be encouraged by another hopeful word of Paul in 1 Corinthians 15. Verse 58 says: "Therefore, my beloved, be steadfast, immovable, always excelling in the work of the Lord, because you know that in the Lord your labor is not in vain." May it be so, through Jesus Christ our Lord, who lives and reigns with the Father in the unity of the Holy Spirit, one God, now and forever. Amen.

* * *

This is also my encouragement to readers of this book who are Baptists, Catholics, and members of other churches that belong to the whole church that God is in the process of transforming into the church that is one, as the Triune God is one, through our shared pilgrim journey that leads to the realization of visible unity. Toward that end, I also encourage readers to walk on further in this book by reading the two appended chapters that address how Baptists especially, but also Catholics and others in the whole church, might envision what the church should be and engage in moral discernment about a wide range of issues that are confronting the church and have often contributed to its further fragmentation.

Appendix One

Envisioning the Whole Church

In 2013, the World Council of Churches Commission on Faith and Order—on which both Baptist and Catholic representatives serve—issued *The Church: Towards a Common Vision* (*TCTCV*), which joined the *Baptism, Eucharist and Ministry* (*BEM*) document the WCC issued in 1982 as the only two documents to be designated as a "convergence texts" among the approximately 300 documents produced by the WCC Faith and Order Commission across its history. The 186 responses to *BEM* from member communions of the WCC had surfaced some ecclesiological themes that needed further study: (1) the role the church plays in God's salvific goals; (2) the implications for ecclesiology of the concept of Trinitarian *koinonia*; (3) the manner in which the church is created by the word of God; (4) the nature of the church as a sacrament by which the world comes to experience God's love; (5) the church's identity as a pilgrim community; and (6) the church as prophetic sign and servant of the coming reign of God.

A new project to address these broader issues of ecclesial vision evolved in several stages, beginning with a draft text titled *The Nature and Purpose of the Church: A Stage on the Way to a Common Statement*. As with *BEM*, again the churches offered responses to this draft document that were taken into account in the next phase of the Commission's work. At the 2006 WCC Assembly in Porto Alegre, Brazil, the Commission presented a new draft, *The Nature and Mission of the Church*, again subtitled *A Stage on the Way to a Common Statement*, and again the Commission submitted the text to the churches for response. Further input came from the Plenary Commission on Faith and Order meeting in Crete in October 2009, in which I participated as the representative of the Baptist World Alliance on the Commission. In addition to feedback offered in plenary addresses, smaller working groups, and general discussions, we recommended that those responsible for drafting "shorten the text and . . . make it more contextual, more reflective of the lives of the churches throughout the world, and more accessible to a wider readership" (from the "Historical Note" appended to *TCTCV*). The drafting committee took this feedback into account along with a 2011 inter-Orthodox consultation on the text and the churches' earlier responses to *The Nature and Mission of the Church*. It underwent three more drafts that made improvements in light of continued feedback, and in September 2012 the WCC Central Committee officially received the new convergence statement, now titled *The Church: Towards a Common Vision*. It was published in 2013, presented at the 10th Assembly of the World Council of Churches in Busan, South Korea, that October, and commended to the churches for study and response.

At its meeting during the 2018 annual gathering of the Baptist World Alliance in Zürich, Switzerland, the BWA Commission on Baptist Doctrine and Christian Unity decided that it should make a response to *The Church: Towards a Common Vision* on behalf of the BWA. I was asked to draft a response on behalf of the Commission.

Appendix One

I presented it during our next BWA annual gathering in Nassau, The Bahamas, in 2018 and incorporated Commission members' feedback into the final text that follows in the remainder of this appended chapter. (Both text and notes—here converted from footnotes to endnotes—are unchanged, as this response now has official status as the response of the BWA Commission on Baptist Doctrine and Christian Unity.) It is included in this book as a Baptist response to this historic effort by representatives of the whole church, including both Baptists and Catholics, to envision together a church in which Baptists, Catholics, and all Christians will live more fully into a unity that is visible to the world.

A Response to *The Church: Towards a Common Vision* by the Baptist World Alliance Commission on Baptist Doctrine and Christian Unity[177]

In response to the invitation of the WCC Commission on Faith and Order to the churches to submit official responses to *The Church: Towards a Common Vision* (hereinafter *TCTCV*), the Baptist World Alliance Commission on Baptist Doctrine and Christian Unity is pleased to make the following contribution to the process of reception of this important convergence text, in the hope that our churches and all churches might live into its vision of an ecclesial communion that receives from the communion of the Triune God "both the gift by which the Church lives and, at the same time, the gift that God calls the Church to offer to a wounded and divided humanity in hope of reconciliation and healing" (*TCTCV* § 1).

1. The Baptist World Alliance and the Status of This Response

1.1. Founded in 1905, the Baptist World Alliance (hereinafter BWA) is a fellowship of 240 Baptist conventions and unions located in 125 countries and territories, including 168,491 local congregations and 47,500,324 members.[178] According to its Constitution, "The Baptist World Alliance, extending over every part of the world, exists as an expression of the essential oneness of Baptist people in the Lord Jesus Christ, to impart inspiration to the fellowship, and to provide channels for sharing concerns and skills in witness and ministry. This Alliance recognizes the traditional autonomy and interdependence of Baptist churches and member bodies." One of the objectives of the BWA articulated in its Constitution is "to promote understanding and cooperation among Baptist bodies and with other Christian groups, in keeping with our unity in Christ."[179]

1.2. One of the Commissions of the BWA is the Commission on Baptist Doctrine and Christian Unity, which is charged with the following work:

> The Commission on Baptist Doctrine and Christian Unity identifies, reflects on, and clarifies issues of doctrine that are important to Baptists. It analyzes the causes of disunity among Baptists and promotes ways to overcome this disunity. It shares in theological conversations between the BWA and other Christian communities, in furtherance of Jesus' prayer for the unity of the church. It also participates in programs to

improve inter-church understanding and cooperation. The Commission makes its findings available to the wide Baptist family.[180]

As an instrument by which the BWA relates to other Christian traditions, the Commission on Baptist Doctrine and Christian Unity supplies the members of Baptist delegations to the joint commissions of international bilateral ecumenical dialogues, receives updates on these dialogues, and offers responses to multilateral proposals for ecumenical convergence such as *Baptism, Eucharist and Ministry* (hereinafter *BEM*) and *TCTCV*.

1.3. While the BWA itself is not a member body of the World Council of Churches (hereinafter WCC), eight Baptist unions were founding members of the WCC in 1948: the Baptist Union of Great Britain, the Northern Baptist Convention (now American Baptist Churches, USA), the National Baptist Convention (USA), the Seventh Day Baptist General Conference (USA), the Baptist Union of New Zealand, the Union of Baptist Congregations in the Netherlands, the Burma Baptist Missionary Convention, and the China Baptist Council.[181] Today twenty-seven Baptist unions are WCC members.[182] Representatives of these Baptist WCC member unions, as well as representatives of the BWA itself, have served on commissions of the WCC, including the WCC Commission on Faith and Order and its working groups that have been responsible for drafting and offering input into the Faith and Order study documents and convergence texts.

1.4. While the WCC Commission on Faith and Order has commended to the churches for study numerous study documents among the more than two hundred Faith and Order Papers issued by that commission since 1948 and has invited the churches to offer responses to them, only two have been designated as "convergence texts": *BEM* (1982) and *TCTCV* (2013). The Introduction to *TCTCV* explains the status of a convergence text in this manner:

> Our aim is to offer a convergence text, that is, a text which, while not expressing full consensus on all the issues considered, is much more than simply an instrument to stimulate further study. Rather, the following pages express how far Christian communities have come in their common understanding of the Church, showing the progress that has been made and indicating work that still needs to be done.[183]

The Preface to *TCTCV* invites both "ecclesial responses" from "the churches that are members of the Commission [on Faith and Order] and the fellowship of churches in the World Council of Churches" and "responses from ecclesial bodies, such as national and regional councils of churches and the Christian World Communions, whose official dialogues among themselves have contributed so much to the convergence reflected in *The Church*" [*TCTCV*].[184] When a similar call accompanied the publication of *BEM*, nine Baptist unions issued official ecclesial responses.[185] In the category of responses from ecclesial bodies such as Christian World Communions, the BWA Commission on Baptist Doctrine and Interchurch Cooperation (now the Commission on Baptist Doctrine and Christian Unity) received an initial response to *BEM* drafted by George Beasley-Murray, Morris West, and Robert Thompson that was subsequently

Appendix One

expanded by William R. Estep.[186] This response detailed Baptist affirmation of aspects of *BEM* along with Baptist concerns about other elements of that convergence text: for example, appreciation for *BEM*'s recognition, informed by ecumenical biblical and historical scholarship, of the biblical, historical, and theological priority of believer's baptism, but also concern about what seemed to be an *ex opere operato* (i.e., automatically conferred) connection between baptism and salvation; an appreciation for the biblically rich development of the meaning of the Eucharist, but again reservations about a stronger connection between the Eucharist and the experience of salvation than Baptists would typically make; and appreciation for the attention to the ministry of the whole people of God in the section on Ministry, but disappointment that *BEM* seemed to make reconciliation with the historic episcopate (i.e., apostolic succession) a condition for visible unity.[187]

1.5. While the present document is presented as a response to *TCTCV* by the BWA Commission on Baptist Doctrine and Christian Unity, it is not the first effort of this commission to participate in the process of reception of *TCTCV*. At the meeting of [the] Commission on Baptist Doctrine and Christian Unity in Ocho Rios, Jamaica, July 1-6, 2013, three responses to different sections of *TCTCV* (in one case, to a section of its 2005 predecessor *The Nature and Mission of the Church: A Stage on the Way to a Common Statement*[188]) were presented to and discussed by the Commission. These responses were subsequently published in the collected papers of the BWA Division of Mission, Evangelism, and Theological Reflection for the quinquennium 2010-2015.[189] In addition, other individual Baptist theologians have published independent responses to *TCTCV*.[190] The present response draws in part on these previous instances of Baptist participation in the reception of *TCTCV* as well as on the input of the current membership of the BWA Commission on Baptist Doctrine and Christian Unity.

1.6. This response is in the category of "responses from ecclesial bodies, such as national and regional councils of churches and the Christian World Communions"[191] solicited by the WCC, but its status as a response from the BWA needs some qualification. It is the product of the work of the BWA Commission on Baptist Doctrine and Christian Unity as an expression of its charge to share "in theological conversations between the BWA and other Christian communities, in furtherance of Jesus' prayer for the unity of the church" and to make "its findings available to the wide Baptist family."[192] As such, it has a status similar to that of the reports written by the joint commissions to the international bilateral ecumenical dialogues with BWA participation. The note on "The Status of This Report" appended to the Preface of the report from Phase II of the dialogue between the BWA and the Catholic Church (2006-2010) also applies to the status of this response in relation to the BWA and its member unions:

> The Report published here is the work of the International Conversations between the Catholic Church and the Baptist World Alliance. It is a study document produced by participants in the Conversations. The authorities who appointed the participants have

Appendix One

allowed the Report to be published so that it may be widely discussed. It is not an authoritative declaration of either the Catholic Church or of the Baptist World Alliance, who will both also evaluate the document.[193]

2. The Church: Towards a Common Vision in Baptist Ecclesiological Perspective

2.1. The Introduction to *TCTCV* invites the churches to respond to this convergence text in light of five questions, the first of which is, "To what extent does this text reflect the ecclesiological understanding of your church?"[194] While the Baptist ecclesiological principle of congregational freedom to follow the leadership of the Spirit in discerning the mind of Christ about what it will mean for the congregation to be the body of Christ in its particular context makes it difficult to generalize about Baptists' ecclesiological self-understanding, there are multiple dimensions of the Baptist ecclesial vision that may be recognized in the vision of church articulated by *TCTCV*.

2.2. Apart from the ecclesial vision expressed in the text of *TCTCV*, Baptists may recognize themselves also in the process that led to it. The previous paragraph mentioned the Baptist ecclesiological principle of congregational freedom to follow the leadership of the Spirit in discerning the mind of Christ about what it will mean for the congregation to be the body of Christ in its particular context. One way in which Baptists have sought to exercise this freedom is the practice of ecclesial discernment. Ideally this practice entails deep listening not only to all voices within the congregation—including (perhaps especially including) minority or marginalized voices—but also to various voices from other contexts beyond the local church.[195] A parallel to this Baptist practice of ecclesial discernment through listening deeply to the input of multiple voices is the process by which the WCC Commission on Faith and Order solicited and received responses from a wide range of ecclesial voices to the successive drafts of the convergence text that became *TCTCV*: *The Nature and Purpose of the Church* (1998), *The Nature and Mission of the Church* (2005), and three successive additional drafts that made continued improvements in light of ongoing input on the way to the reception by the WCC Central Committee in September 2012 of the new convergence text now titled *TCTCV* and published in 2013.[196]

2.3. Baptists may especially see themselves in the way *TCTCV* attended to the voices of those who have been marginalized in their contexts. Baptists began as a persecuted religious minority, and this formative experience has led them historically to be advocates for religious liberty, not only for themselves but for other marginalized minorities, and to work for the just treatment of all persons. We confess that there have been notable Baptist failures to embody these convictions regarding freedom and justice. But at their best, Baptists have sought to live in light of the insistence of Baptist minister and theologian Martin Luther King, Jr. that "injustice anywhere is a threat to justice everywhere."[197] The ongoing commitment of the global Baptist community to seeking liberty and justice for the oppressed and marginalized is reflected in the existence of BWA Commissions devoted to Religious Freedom; Racial, Gender, and Economic Justice; and Human Rights, Peace-

Appendix One

building, and Reconciliation. In addition, the BWA awards an annual Human Rights Award that reflects this commitment.[198] When members of the Plenary Commission on Faith and Order meeting in Crete in October 2009, with Baptist representatives among them, offered their perspectives on the draft statement *The Nature and Mission of the Church* and suggestions for revising it, one speaker critiqued the way that draft text treated biblical images of the church in purely doctrinal terms without sufficient attention to their sociological dimensions and implications for the liberation of the dispossessed and the disempowered.[199] Baptists who pray and work for liberty and justice for the dispossessed and disempowered will rejoice that this critical voice was heard by the drafting committee. It is reflected in the insistence of *TCTCV* that "the Church needs to help those without power in society to be heard," "must become a voice for those who are voiceless," and is impelled "to work for a just social order, in which the goods of this earth may be shared equitably, the suffering of the poor eased and absolute destitution one day be eliminated" (§ 64), as well as in its assertion that "after the example of Jesus, the Church is called and empowered in a special way to share the lot of those who suffer and to care for the needy and the marginalized" (§ 66).

2.4. Baptists welcome one feature of *TCTCV* that seems most obviously an advance beyond *BEM*: its reengagement of the roots of the modern ecumenical movement in the modern missions movement. The 1910 Edinburgh World Missionary Conference that led to the founding of the ongoing International Missionary Conference in 1921 was in some sense anticipated a century earlier by pioneering Baptist missionary to India William Carey (1761-1834), who in 1806 suggested that "a general association of all denominations of Christians from the four quarters of the earth" meet each decade at the Cape of Good Hope.[200] In *TCTCV*, the quest for Christian unity is framed as a participation in God's mission in the world in its opening chapter, "God's Mission and the Unity of the Church." The opening paragraph ends with these two sentences:

> The Church, as the body of Christ, acts by the power of the Holy Spirit *to continue his life-giving mission in prophetic and compassionate ministry and so participates in God's work of healing a broken world*. Communion, whose source is the very life of the Holy Trinity, is both the gift by which the Church lives and, at the same time, the gift that God calls the Church to offer to a wounded and divided humanity in hope of reconciliation and healing (*TCTCV* § 1 [emphasis added]).

This first chapter sees the *missio dei* as carried out in the sending of the Son, defined by the earthly ministry of Jesus, extended in the church as the body of Christ that continues his mission, and empowered by the Holy Spirit sent upon the church and into the world. In the next chapter on "The Church of the Triune God," the church "is by its very nature missionary, called and sent to witness in its own life to that communion which God intends for all humanity and for all creation in the kingdom" (§ 13). Whereas the title of the earlier text on "The Nature *and Mission* of the Church" suggested that one could somehow differentiate the church's nature and the church's mission, *TCTCV* now conceives of mission as essential to the nature of the church—a strengthening of a long-developing trajectory in ecclesiology and ecumenical theology that appropriates the missiological concept of the *missio dei* in which the church participates and becomes more fully the church whenever it does so. Johann Gerhard Oncken (1800-84), the German "Father of Continental Baptists" who adopted as his motto "Every Baptist a Missionary," would have been pleased by this aspect of *TCTCV*.[201]

2.5. A second notable advance beyond *BEM* is the way *TCTCV* roots the unity of the church in the unity of the Triune God: "Communion, whose source is the very life of the Holy Trinity, is both the gift by which the Church lives and, at the same time, the gift that God calls the Church to offer to a wounded and divided humanity in hope of reconciliation and healing" (§ 1). The text advances this Trinitarian rationale and framework for conceiving of the church and its unity not only in its second chapter, titled "The Church of the Triune God," but throughout the document. It does so especially in terms of the biblical concept of *koinonia*, which the subsequent Christian theological tradition has developed both as Trinitarian concept and as an ecclesiological concept, and it is influenced in particular by recent constructive retrievals of these developments.[202] *TCTCV* reaps the harvest of this Trinitarian ecclesiological ferment as a deepening of a theme long present in ecumenical theology,[203] but it is also a theme that had already featured prominently in international bilateral ecumenical dialogues with Baptist participation—in particular, Phase II of the dialogue between the BWA and the Catholic Church (2006-2010). A "common language" of an ecclesiology rooted in Trinitarian *koinonia* enabled Baptists and

Catholics together to make affirmations such as the following in the report of this dialogue, *The Word of God in the Life of the Church*:[204]

> Jesus Christ is thus God's self-revelation who draws us into the communion of God's own triune life and into communion (*koinonia*) with each other (§ 7).
>
> The church is thus to be understood as a *koinonia* . . . which is grounded in the *koinonia* of the triune God. Believers are joined in *koinonia* through participation in the communion of Father, Son and Holy Spirit. . . . [and] are in *koinonia* through their participation in the community of believers gathered by Christ in his church (§ 11).
>
> The principle of *koinonia* applies both to the church gathered in a local congregation and to congregations gathered together. . . . We agree that the local fellowship does not derive from the universal church, nor is the universal a mere sum of various local forms, but that there is mutual existence and coinherence between the local and universal church of Christ (§ 12).

The Baptists recognized in such an ecclesiology of *koinonia* a convergence with the concept of "covenant" emphasized in Baptist ecclesiology, in which the church is constituted by participatory divine-human and human-human relationships that extend beyond the local church to include trans-local ecclesial relationships (§§ 16-19). While *TCTCV* does not make this connection between *koinonia* and covenant, it is in particular the communion ecclesiology of *TCTCV* that makes it possible for Baptists to see *TCTCV* as a basis for growth in unity, a matter addressed in the next major section of this response.

2.6. Baptists are also able to appreciate a third strand in this ecumenical vision that *TCTCV* brings into sharper focus: its development more strongly than *BEM* of the church's ecumenical imperative in eschatological terms, which *TCTCV* sees as inseparable from the mission of the Triune God, who is the source of ecclesial unity. The three strands come together in the opening paragraph of *TCTCV*, which concludes with the insistence that "Communion, whose source is the very life of the Holy Trinity, is both the gift by which the Church lives and, at the same time, the gift that God calls the Church to offer to a wounded and divided humanity *in hope of reconciliation and healing*" (§ 1 [emphasis added]). *TCTCV* portrays the church that has this eschatological hope as "an eschatological reality, already anticipating the kingdom, but not yet its full realization." Therefore, it is also "a pilgrim community" on a "journey towards the full realization of God's gift of communion" (§§ 33, 35, 37).[205] This vision of a pilgrim church articulated by *TCTCV* may be the feature of this convergence text that most fully reflects the ecclesiological self-understanding of Baptists. The Baptist ecclesial ideal is the church that is fully under the rule of Christ, which Baptists locate somewhere ahead of them in a not-yet-arrived-at future rather than in any past or present instantiation of the church.[206] Baptists are relentlessly dissatisfied with the present state of the church in their pilgrim journey toward the community that will be fully under the reign of Christ, and *TCTCV* gives expression to the same sort of holy dissatisfaction with the ecclesial status quo. The acknowledgement that the whole church both shares in past and present ecclesial failures to realize God's gift of communion and shares in a pilgrim journey toward a visible manifestation of communion that has yet to be fully realized makes it possible for Baptists to see the vision of *TCTCV* as a basis for mutual growth toward a more fully visible unity.

3. *The Church: Towards a Common Vision* as Basis for Growth in Unity

3.1 *TCTCV* also invites response to the question, "To what extent does this text offer a basis for growth in unity among the churches?" In Baptist perspective, the communion ecclesiology developed within the framework of Trinitarian *koinonia* noted in the previous section makes it possible to envision a movement toward visible unity that has a place not only for Baptists and their own ecclesiological convictions but also for all the other churches with which Baptists do not currently have full communion, without any of the traditions being required to surrender the distinctive ecclesial gifts that have been uniquely preserved in each of the divided traditions. Without the exchange of these gifts, none of the divided churches can become fully catholic (in the sense not only of quantitative catholicity, which describes the totality of the one church to which all who belong to Christ belong, but also of qualitative catholicity, which describes the fullness of certain qualities of faith and faithfulness that mark the one church fully under the rule of Christ).[207]

3.2. *TCTCV* insists that "each local church contains within it the fullness of what it is to be the Church" (§ 31). This emphasis of *TCTCV* on the presence in the local church of the catholic fullness of what it means to be church (in both senses of catholicity noted in the preceding paragraph of this response), without prioritizing the universal church over the local church, invites a growth toward unity that happens at the grassroots. This develops further the locality of growth toward visible unity envisioned by the 1962 New Delhi assembly of the WCC in its definition of "The Unity We Seek": "We believe that the unity which is both God's will and [God's] gift to [God's] Church is being made visible as *all in each place* who are baptized into Jesus Christ and confess him as Lord and Savior are brought by the Holy Spirit into one fully-committed fellowship. . . . "[208] This emphasis on the local church makes space for the contributions of difference and diversity to the growth toward unity, and it helps ensure that growth toward unity is not merely a matter of negotiating mergers between trans-local unions of churches, which themselves play an important role in the traditioning of healthy diversity within the body of Christ.

3.3. The affirmation of *TCTCV* that "each local church contains within it the fullness of what it is to be the Church" quoted in the preceding paragraph of this response continues, "It [the local church] is wholly Church, but not the whole Church. Thus, the local church should not be seen in isolation from but in dynamic relation with other local churches" (§ 31).[209] This application of the *koinonia* ecclesiology of *TCTCV* helps the churches to imagine the possibility of a form of future visible unity that is neither ecclesial merger nor a movement "home to Rome" (or Constantinople), but rather a communion of communions in which each communion is able to conserve and offer to the whole church its diversity of distinctive ecclesial gifts while having full communion with the other communions. Such "full communion" would entail the conditions envisioned by the New Delhi statement referenced above: a full communion of the churches with each other in which all baptized Christians fully belong to one another in a covenanted community that is both local and worldwide, marked by common confession of the broad contours of the historic faith of the church, common celebration of the Eucharist in which table fellowship is fully extended to all members of all churches, joint engagement in mission and service, mutual recognition of the baptisms and ordinations performed by one another's churches, and a unified prophetic voice. The communion ecclesiology of *TCTCV* offers a theological framework within which such full communion may more easily be envisioned, and in a manner that may seem much more inviting to the churches that have a history of reticence about Faith and Order ecumenical proposals.

3.4. The *koinonia* ecclesiology of *TCTCV* also makes ecclesial space for the practice of "receptive ecumenism" as a paradigm for ecumenical convergence. It invites the churches "not only to work untiringly to overcome divisions and heresies but also to preserve and treasure their legitimate differences in liturgy, custom, and law and to foster legitimate diversities of spirituality, theological method and formulation in such a way that they contribute to the unity and catholicity of the Church as a whole"

(§ 30). While the language of receptive ecumenism is recent in ecumenical theology,[210] as a practice it has long been practiced in the recognition that there are gifts of liturgy, spirituality, theology, and other ecclesial practices present in other traditions that may be received into one's own tradition to help it become more fully catholic, more fully under the rule of Christ, without relinquishing the good gifts that have been distinctively stewarded in one's own tradition. The reception of *TCTCV* by the churches can help the practice of receptive ecumenism become more intentional. When practiced over time by the churches, it may lead to the future realization that our churches have so remarkably converged toward one another through the exchange of these gifts that full communion is now possible in ways not previously envisioned, as the gift of the Spirit at work in the churches rather than a blueprint for convergence engineered by ecumenists.

4. Challenges to Baptists

4.1. The next question which *TCTCV* poses to the churches is, "What adaptations or renewal in the life of your church does this statement challenge your church to work for?" Receptive ecumenism is not merely the addition of gifts received from other churches to the store of gifts already possessed by one's own church. Sometimes the recognition of the desirability of these gifts carries with it the realization of deficiencies in one's own church that must be rectified by altering aspects of faith and practice in light of a current shortcoming that another tradition's gift reveals. At other times, a gift recognized in another tradition leads to the re-reception of a gift that has previously marked the life of one's own communion but that has been neglected or forgotten and therefore must be renewed.

4.2 After noting the interdependence that marked the first-century Christian communities described in the New Testament, *TCTCV* rightly insists:

> This communion of local churches is thus not an optional extra. The universal Church is the communion of all local churches united in faith and worship around the world. It is not merely the sum, federation or juxtaposition of local churches, but all of them together are the same Church present and acting in this world. Catholicity . . . refers not simply to geographic extension but also to the manifold variety of local churches and their participation in the fullness of faith and life that unites them in the one *koinonia* (§ 31).

While Baptists are able to recognize their emphasis on the primacy of the local church in the refusal of *TCTCV* to prioritize the universal church over the local church, serious consideration of the *koinonia* ecclesiology of *TCTCV* will remind Baptists that while "the local church is wholly church, it is not the whole church" and that there is therefore something intrinsically deficient about the local church when it is not living into the fullest possible extension of its interdependence with the whole church.

4.3. Baptists have often seen themselves as ecumenical in the sense that they value their spiritual connection that they already have with other followers of Jesus Christ in other churches from which Baptists are visibly divided.

Appendix One

They recognize that with these other Christians they share "one body and one Spirit . . . one hope . . . one Lord, one faith, one baptism, one God" (Eph. 4:4-6 NRSV) in what has been termed a "spiritual ecumenism." While this is an important recognition as a starting point for ecumenical engagement, Baptists have too often been content with affirming spiritual ecumenism and neglecting or even disavowing the visible unity of the followers of Jesus, which is the clear implication of Jesus' prayer "that they may all be one . . . so that the world may believe that you have sent me" (John 17:21 NRSV). The insistence of *TCTCV* that visible unity is the goal of ecumenical convergence challenges Baptists beyond being content with the spiritual ecumenism they already affirm.

5. Opportunities for *Koinonia* in Life and Mission

5.1. The Introduction to *TCTCV* asks, "How far is your church able to form closer relationships in life and mission with those churches which can acknowledge in a positive way the account of the Church described in this statement?" While Baptist ecclesial diversity precludes generalizing about Baptists' perspectives on particular ecclesiological proposals, in general Baptists will be able both to affirm the vision of the church articulated by *TCTCV* and to recognize churches that can join them in affirming this vision as churches with which "closer relationships in life and mission" can be formed.

5.2. The "Lund Principle" proposed at the Third World Conference on Faith and Order in Lund, Sweden in 1952, according to which churches should "act together in all matters except those in which deep difference of conviction compel them to act separately," serves as a useful means of self-examination regarding the extent to which Baptist churches have developed missional partnerships with other churches in living into the vision of *TCTCV* for a more visible unity.[211]

5.3. In the context of international bilateral dialogue, delegated representatives of the BWA have already affirmed the "Lund Principle" as a guideline for entering into missional partnerships with other churches. The first of eleven recommendations at the conclusion of the report from the dialogue between the BWA and the World Methodist Council is this:

> Around the world Baptists and Methodists share joint work through theological education, social ministry, youth programs, evangelistic meetings, joint communion services, and they often participate in each other's churches when there is no congregation of their own denomination in the area. Because such widespread shared life already exists, we recommend that at every geographical level from the global to the local congregation, Baptists and Methodists always seek to follow the Lund principle that "to manifest the oneness of the people of God [they should] act together in all matters except those in which deep differences of conviction compel them to act separately."[212]

Therefore, inasmuch as there are other churches beyond Baptist churches and Methodist churches that embrace the ecclesial vision of *TCTCV* in which Baptists can recognize themselves and which Baptists can affirm, this application

Appendix One

of the "Lund Principle" to Baptist-Methodist relationships can be applied to Baptist relationships with these other Christian churches as well.

6. Baptist Questions and Suggestions for the Commission on Faith and Order

6.1. Finally, *TCTCV* invites response to the question, "What aspects of the life of the Church could call for further discussion and what advice could your church offer for the ongoing work by Faith and Order in the area of ecclesiology?" While there is much that Baptists could propose for work by the Commission on Faith and Order, in this response we focus on some ways in which from our perspective the *koinonia* ecclesiology of *TCTCV* could be fruitfully applied to matters not sufficiently developed in this convergence text.

6.2. Although *One Baptism: Towards Mutual Recognition* (2011) represented a fuller development of *BEM*'s recognition of the historical and theological priority of believer's baptism that Baptists were able to appreciate,[213] this did not receive as thorough an exploration as might have been desired in *TCTCV*. This convergence text also did not apply the insights of its emphasis on *koinonia* to the ongoing divisions between churches that baptize only believers and those that also baptize the infant children of believing parents. Proposals that focus on the "mutual recognition of baptism," which is the language employed also by *TCTCV* (§ 41), remain problematic from a Baptist perspective. However, the international bilateral dialogues which the BWA has held with the Anglican Communion, the Catholic Church, and the World Methodist Council have explored the possibilities for a mutual recognition of journeys of initiation in which the emphasis is shifted from chronological orderings of faith, baptism, and formation in faith to a focus on the whole journey of Christian initiation in the company of the church.[214] As one response to *TCTCV* by an individual Baptist theologian has suggested, a theology of *koinonia* makes it possible to appreciate the manner in which different orderings of events in whole journeys of initiation nonetheless draw those who are baptized into participation in the communion of the Triune God in the communion of the church.[215] We believe that a fully ecumenical exploration of these possibilities for a mutual recognition of journeys of initiation in light of the *koinonia* ecclesiology expressed in *TCTCV* would be a fruitful endeavor for future work by the WCC Commission on Faith and Order.

6.3. In light of the convergence between an ecclesiology rooted in Trinitarian *koinonia* and a Baptist covenantal ecclesiology explored in bilateral dialogues with BWA participation noted earlier in this response (2.5), we suggest that further study of the parallels between covenantal ecclesiologies and communion ecclesiology would invite a wider embrace of the vision of *TCTCV* not only by Baptists but also by other churches in the broader Free Church tradition.

6.4. The WCC Commission on Faith and Order recently has been giving attention to the matter of ecclesial moral discernment, which is becoming a concern for Faith and Order ecumenism because disagreements over ethical issues are increasingly a cause of ecclesial division.[216] It has been noted that the section of *TCTCV* on "The Moral Challenge of the Gospel" (§§ 61-63) lacks any connection with the overarching theme of *koinonia*. The application of the framework of Trinitarian *koinonia* to moral discernment in the churches might supply this ecclesial practice with a theological framework that "can point all people towards the possibility of a life in which relations are the most important thing, where all persons and even the natural environment are interconnected, and where human beings can actively and intentionally participate more deeply in movements of love and justice in which they are already immersed by living in the world."[217]

7. Recommendations for Baptist Reception of *The Church: Towards a Common Vision*

Toward the end of facilitating reception of *TCTCV* among Baptists, the BWA Commission on Baptist Doctrine and Christian Unity makes the following recommendations:

7.1.1. The text of *TCTCV* and this response to it need to be disseminated widely in the global Baptist community if there is to be a Baptist reception of what is proposed by this convergence text. Links to the electronic version of *TCTCV* on the web site of the WCC Commission on Faith and Order and to this response from the BWA Commission on Baptist Doctrine and Christian Unity should be posted on the web sites of the BWA and its regional fellowships.

7.1.2. The Baptist reception of the ecumenical ecclesiology articulated by *TCTCV* will be aided by posting the statement from the 2007 Elstal Symposium on Baptist Identity and Ecclesiology once again on the BWA web site (see 3.3 above).

7.2. In the absence of ecumenical officers and other structures tasked with promoting ecumenical engagement, in the Baptist tradition it is institutions of theological education that have the greatest opportunity for facilitating Baptist reception of *TCTCV*. We recommend that the BWA encourage Baptist theological educators to make use of *TCTCV* and this response to it as texts in courses that include attention to ecclesiology and that institutions of theological education provide continuing education opportunities for ministers that introduce them to *TCTCV*.

7.3. At the local level, we encourage Baptist ministers to study *TCTCV* themselves and to form local study groups with ministers of neighboring churches from other traditions to read and discuss *TCTCV* and to contemplate the possibilities for living into its vision locally in the relationships between their churches.

7.4. We appeal to local Baptist churches, to Baptist associations and unions, and to the BWA itself to give serious, prayerful consideration to the Lund principle, according to which churches should "act together in all matters except those in which deep difference of conviction compel them to act separately," as a call to seek a fuller, more visible participation in the Trinitarian *koinonia* imagined by *TCTCV* wherever manifestations of this *koinonia* are recognized.

Appendix Two

Moral Discernment with the Whole Church

As Baptists, Catholics, and the whole church have continued to work on the matters of faith and order that continue to divide the churches, it has become increasingly clear that many of these matters are now related to the differing perspectives on ethical issues formed by the churches on the basis of the Scriptures and the Christian tradition. These divisions related to ethics have been within particular Christian communions as well as between them. The World Council of Churches Commission on Faith and Order has been involved in an ongoing study project on Moral Discernment in the Churches to address the roots of these divisions and envision ways of overcoming them. An early stage of that project involved commissioning case studies from different Christian traditions that would illustrate how each approaches the task of moral discernment. I participated in a meeting of the WCC Plenary Commission on Faith and Order that met in Crete in October 2009 as a representative of the Baptist World Alliance and offered responses to these case studies in smaller working groups. (My own working group included Catholic and Orthodox theologians as well as representatives from various Protestant traditions.) Drawing on the Plenary Commission's discussion of the case studies and further work by a standing Moral Discernment Working Group, in 2013 the WCC issued *Moral Discernment in the Churches: A Study Document*. When the Moral Discernment Working Group held a meeting in Erfurt, Germany, in July 2016 to hear and discuss papers from different Christian traditions summarizing how their own churches engaged in the task outlined in the study document, I presented (via Skype) a paper on "Authority for Ecclesial Moral Discernment in Baptist Perspective" on behalf of the BWA that characterized Baptist moral discernment as a congregationally-located exercise of something that parallels the function of magisterium in the Catholic tradition. A revision of that paper follows in the remainder of this appended chapter, which like Appendix One is included in this book as a Baptist contribution to an ongoing effort by Baptists, Catholics, and the whole church to walk together on the pilgrimage of unity.

Baptist Moral Discernment: Congregational Hearing and Weighing

In September 2003 I served as a member of the Baptist delegation to the North American phase of a dialogue between the Anglican Communion and the Baptist World Alliance (BWA).[218] One of my responsibilities was to present a paper offering a Baptist perspective on authority. I began with the qualification that "there is not a singular Baptist understanding of authority, nor are there universally authoritative sources in the Baptist world to which one might look for expressions of such an understanding"; instead I would present "an overview of Baptist understandings (plural) of authority."[219] The need to make such qualifications is not limited to Baptists, for my counterpart on the Anglican delegation began his paper on an Anglican perspective on authority by offering precisely the same qualification about the Anglican tradition.[220] What is true for the question of authority in the abstract is true for the particular question of authority for moral discernment in ecclesial traditions as diverse as Baptist churches on the one hand and Anglican churches on the other, as a recent journal article examining former Archbishop of Canterbury Rowan Williams's approach to moral discernment in Christian community suggests. One of its quotations from Williams would be just as applicable to Baptists as to the Anglicans he addresses: "In a 2006 letter to the Anglican Communion, Williams argued that the main issue for the Church 'is a question, agonisingly difficult for many, as to what kinds of behaviour a Church that seeks to be loyal to the Bible can bless, and what kinds of behaviour it must warn against—and so it is a question about how we make decisions corporately with other Christians, looking together for the mind of Christ as we share the study of the scriptures.'"[221]

The Baptist counterpart to the Archbishop of Canterbury, in the sense of functioning as the leader of a Christian world communion, is the General Secretary of the BWA. Current General Secretary Neville Callam recently offered reflections on the necessity and complexity of moral discernment: "[W]e should not fail to recognize the complexity of the process by which we can hear the voice of God as we seek to relate the teaching of Scripture to the vexed issues of contemporary life."[222] Williams and Callam both point to a common authorizing source for the church's task of moral discernment—the normativity of Scripture—and recognize the complexity of the church's efforts to apply the authority of Scripture to issues faced by the church today in relation to various other sources that play some authoritative role in ecclesial moral discernment.

In offering an account of how Baptist communities approach moral discernment, I will distinguish between two differing types of authoritative sources for this task: first, *theological* sources that function in a pattern of authority for the practice of the church as well as its faith, and second, *ecclesiological* sources that are essentially a community's socially embodied efforts to discern what the mind of Christ is for their life together in the world. Though this twofold typology differs from the classification of various sources of authority as "faith sources" and "sapiential sources" in the Faith and Order study document *Moral Discernment in the Churches*, all fourteen sources identified there as "Sources for Moral Discernment" inform Baptist communities in the task of moral discernment, even when they are not explicitly acknowledged.[223]

1. "Theological" Authority for Moral Discernment[224]

Baptists have emphasized the primacy and sufficiency of the Scriptures as their authority for faith and practice, but their confessions of faith make it clear that they ascribe ultimate authority to the Triune God.[225] With few exceptions, early Baptist confessions issued in the Netherlands and England begin not with statements about the authority of the Bible (and frequently lacked such statements) but rather with articles on the nature and attributes of the one God who is Father, Son, and Holy Spirit. It is not making too much of this ordering of confessional statements to discern in it the conviction that the God whose story Scripture tells is the ultimate authority for Christian faith and practice. Confessions issued in North America during the nineteenth and twentieth centuries, however, have normally begun with an article on the inspiration and authority of the Scriptures, yet this shift does not indicate a reversal of ultimate authorities. Even if these confessions emphasize Scripture as the means by which God is known, the Baptists who adopted and affirmed them would agree that any legitimate source of religious authority derives from the God who is revealed in the person of Jesus Christ to whom the Spirit bears witness.[226]

While Baptists ascribe ultimate authority to the Triune God, they identify Scripture as the supreme earthly source of authority that derives its authority from the Triune God. Many early Baptist confessions lacked articles on the Scriptures, but they evidenced a radical biblicism in their copious prooftexting of confessional statements with parenthetical and marginal biblical references. Most Baptist confessions adopted in North America have contained an article specifically addressing the inspiration and authority of the Scriptures.

The most widely influential article on the Scriptures in Baptist confessions issued in the United States is the article with which the *New Hampshire Confession* of 1833 begins.[227] This article was incorporated in or adapted by confessions printed in numerous Baptist church manuals and issued by various Baptist unions in the United States, notably the Southern Baptist Convention, which made the *New Hampshire Confession* the basis of the statement of the

Baptist Faith and Message that the SBC adopted in 1925, revised in 1963, amended in 1998, and revised yet again in 2000. The successive modifications of the article on the Scriptures in the *Baptist Faith and Message*, which reflect a movement from a perspective that was arguably more open to the contributions of historical-critical biblical scholarship and limited the scope of the Bible's authority to matters of faith and practice toward a more restrictive theory of biblical inerrancy,[228] illustrate the diversity that has characterized recent understandings of biblical authority in Baptist life in North America. In the larger Baptist context, some Baptists would affirm this recent more restrictive understanding of the inspiration and authority of the Bible;[229] some Baptists would affirm standard historical-critical conclusions about the formation of the Bible and their usefulness for biblical interpretation;[230] and some Baptists would view these battles as vestiges of a dying modernity and would prefer to move beyond them by focusing instead on the manner in which Scripture functions authoritatively for the Baptist communities that are gathered by its proclamation and study.[231]

A focus on the authoritative function of Scripture in the life of the community implies a relationship between Scripture and other possible sources of authority to which members of the community may turn, consciously and unconsciously, when they interpret the Scriptures together. Baptist confessions have tended toward a *Sola Scriptura* understanding of authority in that they specify Scripture as the supreme authority but do not explicitly identify other subordinate sources of authority.[232] Yet the actual hermeneutical practice of Baptists might be better described as *Suprema Scriptura*.[233] Baptist confessions contain numerous echoes of the doctrinal formulations of Nicaeno-Constantinopolitan trinitarianism and Chalcedonian Christology, employing theological terminology with origins in the fourth century and later.[234] When Baptists affirm doctrinal formulations with patristic origins or embrace the authority of a biblical canon, they are at least unconsciously granting some degree of authority to tradition in the interpretation of Scripture.

Explicit Baptist recognition of tradition or other sources of theological authority in addition to Scripture exists almost exclusively in the context of academic theological discourse;[235] extrabiblical sources of authority are seldom referenced by Baptist confessions of faith. A major exception to this generalization is the 1678 confession issued by General (i.e., non-Calvinistic) Baptists in England under the title *An Orthodox Creed*, which commends the reception and belief of the Nicene, (pseudo-) Athanasian, and Apostles' Creeds, subordinating their authority to that of Scripture but regarding them as reliable summaries of biblical teaching.[236] In addition, at least two recent European Baptist confessions of faith likewise make positive reference to the Apostles' Creed. The first paragraph of the confession adopted in 1977 by German-speaking Baptist unions in Germany, Austria, and Switzerland "presupposes the Apostles' Creed as a common confession of Christendom,"[237] and the initial paragraph of the confession approved by the Swedish-Speaking Baptist Union of Finland in 1979 "accepts the Apostolic Creed as the comprehensive creed for the union."[238] While these affirmations of a traditional rule of faith that summarizes the Bible and provides broad guidance for its proper interpretation suggest openings for a Baptist convergence with other Christian traditions that have more explicitly affirmed tradition as authoritative, most Baptists profess adherence to a *Sola Scriptura* theological hermeneutic. Yet Baptist laypeople and Baptist clergy alike are in fact reading the Bible through the lenses of all sorts of tradition and engaging in moral discernment on the basis of what seems reasonable to them and what best accords with Christian experience, in a manner comparable to the "Wesleyan Quadrilateral." The actual hermeneutical practice of Baptists is therefore *Suprema Scriptura*, with Scripture functioning as the supreme source of authority in a larger pattern of authority.

2. "Ecclesiological" Authority for Moral Discernment

The foregoing description of "theological" authority for Baptist moral discernment could be applied to what individual Baptists do when they wrestle with moral issues, whether as laypersons, ministers, or theologians and ethicists. But while there have been individualistic tendencies in Baptist life, for Baptists moral discernment is also an ecclesial matter. To frame Baptist efforts at moral discernment in ecclesiological terms is to recognize that teaching authority, which *Moral Discernment in the Churches* identifies as an ecumenically-shared "faith source" of moral discernment,[239] has this function also for Baptists.

In other words, Baptists have their own form of "magisterium," though differently configured from the forms of magisterium recognized more explicitly as such in other Christian traditions.[240] Beyond the Catholic[241] and Magisterial Protestant[242] configurations of magisterium, there is yet a third major pattern according to which the church "teaches as she must teach if she is to be the church here and now."[243] This configuration might be called "Free Church magisterium."[244]

In one sense, Free Church magisterium functions as a magisterium of the whole. Inasmuch as Baptists have historically granted that local churches gathered under the Lordship of Christ possess an authority that derives from Christ as Lord, this authority can also be extended to the communion of saints, who constitute a real community under the Lordship of Christ that transcends space and time.[245] The church's teaching authority can be located most broadly in the communion of saints in its entirety in its ongoing argument[246] about what the church "must teach in order to be the church here and now."[247] But who decides how the argument should be decided, however provisionally, at various points in the historical extension of the argument? If all members of the communion of saints are participants in this ongoing argument, do they all participate in the same way? Do the voices of all participants carry the same weight, so that the argument is decided by majority? This magisterium of the whole offers a way for Baptists and other historic dissenters to appreciate the place their dissent has within the larger argument that constitutes the Christian tradition, making positive contributions to the health of the living tradition through their dissent,[248] but it needs greater specificity in its location of socially-embodied ecclesial authority.

Free Church magisterial authority is located primarily in the gathered congregation. One might call this the "magisterium-hood of all believers." But in the Free

Church practice of teaching authority it is not the local congregation alone that authorizes its teaching, nor is the membership of the congregation undifferentiated in its participation in this practice. In Baptist ecclesiology, the independence of local congregations is not absolute. Local Baptist congregations are interdependent in their relations with one another, in local associations but also in various national and international associations of Baptists. The rule of Christ in the local congregations in the plural has implications for the efforts of any single local congregation to discern the mind of Christ, and vice versa. Together in their mutual relations they seek to walk under the government of Christ, seeking from him a fuller grasp of the truth, as one ecclesial communion—a communion which, the earliest Baptist confession issued by an association of Baptist churches hopefully suggested, might extend beyond Baptist churches in association to include all the saints.[249]

Within local congregations, discerning the mind of Christ is not a matter of simple majority vote of the congregation, nor is it determined by acquiescence to the will of the congregation's pastor. Baptist theologian Paul Fiddes explains the embodied "Baptist experience" that informs Baptist efforts to bring their faith and practice under the rule of Christ:

> The liberty of local churches to make decisions about their own life and ministry is not based in a human view of autonomy or independence, or in selfish individualism, but in a sense of being under the direct rule of Christ who relativizes other rules. This liberating rule of Christ is what makes for the distinctive 'feel' of

Appendix Two

> Baptist congregational life, which allows for spiritual oversight (*episkopē*) both by the *whole* congregation gathered together in church meeting, and by the minister(s) called to lead the congregation. . . . Since the same rule of Christ can be experienced in assemblies of churches together, there is also the basis here for Baptist associational life, and indeed for participating in ecumenical clusters.[250]

Elsewhere Fiddes fleshes out what it means for the whole congregation to seek together the mind of Christ in what British Baptists call "church meeting":

> Upon the whole people in covenant there lies the responsibility of finding a common mind, of coming to an agreement about the way of Christ for them in life, worship and mission. But they cannot do so unless they use the resources that God has given them, and among those resources are the pastor, the deacons and (if they have them) the elders. The church meeting is not 'people power' in the sense of simply counting votes and canvassing a majority. . . . The aim is to search for consent about the mind of Christ, and so people should be sensitive to the voices behind the votes, listening to them according to the weight of their experience and insight. As B[arrington] White puts it, 'One vote is not as good as another in church meeting,' even though it has the same strictly numerical value.[251]

"In all this," Fiddes writes, "the pastor's voice is the one that carries weight"—provided that pastors have created trust in their leadership through service. In this paradigm, pastors play a distinctive role in the shared exercise of *episkopē*, which carries with it the catechetical task of equipping the members of the congregation with the resources they need from beyond the congregation for seeking the mind of Christ, resources which include the doctrine, worship, and practice of other congregations, other Christian traditions, and indeed the whole Christian tradition.[252]

In 1997 a group of Baptist theologians issued a statement titled "Re-envisioning Baptist Identity: A Manifesto for Baptist Communities in North America." It proposed five affirmations regarding the nature of freedom, faithfulness, and community, the first of which follows in part:

> *We affirm Bible Study in reading communities* rather than relying on private interpretation or supposed 'scientific' objectivity. . . . We thus affirm an open and orderly process whereby faithful communities deliberate together over the Scriptures with sisters and brothers of the faith, excluding no light from any source. When all exercise their gifts and callings, when every voice is heard and weighed, when no one is silenced or privileged, the Spirit leads communities to read wisely and to practice faithfully the direction of the gospel.[253]

Beyond an undifferentiated magisterium of the whole, this way of framing the process by which the church discerns what it must teach regarding its faith and practice on the basis of the Word of God summarizes well how this more nuanced configuration of congregational Free Church magisterium functions. In its ideal exercise, the moral discernment of a Baptist community in which "no light from any source" is excluded and "every voice is heard and weighed" and "no one is silenced or privileged" would give consideration to the full range of "faith sources" and "sapiential sources" treated in *Moral Discernment in the Churches*.[254]

3. Moral Discernment and Congregational Ecclesiology

The congregational ecclesiology of Baptists means, however, that the moral discernment of Baptist communities will result in widely varying decisions as to how they will address a specific moral issue.[255] Furthermore, Baptist congregational governance means that while a local association of Baptist churches, a national union of Baptist churches, a world communion of Baptists, or an ecumenical council to which Baptist churches and unions may belong will also function as ecclesial communities that seek to bring their life together under the rule of Christ[256] and may adopt resolutions or implement policies that are expressions of their communal efforts at moral discernment, these resolutions and policies are not binding on local Baptist churches. But just as local Baptist churches may make their own decisions about the associations or unions of churches with which they will affiliate, Baptist associations and unions too may make their own decisions about the local churches they will consider members in good standing, and sometimes these decisions have been based on stances on moral issues adopted by local Baptist churches.

Authority for Baptist ecclesial moral discernment is primarily located in the local Baptist congregation. Yet when they engage in congregational moral discernment, local Baptist churches can and should take into consideration the efforts at ecclesial moral discernment undertaken by other local Baptist churches and national and international Baptist unions, as well as by churches belonging to other Christian communions. Whenever Baptist communities recognize and approach ecclesial moral discernment as a fully ecumenical undertaking, they are ensuring that "no light from any source" is excluded, "every voice is heard and weighed," and "no one is silenced." When they do so, Baptists are both being true to their own best ecclesial gifts and are joining the pilgrimage of the whole church toward the church fully under the rule of Christ.

Bibliography

Abramov, Alexander, Alexander Geichenko, and Mary Raber. "The Importance, Relevance, and Challenge of 'The Church: Towards a Common Vision.'" *Journal of European Baptist Studies* 15, no. 2 (January 2015): 28-33.

Alberigo, Giuseppe and Joseph A. Komonchak, eds. *History of Vatican II*. 5 vols. Translated by Matthew J. O'Connell. Maryknoll, NY: Orbis, 1995-2006.

Allen, Bob. "Catholics in Nagaland Claiming Persecution at Hands of Baptists." *Baptist News Global* (July 27, 2010). Online https://baptistnews.com/article/catholics-in-nagaland-claiming-persecution-at-hands-of-baptists/#.Xe6N1qeZNQI (accessed November 30, 2020).

Allison-Glenny, Beth, Andy Goodliff, Ruth Gouldbourne, Steve Holmes, David Kerrigan, Glen Marshall, and Simon Woodman. "The Courage to be Baptist: A Statement on Baptist Ecclesiology and Human Sexuality." Online http://www.somethingtodeclare.org.uk/statement.html (accessed February 18, 2017).

American Baptist Churches, USA and United States Conference of Catholic Bishops. "Growing in Understanding: A Progress Report on American Baptist-Roman Catholic Dialogue." In *Building Unity: Ecumenical Dialogues with Roman Catholic Participation in the US*, ed. Joseph Burgess and Jeffrey Gros, 39-44. Mahwah, NJ: Paulist Press, 1989.

Baban, Octavian D. "Four Views and a Response on WCC Church Vision," *Journal of European Baptist Studies* 15, no. 2 (January 2015): 34-45.

Baptist Union of Great Britain and Church of England. *Pushing at the Boundaries of Unity: Anglicans and Baptists in Conversation*. London: Church House Publishing, 2005.

Baptist World Alliance. "Commissions of Mission and Evangelism." Online https://www.bwanet.org/images/MissionEvangelism.pdf (downloaded July 1, 2019).

———. "Constitution of the BWA." Online https://secureservercdn.net/166.62.112.219/o7e.4a3.myftpupload.com/wp-content/uploads/2020/08/BWA-Constitution-and-Bylaws-2020.pdf (downloaded March 3, 2021).

———. "Statistics." Online https://www.bwanet.org/about-us2/stats (accessed July 1, 2019).

Baptist World Alliance and Anglican Consultative Council. *Conversations Around the World 2000-2005: The Report of the International Conversations between the Anglican Communion and the Baptist World Alliance*. London: Anglican Communion Office, 2005.

Baptist World Alliance and Catholic Church. "Summons to Witness to Christ in Today's World: A Report on Conversations 1984-1988." In *Growth in Agreement II: Reports and Agreed Statements of Ecumenical Conversations on a World Level, 1982-1998*, ed. Jeffrey Gros, Harding Meyer, and William G. Rusch, 373-85.

Geneva: WCC Publications and Grand Rapids, MI: William B. Eerdmans, 2000.

_____. "Summons to Witness to Christ in Today's World: A Report on Conversations 1984-1988." Online http://www.christianunity.va/content/unitacristiani/en/dialoghi/sezione-occidentale/alleanza-battista-mondiale/dialogo-internazionale-tra-la-chiesa-cattolica-e-l-alleanza-batt/documenti-di-dialogo/1988-chiamati-ad-essere-testimoni-di-cristo-nel-mondo-di-oggi-/testo-del-documento-in-inglese.html (accessed October 27, 2020).

_____. "Summons to Witness to Christ in Today's World: A Report on Conversations 1984-1988." *The Pontifical Council for Promoting Christian Unity Information Service* 72 (1990): 5-13.

_____. *The Word of God in the Life of the Church: A Report of International Conversations between the Catholic Church and the Baptist World Alliance 2006-2010. American Baptist Quarterly* 31, no. 1 (Spring 2012): 28-122.

_____. "The Word of God in the Life of the Church: A Report of International Conversations between the Catholic Church and the Baptist World Alliance 2006-2010." Online http://www.christianunity.va/content/unitacristiani/en/dialoghi/sezione-occidentale/alleanza-battista-mondiale/dialogo-internazionale-tra-la-chiesa-cattolica-e-l-alleanza-batt/documenti-di-dialogo/2010-la-parola-di-dio-nella-vita-della-chiesa/testo-del-documento-in-inglese.html (accessed October 27, 2020).

———. "The Word of God in the Life of the Church: A Report of International Conversations between the Catholic Church and the Baptist World Alliance 2006-2010." *Pontifical Council for Promoting Christian Unity Information Service* 142 (2013): 20-65.

Baptist World Alliance and Lutheran World Federation. "A Message to Our Churches." In *Growth in Agreement II: Reports and Agreed Statements of Ecumenical Conversations on a World Level, 1982-1998*, ed. Jeffrey Gros, Harding Meyer, and William G. Rusch, 155-75. Faith and Order Paper no. 187. Geneva: WCC Publications and Grand Rapids, MI: William B. Eerdmans, 2000.

Baptist World Alliance and World Methodist Council. *Faith Working through Love: Report of the International Dialogue between the Baptist World Alliance and the World Methodist Council* (2018). Online https://www.bwanet.org/images/MEJ/Final-Report-of-the-International-Dialogue-between-BWA-and-WMC.pdf (downloaded July 1, 2019).

Barth, Karl. *Ad Limina Apostolorum: An Appraisal of Vatican II*. Translated by Keith B. Crim. Richmond, VA: John Knox Press, 1968.

Best, Thomas F., Lorelei F. Fuchs, John Gibaut, Jeffrey Gros, and Despina Prassas, eds. *Growth in Agreement IV: International Dialogue Texts and Agreed Statements, 2004-2014, Books 1 and 2*. 2 vols. Faith and Order Paper no. 219. Geneva: WCC Publications, 2017.

Boswell, W. Benjamin. "Liturgy and Revolution Part 1: Georgian Baptists and the Non-violent Struggle for

Democracy." *Religion in Eastern Europe* 27, no. 2 (May 2007): 48-71.

Broach, Claude U. *Before It Slips My Mind*. Charlotte, NC: Delmar Printing Co., 1974.

Broadway, Mikael, Curtis W. Freeman, Barry Harvey, James Wm. McClendon, Jr., Elizabeth Newman, and Philip E. Thompson. "Re-envisioning Baptist Identity: A Manifesto for Baptist Communities in North America." *Baptists Today* (June 1997): 8-10.

————. "Re-envisioning Baptist Identity: A Manifesto for Baptist Communities in North America." Online http://divinity.duke.edu/sites/divinity.duke.edu/files/documents/faculty-freeman/reenvisioning-baptist-identity.pdf (accessed July 1, 2019).

————. "Re-envisioning Baptist Identity: A Manifesto for Baptist Communities in North America." *Perspectives in Religious Studies* 24, no. 3 (Fall 1997): 303-10.

Brunk, Timothy. "Serious Spiritual Need?" *Horizons: The Journal of the College Theology Society* 45, no. 2 (December 2018): 394-99.

Bush, L. Russ and Thomas J. Nettles. *Baptists and the Bible*. Rev. ed. Nashville: Broadman & Holman, 1999.

Buttry, Daniel. "Baptists Amid Georgian Revolutions." *Baptists Today* 23, no. 8 (August 2005): 9.

Callam, Neville. "When the Churches Present Inconsistent Moral Teachings." *Baptist World Alliance General Secretary's Blog*, March 1, 2016. Online http://www.bwanet.org/dialogue/entry/when-the-churches-present-inconsistent-moral-teachings (accessed July 15, 2016).

Catholic Church and Mennonite World Conference. *Called Together to Be Peacemakers: Report of the International Dialogue between the Catholic Church and Mennonite World Conference 1998-2003* (August 2003). Online http://www.vatican.va/roman_curia/ pontifical_councils/chrstuni/mennonite-conference-docs/rc_pc_chrstuni_doc_20110324_mennonite_en.html#_ftn170 (accessed November 30, 2020).

Catholic Church and World Methodist Council. *The Grace Given You in Christ: Catholics and Methodists Reflect Further on the Church.* Lake Junaluska, NC: World Methodist Council, 2006.

Catholic Church, Lutheran World Federation, and Mennonite World Conference. "Communiqué: Lutheran, Mennonite, Catholic Trilateral Dialogue" (Strasbourg, France, 15-19 September 2017). Online http:// www.christianunity.va/content/unitacristiani/en/ dialoghi/sezione-occidentale/dialoghi-multilaterali/ dialogo-trilaterale-cattolico-mennonita-luterano/ comunicati-stampa/2017-strasbourg/en.html (accessed November 30, 2020).

Catholic Diocese of Dallas. "The Dallas Connection: Albert Outler, Dean of Observers." *The Texas Catholic: The Official Newspaper of the Diocese of Dallas* (January 30, 2013). Online http://www.texascatholic. com/2013/01/30/the-dallas-connection-albert-outler-dean-of-observers/ (accessed November 29, 2020).

Chilton, Amy L. and Steven R. Harmon, eds. *Sources of Light: Resources for Baptist Churches Practicing Theology.* Perspectives on Baptist Identities, no. 3. Macon, GA: Mercer University Press, 2020.

Clifford, Catherine E. and James F. Puglisi, eds. *A Century of Prayer for Christian Unity*. Grand Rapids, MI: William B. Eerdmans, 2009.

Coggins, James Robert. *John Smyth's Congregation: English Separatism, Mennonite Influence, and the Elect Nation*. Studies in Anabaptist and Mennonite History, no. 32. Waterloo, Ontario: Herald Press, 1991.

Coleman, John A. "Vatican II as a Social Movement." In *The Belgian Contribution to the Second Vatican Council: International Research Conference at Mechelen, Leuven and Louvain-la-Neuve (September 12-16, 2005)*, ed. Doris Donnelly, 5-28. Bibliotheca Ephemeridum theologicarum Lovaniensium, no. 216. Leuven and Dudley, MA: Peeters, 2008.

Comité mixte baptiste-catholique en France. *Du Baptême à l'Eglise: Accords et divergences actuels*. Documents d'Église; Paris: Les Éditions du Cerf, 2006.

_____. *Marie*. Documents episcopat, no. 10. Paris: Le secretariat général de la conférence des évêques de France, 2009.

_____. *Rendre témoinage au Christ*. Documents d'Église; Paris: Les Éditions du Cerf, 1992.

Conference on Biblical Inerrancy. *The Proceedings of the Conference on Biblical Inerrancy, 1987*. Nashville: Broadman Press, 1987.

Congar, Yves. *Chrétiens désunis: principes d'un "oecuménisme" catholique*. Unum Sanctam, no. 1. Paris: Éditions du Cerf, 1937.

_____. *Divided Christendom: A Catholic Study of the Problem of Reunion.* Translated by M. A. Bousfield. London: Geoffrey Bles/Centenary Press, 1939.

_____. *My Journal of the Council.* Translated by Mary John Ronayne and Mary Cecily Boulding. Edited by Denis Minns. Collegeville, MN: Liturgical Press, 2012.

Congregation for the Doctrine of the Faith. "Declaratio *Dominus Iesus* de Iesu Christi atque Ecclesiae Unicitate et Universalitate Salvifica." Online http://www.vatican.va/roman_curia/congregations/cfaith/documents/rc_con_cfaith_doc_20000806_dominus-iesus_lt.html (accessed November 29, 2020).

_____. "Declaration '*Dominus Iesus*' On the Unicity and Salvific Universality of Jesus Christ and the Church." Online http://www.vatican.va/roman_curia/congregations/cfaith/documents/rc_con_cfaith_doc_20000806_dominus-iesus_en.html (accessed November 29, 2020).

_____. "Responsa ad Quaestiones de Aliquibus Sententiis ad Doctrinam de Ecclesia Pertinentibus." Online http://www.vatican.va/roman_curia/congregations/cfaith/documents/rc_con_cfaith_doc_20070629_responsa-quaestiones_lt.html#_ftnref20 (accessed November 29, 2020).

_____. "Responses to Some Questions Regarding Certain Aspects of the Doctrine of the Church." Online http://www.vatican.va/roman_curia/congregations/cfaith/documents/rc_con_cfaith_doc_20070629_ responsa-quaestiones_en.html (accessed November 29, 2020).

Coorilos, Geevarghese Mar. "The Nature and Mission of the Church: An Indian Perspective." In *Called to Be the One Church: Faith and Order at Crete*, ed. John Gibaut, 188-92. Faith and Order Paper no. 212. Geneva: WCC Publications, 2012.

D'Ambrosio, Marcellino. "Ressourcement Theology, Aggiornamento, and the Hermeneutics of Tradition." *Communio* 18 (Winter 1991): 530-55.

Dayspring Baptist Church. Online http://ourdayspring.org (accessed November 27, 2020).

Department of Interfaith Witness of the Home Mission Board of the Southern Baptist Convention and United States Conference of Catholic Bishops. "How We Agree/How We Differ: Roman Catholic-Southern Baptist Scholars' Dialogue (1986-88)." In *Growing Consensus: Church Dialogues in the United States, 1962-1991*, ed. Joseph A. Burgess and Jeffrey Gros, 557-65. Ecumenical Documents, no. 5. New York: Paulist Press, 1995.

————. "Report on Sacred Scripture: Southern Baptist-Roman Catholic Conversation, 1999." In *Growing Consensus II: Church Dialogues in the United States, 1992-2004*, ed. Lydia Veliko and Jeffrey Gros, 334-38. Washington, DC: Bishops' Committee for Ecumenical and Interreligious Affairs, United States Conference of Catholic Bishops, 2005.

_____. "Summary Statement of the Second Triennium in the Dialogue between Southern Baptist and Roman Catholic Scholars (1982-1984)." In *Building Unity: Ecumenical Dialogues with Roman Catholic Participation in the US*, ed. Joseph Burgess and Jeffrey Gros, 45-51. Mahwah, NJ: Paulist Press, 1989.

Dick, John A. *The Malines Conversations Revisited.* Bibliotheca Ephemeridum theologicarum Lovaniensium, no. 85. Leuven: Leuven University Press, 1989.

Dulles, Avery. "Eucharistic Sharing as an Ecumenical Problem." Chapter in *The Resilient Church*, 153-71. Garden City, NY: Doubleday, 1977.

Durnbaugh, Donald F. *The Believer's Church: The History and Character of Radical Protestantism.* New York: Macmillan, 1968.

Ellis, Christopher J. *Gathering: A Theology and Spirituality of Worship in Free Church Tradition.* London: SCM Press, 2004.

Estep, William R. *Baptists and Christian Unity.* Nashville: Broadman Press, 1966.

_____. "A Response to *Baptism, Eucharist and Ministry*: Faith and Order Paper No. 111." In *Faith, Life and Witness: The Papers of the Study and Research Division of the Baptist World Alliance 1986-1990*, ed. William H. Brackney and R. J. Burke, 2-16. Birmingham, AL: Samford University Press, 1990.

Evangelical Baptist Church of Georgia. Online: http://www.ebcgeorgia.org/Neue_Dateien/start.html (accessed November 27, 2020).

Fiddes, Paul S. "'*Koinonia*: The Church in and for the World': Comment on the Final Part of *The Church: Towards a Common Vision* (Faith and Order Paper 214)." In *Baptist Faith & Witness, Book 5: Papers of the Commission on Mission, Evangelism and Theological Reflection of the Baptist World Alliance 2010-2015*, ed. Eron Henry, 37-47. Falls Church, VA: Baptist World Alliance, 2015.

———. "Learning from Others: Baptists and Receptive Ecumenism." *Louvain Studies* 33, nos. 1-2 (2008): 54-73.

———. *Participating in God: A Pastoral Doctrine of the Trinity*. Louisville, KY: Westminster John Knox Press, 2000.

———. *Tracks and Traces: Baptist Identity in Church and Theology*. Studies in Baptist History and Thought, vol. 13. Milton Keynes, UK: Paternoster, 2003.

Fiddes, Paul S., Brian Haymes, and Richard Kidd. *Baptists and the Communion of Saints: A Theology of Covenanted Disciples*. Waco, TX: Baylor University Press, 2014.

Forbis, Wesley L., ed. *The Baptist Hymnal*. Nashville: Convention Press, 1991.

Freeman, Curtis W. "Can Catholics and Baptists Share Communion without Breaking the Rules?" *Horizons: The Journal of the College Theology Society* 45, no. 2 (December 2018): 375-94.

———. "'The Church of the Triune God': A Baptist Response to *The Nature and Mission of the Church: A*

Stage on the Way to a Common Statement (Faith and Order Paper 198)." In *Baptist Faith & Witness, Book 5: Papers of the Commission on Mission, Evangelism and Theological Reflection of the Baptist World Alliance 2010-2015*, ed. Eron Henry, 7-24. Falls Church, VA: Baptist World Alliance, 2015.

_____, ed. "Congregational Independence—Associational Interdependence." Thematic issue of *American Baptist Quarterly* 38, no. 1 (Spring 2019).

Fuchs, Lorelei F. *Koinonia and the Quest for an Ecumenical Ecclesiology: From Foundations through Dialogue to Symbolic Competence for Communionality*. Grand Rapids, MI: William B. Eerdmans, 2008.

Garrett, James Leo Jr., ed. *The Concept of the Believers' Church: Addresses from the 1967 Louisville Conference*. Scottdale, PA: Herald Press, 1969.

_____. "Sources of Authority in Baptist Thought." *Baptist History and Heritage* 13 (1978): 41-49.

_____. *Systematic Theology: Biblical, Historical, and Evangelical*. 2 vols. Grand Rapids, MI: William B. Eerdmans, 1990-1995.

Garrett, W. Barry. "Council Adjourns with Unfinished Business." *Baptist Press* (November 25, 1964). Online http://media.sbhla.org.s3.amazonaws.com/1981,25-Nov-1964.pdf (accessed September 28, 2020).

George, Timothy F. *Faithful Witness: The Life and Mission of William Carey*. Birmingham, AL: New Hope, 1991.

Graymoor Ecumenical & Interreligious Institute. "2012 Week of Prayer Materials." Online https://geii.org/

week_of_prayer_for_christian_unity/week_of_prayer_materials.html (accessed December 7, 2020).

Gros, Jeffrey, Harding Meyer, and William G. Rusch, eds. *Growth in Agreement II: Reports and Agreed Statements of Ecumenical Conversations on a World Level, 1982-1998*. Faith and Order Paper no. 187. Geneva: WCC Publications and Grand Rapids, MI: William B. Eerdmans, 2000.

Gros, Jeffrey, Thomas F. Best, and Lorelei F. Fuchs, eds. *Growth in Agreement III: International Dialogue Texts and Agreed Statements, 1998-2005*. Faith and Order Paper no. 204. Geneva: WCC Publications and Grand Rapids, MI: William B. Eerdmans, 2007.

Halifax, Charles Lindley Wood. *The Conversations at Malines, 1921-1925: Original Documents*. London: Philip Allan, 1930.

Harmon, Steven R. *Baptist Identity and the Ecumenical Future: Story, Tradition, and the Recovery of Community*. Waco, TX: Baylor University Press, 2016.

_____. "Baptist Confessions of Faith and the Patristic Tradition." *Perspectives in Religious Studies* 29, no. 4 (Winter 2002): 349-58.

_____. "Baptist Moral Discernment: Congregational Hearing and Weighing." In *Churches and Moral Discernment, Volume 1: Learning from Traditions*, ed. Myriam Wijlens and Vladimir Shmaliy, 99-114. Faith and Order Paper no. 228. Geneva: WCC Publications, 2021.

_____. "Baptist Understandings of Theological Authority: A North American Perspective." *International Journal for the Study of the Christian Church 4, no. 1 (2004): 50-63.

———. "Baptist World Alliance Commission on Baptist Doctrine and Christian Unity." Chapter in *Churches Respond to The Church: Towards a Common Vision*, ed. Ellen Wondra, Stephanie Dietrich, and Ani Ghazaryan Drissi, vol. 2, 279-95. Faith and Order Paper No. 232. Geneva: World Council of Churches Publications, 2021.

———. "Baptists and Catholics Together—Twitter Edition," *Baptist News Global* (February 13, 2014). Online https://baptistnews.com/article/baptists-and-catholics-together-twitter-edition/#.W4Q-fi-ZOgQ (accessed September 21, 2020).

———. "'Catholic Baptists' and the New Horizon of Tradition in Baptist Theology." In *New Horizons in Theology*, ed. Terrence W. Tilley, 117-43. Maryknoll, NY: Orbis Books, 2005.

———. "*Dei Verbum* § 9 in Baptist Perspective." *Ecclesiology* 5, no. 3 (September 2009): 299-321.

———. *Ecumenism Means You, Too: Ordinary Christians and the Quest for Christian Unity*. Eugene, OR: Cascade Books, 2010.

———. "A Eucharistically-Malnourished Baptist's Desire for Intercommunion." *Horizons: The Journal of the College Theology Society* 45, no. 2 (December 2018): 399-402.

———. "From Anti-Catholicism to Fellow Pilgrims: Baptist Identity, *Unitatis Redintegratio*, and the Ecumenical Future." *The South African Baptist Journal of Theology* 26 (2017): 139-56.

_____. "The Healing of Memories in Bilateral Dialogues with Anabaptist (and Baptist) Participation." *Journal of Baptist Theology in Context* no. 2 (Autumn 2020): 34-56. Online https://www.jbtc.org.uk/wp-content/uploads/2020/11/Journal-of-Baptist-Theology-Issue-2.pdf (accessed November 29, 2020).

_____. "How Baptists Receive the Gifts of Catholics and Other Christians." *Ecumenical Trends* 39, no. 6 (June 2010): 1/81-5/85.

_____. "How Might We Envision the Unity We Have? Engaging *The Church: Towards a Common Vision*, Part 1." Keynote address presented to the annual assembly of the Louisiana Interchurch Conference, The Wesley Center, Woodworth, Louisiana, March 2-3, 2015. Online http://www.lainterchurch.org/documents/Speaker-Harmon-SessionOne-3-3-15.pdf (accessed July 1, 2019).

_____. "'One Baptism': A Study Text for Baptists." *Baptist World: A Magazine of the Baptist World Alliance* 58, no. 1 (January/March 2011): 9-10.

_____. "Scripture in the Life of the Baptist Churches: Openings for a Differentiated Catholic-Baptist Consensus on Sacred Scripture." *Pro Ecclesia* 18, no. 2 (Spring 2009): 187-215.

_____. *Towards Baptist Catholicity: Essays on Tradition and the Baptist Vision*. Studies in Baptist History and Thought, vol. 27. Milton Keynes, UK: Paternoster, 2006.

———. "The Traditioned Word in the Life of the Church: The Influence of the NABPR Region-at-Large/CTS Partnership on the Second Baptist–Catholic International Dialogue (2006–2010)." In *American Catholicism in the 21st Century: Crossroads, Crisis, or Renewal?*, ed. Benjamin Peters and Nicholas Rademacher, 177-88. Maryknoll, NY: Orbis Books, 2018.

———. "What Can We Do About the Unity We Envision? Engaging *The Church: Towards a Common Vision*, Part 2." Keynote address presented to the annual assembly of the Louisiana Interchurch Conference, The Wesley Center, Woodworth, Louisiana, March 2-3, 2015. Online http://www.lainterchurch.org/documents/Speaker-Harmon-SessionTwo-3-3-15.pdf (accessed July 1, 2019).

———. "What Have Baptist Professors of Religion to Do with Magisterium?" *Perspectives in Religious Studies*, 45, no. 1 (Spring 2018): 37-48.

———. "A Word About…Claude Broach, Pastoral Ecumenical Activist." *Review and Expositor* 118, no. 1 (February 2021): 11-17.

Hatch, Derek C. "Discerning the Questions." *Horizons: The Journal of the College Theology Society* 45, no. 2 (December 2018): 409-11.

———. "*Koinonia* as Ecumenical Opening for Baptists." *The Ecumenical Review* 71, nos. 1-2 (January-April 2019): 175-88.

Hinson, E. Glenn. "William Carey and Ecumenical Pragmatism." *Journal of Ecumenical Studies* 17, no. 2 (Spring 1980): 73-83.

Hjelm, Norman A., ed. *Faith and Order: Toward a North American Conference. Study Guide*. Grand Rapids, MI: William B. Eerdmans, 2005.

International Council on Biblical Inerrancy. "Chicago Statement on Biblical Inerrancy." *Journal of the Evangelical Theological Society* 21 (December 1978): 289-96.

Jackson, J. H. *Many but One: The Ecumenics of Charity*. New York: Sheed and Ward, 1964.

James, Robison B. ed. *The Unfettered Word: Southern Baptists Confront the Authority-Inerrancy Question*. Waco, TX: Word Books, 1987.

John Paul II (Pope). "On Commitment to Ecumenism (*Ut Unum Sint*)" (May 25, 1995). Online http://www.vatican.va/holy_father/john_paul_ii/encyclicals/documents/hf_jp-ii_enc_25051995_ut-unum-sint_en.html (downloaded September 29, 2020).

Justin Martyr. *1 Apology*. English translation in *Ante-Nicene Fathers*, ed. Alexander Roberts and James Donaldson, 1:163-87. New York: Christian Literature Publishing Co., 1885.

Kasper, Walter Cardinal. "The Decree on Ecumenism—Read Anew After Forty Years." In *Searching for Christian Unity*, ed. Walter Cardinal Kasper, 18-36. Hyde Park, NY: New City Press, 2007.

_____. "The Week of Prayer for Christian Unity: Origin and Continuing Inspiration of the Ecumenical Movement." In *A Century of Prayer for Christian Unity*, ed. Catherine E. Clifford, 25-40. Grand Rapids, MI: William B. Eerdmans, 2009.

Kayser, Undine. "Creating a Space for Encounter and Remembrance: The Healing of Memories Process." Research Report Written for the Centre for the Study of Violence and Reconciliation and the Institute for Healing of Memories (January 2000). Online http://www.csvr.org.za/docs/reconciliation/creatingaspace.pdf (accessed November 30, 2020).

Kerstan, R. J. and R. J. Burke, eds. *Out of Darkness into the Light of Christ: Official Report of the Fifteenth Baptist World Congress, Los Angeles, California, USA July 2-7, 1985*. McLean, VA: Baptist World Alliance, 1985.

King, Martin Luther Jr. "Letter from Birmingham Jail" (April 16, 1963). Online http://okra.stanford.edu/transcription/document_images/undecided/630416-019.pdf (accessed July 1, 2019).

Kinnamon, Michael. *Can a Renewal Movement Be Renewed? Questions for the Future of Ecumenism*. Grand Rapids, MI: William B. Eerdmans, 2014.

Kobler, John F. "On D'Ambrosio and Ressourcement Theology." *Communio* 19 (Summer 1992): 321-25.

Kolb, Robert and Timothy J. Wengert, eds. *The Book of Concord: The Confessions of the Evangelical Lutheran Church*. Translated by Charles P. Arand et al. Minneapolis: Augsburg Fortress, 2000.

Lewis, Charlton T. and Charles Short, eds. *A Latin Dictionary.* Rev. ed. Oxford: Clarendon Press, 1955.

Littell, Franklin H. *The Anabaptist View of the Church.* Boston: Starr King, 1952.

Luckey, Hans. *Johann Gerhard Oncken und die Anfänge des deutschen Baptismus*, 3rd ed. Kassel: Oncken Verlag, 1958.

Lumpkin, William L., ed. *Baptist Confessions of Faith.* Rev. ed. Valley Forge, PA: Judson Press, 1969.

⸻, ed. *Baptist Confessions of Faith.* 2nd rev. ed. Revised by Bill J. Leonard. Valley Forge, PA: Judson Press, 2011.

Lutheran World Federation and Catholic Church. *Joint Declaration on the Doctrine of Justification.* Grand Rapids, MI: William B. Eerdmans, 2000.

Lutheran World Federation and Mennonite World Conference. *Healing Memories: Reconciling in Christ. Report of the Lutheran-Mennonite International Study Commission.* Geneva and Strasbourg: Lutheran World Federation and Mennonite World Conference, 2010. Online https://www.lutheranworld.org/sites/default/files/OEA-Lutheran-Mennonites-EN-full.pdf (accessed November 29, 2020).

MacIntyre, Alasdair. *After Virtue: A Study in Moral Theory.* 2nd ed. Notre Dame, IN: University of Notre Dame Press, 1984.

Manley, Ken. "A Survey of Baptist World Alliance Conversations with Other Churches and Some Implications for Baptist Identity." Paper presented to the joint meeting of the BWA Baptist Heritage and Identity Commission and Doctrine and Interchurch Cooperation Commission, Seville, Spain, July 11, 2002. Online http://bwa-baptist-heritage.org/wp-content/uploads/2016/07/Survey-of-Conversations-with-Other-Churches.pdf (accessed July 1, 2019).

Mannion, Gerard. "Retrieving a Participatory Teaching 'Office': A Comparative and Ecumenical Analysis of Magisterium in the Service of Moral Discernment." *Journal of the Society of Christian Ethics* 34, no. 2 (2014): 61-86.

McAfee, Tom, John Simons, David Music, Milburn Price, Stanley Roberts, and Mark Edwards, eds. *Celebrating Grace Hymnal*. Macon, GA: Celebrating Grace, Inc., 2010.

McClendon, James Wm. Jr. *Systematic Theology*. 3 vols. Waco, TX: Baylor University Press, 2012.

Meyer, Harding. "Die Prägung einer Formel: Ursprung und Intention." In *Einheit—Aber Wie? Zur Tragfähigkeit der ökumenischen Formel vom "Differenzierten Konsens,"* ed. Harald Wagner, 36-58. Quaestiones Disputatae, ed. Peter Hünermann and Thomas Söding, vol. 184. Freiburg: Herder, 2000.

Meyer, Harding and Lukas Vischer, eds. *Growth in Agreement: Reports and Agreed Statements of Ecumenical Conversations on a World Level*. Faith and Order Paper no. 108. New York: Paulist Press and Geneva: World Council of Churches, 1984.

Minnich, Nelson H. "'Wie in dem basilischen concilio den Behemen gescheen'? The Status of the Protestants at the Council of Trent." In *The Contentious Triangle: Church, State, and University. A Festschrift in Honor of Professor George Hunston Williams*, ed. Rodney L. Peterson and Calvin Augustine Pater, 201-19. Sixteenth Century Essays & Studies, vol. 51. Kirksville, MO: Truman State University Press, 1999.

Moorman, John R. H. "Observers and Guests at the Council." In *Vatican II: By Those Who Were There*, ed. Alberic Stacpoole, 155-69. London: G. Chapman, 1986.

Moses, Sarah. "The Ethics of 'Recognition': Rowan Williams's Approach to Moral Discernment in the Christian Community." *Journal of the Society of Christian Ethics* 35, no. 1 (2015): 147-65.

Murray, Paul D., ed. *Receptive Ecumenism and the Call to Catholic Learning: Exploring a Way for Contemporary Ecumenism*. Oxford: Oxford University Press, 2008.

Newman, Elizabeth. "Are Local Baptist Churches Wholly Autonomous?" *Baptist News Global* (June 12, 2007). Online http://baptistnews.com/archives/item/2582-opinion-are-local-baptist-churches-wholly-autonomous (accessed July 1, 2019).

―――. "'The Church: Growing in Communion': Response to Chapter III of *The Church: Towards a Common Vision* (Faith and Order Paper 214)." In *Baptist Faith & Witness, Book 5: Papers of the Commission on Mission, Evangelism and Theological Reflection of the Baptist World Alliance 2010-2015*, ed. Eron

Henry, 25-36. Falls Church, VA: Baptist World Alliance, 2015.

Norwood, Donald W. "The Impact of Non-Roman Catholic Observers at Vatican II." *Ecclesiology* 10 (2014): 293-312.

Nugent, Robert. *Silence Speaks: Teilhard de Chardin, Yves Congar, John Courtney Murray, and Thomas Merton.* New York: Paulist Press, 2010.

Orians, Thomas. "Brief History of the Week of Prayer for Christian Unity." Online https://geii.org/week_of_prayer_for_christian_unity/week_of_prayer_history.html (accessed December 7, 2020).

Parker, G. Keith. *Baptists in Europe: History & Confessions of Faith.* Nashville: Broadman Press, 1982.

Payne, Ernest. "Baptists and the Ecumenical Movement." *Baptist Quarterly* 8: 258-67.

———. *The Fellowship of Believers: Baptist Thought and Practice Yesterday and Today.* London: Carey Kingsgate Press, 1952.

Pontifical Council for Promoting Christian Unity. "Ecumenical Relations." Online http://www.christianunity.va/content/unitacristiani/en/dialoghi.html (accessed October 27, 2020).

Ratzinger, Joseph. "Dogmatic Constitution on Divine Revelation: Chapter II, The Transmission of Divine Revelation." Translated by William Glen-Doepel. In *Commentary on the Documents of Vatican II*, ed. Herbert Vorgrimler, vol. 3, 181-98. New York: Herder and Herder, 1967-69.

Rippon, John. *A Selection of Hymns from the Best Authors, intended to be an appendix to Dr. Watts's Psalms and Hymns*. London: 1787.

Rösler, Klaus. "Italy: When Baptists Marry Catholics," *European Baptist Federation News* (July 7, 2009). Online http://ebf.org/italy-when-baptists-marry-catholics (accessed November 27, 2020).

Searle, Joshua T. "Moving towards an Ecumenism of *Koinonia*: A Critical Response to 'The Church: Towards a Common Vision' from a Baptistic Perspective." *Journal of European Baptist Studies* 15, no. 2 (January 2015): 17-27.

Songulashvili, Malkhaz. *Evangelical Christian Baptists of Georgia: The History and Transformation of a Free Church Tradition*. Studies in World Christianity. Waco, TX: Baylor University Press, 2015.

Sullivan, Francis A. "The Impact of *Dominus Iesus* on Ecumenism." *America* (October 28, 2000). Online https://www.americamagazine.org/issue/386/article/impact-dominus-iesus-ecumenism (accessed November 30, 2020).

Thompson, Philip E. "Being Made a Patient People." *Horizons: The Journal of the College Theology Society* 45, no. 2 (December 2018): 402-06.

Thurian, Max, ed. *Churches Respond to Baptism, Eucharist and Ministry*. 6 vols. Geneva: World Council of Churches, 1986-88.

Toom, Tarmo. "Baptists on Justification: Can We Join the Joint Declaration on the Doctrine of Justification?" *Pro Ecclesia* 13, no. 3 (Summer 2004): 289-306.

Van der Leer, Teun. "*The Church: Towards a Common Vision*: A Believers Church Response." *Journal of European Baptist Studies* 15, no. 3 (May 2015): 21-31.

Von Allmen, Jean-Jacques. "L'Église locale parmi les autres Eglises locales." *Irénikon* 43 (1970): 512-37.

Vatican Council II. "Constitutio Dogmatica de Ecclesia *Lumen Gentium*" (21 November 1964). Online http://www.vatican.va/archive/hist_councils/ii_vatican_council/documents/vat-ii_const_19641121_lumen-gentium_lt.html (accessed November 29, 2020).

———. Decree on Ecumenism *Unitatis Redintegratio* (21 November 1964). Online http://www.vatican.va/archive/hist_councils/ii_vatican_council/documents/vat-ii_decree_19641121_unitatis-redintegratio_en.html (accessed September 28, 2020).

———. Decree on the Catholic Churches of the Eastern Rite *Orientalium Ecclesiarum* (21 November 1964). Online http://www.vatican.va/archive/hist_councils/ii_vatican_council/documents/vat-ii_decree_19641121_orientalium-ecclesiarum_en.html (accessed November 29, 2020).

———. Decretum de Oecumenismo *Unitatis Redintegratio* (21 November 1964). Online http://www.vatican.va/archive/hist_councils/ii_vatican_council/documents/vat-ii_decree_19641121_unitatis-redintegratio_lt.html (accessed November 29, 2020).

_____. Dogmatic Constitution on the Church *Lumen Gentium* (21 November 1964). Online http://www.vatican.va/archive/hist_councils/ii_vatican_council/documents/vat-ii_const_19641121_lumen-gentium_en.html (accessed November 29, 2020).

_____. Dogmatic Constitution on Divine Revelation *Dei Verbum* (18 November 1965). Translated by Robert Murray. In *Decrees of the Ecumenical Councils*, ed. Norman P. Tanner, vol. 2, *Trent to Vatican II*. London: Sheed & Ward and Washington, DC: Georgetown University Press, 1990.

Weaver, C. Douglas. *In Search of the New Testament Church: The Baptist Story*. Macon, GA: Mercer University Press, 2008.

Westin, Gunnar. *The Free Church through the Ages*. Translated by Virgil Olson. Nashville: Broadman Press, 1954.

Whitley, W. T., ed. *The Works of John Smyth, Fellow of Christ's College, 1594-8*. 2 vols. Cambridge: Cambridge University Press, 1915.

Wilde, Melissa J. *Vatican II: A Sociological Analysis of Religious Change*. Princeton, NJ: Princeton University Press, 2007.

Williams, George Huntston. *The Radical Reformation*. Philadelphia: Westminster Press, 1962.

Williams, Rowan. "The Challenge and Hope of Being an Anglican Today: A Reflection for the Bishops, Clergy, and Faithful of the Anglican Communion" (June 27, 2006). Online http://rowanwilliams.archbishopofcanterbury.org/articles.php/1478/the-challenge-and-hope-of-being-an-anglican-today-a-reflection-for-the-bishops-clergy-and-faithful-o (accessed July 15, 2016).

Wittgenstein, Ludwig. *Philosophical Investigations*. Rev. 4th ed. Translated by G. E. M. Anscombe, P. M. S. Hacker, and Joachim Schulte. Chichester, UK: Wiley-Blackwell, 2009.

World Council of Churches. *Baptism, Eucharist and Ministry*. Faith and Order Paper no. 111. Geneva: World Council of Churches, 1982.

―――. *The Church: Towards a Common Vision*. Faith and Order Paper no. 214. Geneva: World Council of Churches, 2013.

―――. "Church Families: Baptist Churches." Online https://www.oikoumene.org/en/church-families/baptist-churches (downloaded July 1, 2019).

―――. *Moral Discernment in the Churches: A Study Document*. Faith and Order Paper no. 215. Geneva: WCC Publications, 2013.

―――. *The Nature and Mission of the Church: A Stage on the Way to a Common Statement*. Faith and Order Paper no. 198. Geneva: World Council of Churches Publications, 2005.

―――. *The Nature and Purpose of the Church: A Stage on the Way to a Common Statement*. Faith and Order Paper no. 181. Geneva: World Council of Churches Publications, 1998.

―――. *The New Delhi Report: The Third Assembly of the World Council of Churches, 1961*. New York: Association Press, 1962.

―――――. *The Third World Conference on Faith and Order, Lund 1952*. Edited by Oliver S. Tomkins. London: SCM Press, 1953.

―――――. "Week of Prayer for Christian Unity Asks What Victory Means for Unity." Online https://www.oikoumene.org/news/week-of-prayer-2012-asks-what-victory-means-for-unity (accessed December 7, 2020).

Yocum, Sandra. "Fulfilling the Rules." *Horizons: The Journal of the College Theology Society* 45, no. 2 (December 2018): 406-09.

Young, Richard L. and J. Kenneth Sanford. *Fifty Favored Years: A History of St. John's Baptist Church*. Charlotte, NC: St. John's Baptist Church, 1972.

Endnotes

1. Steven R. Harmon, *Towards Baptist Catholicity: Essays on Tradition and the Baptist Vision* (Studies in Baptist History and Thought, vol. 27; Milton Keynes, UK: Paternoster, 2006).
2. Steven R. Harmon, *Baptist Identity and the Ecumenical Future: Story, Tradition, and the Recovery of Community* (Waco, TX: Baylor University Press, 2016).
3. A version of my address for this symposium, part of a four-year celebration of the legacy of Vatican II by Creighton University, 2012-2015, was published as Steven R. Harmon, "From Anti-Catholicism to Fellow Pilgrims: Baptist Identity, *Unitatis Redintegratio*, and the Ecumenical Future," *The South African Baptist Journal of Theology* 26 (2017): 139-56. It has been adapted for publication in this book with permission from *The South African Baptist Journal of Theology*.
4. The lecture that served as the basis for chapter 2 incorporated material originally summarized in Steven R. Harmon, "Baptists and Catholics Together—Twitter Edition," *Baptist News Global* (February 13, 2014), online https://baptistnews.com/article/baptists-and-catholics-together-twitter-edition/#.W4Q-fi-ZOgQ (accessed September 21, 2020). It has been adapted for publication in this book with permission from *Baptist News Global*.
5. The lecture was published initially as Steven R. Harmon, "How Baptists Receive the Gifts of Catholics and Other Christians," *Ecumenical Trends* 39, no. 6 (June 2010): 1/81-5/85. It has been adapted for publication in this book with permission from *Ecumenical Trends*.
6. A revised version of the paper was published as Steven R. Harmon, "The Healing of Memories in Bilateral Dialogues with Anabaptist (and Baptist) Participation," *Journal of Baptist Theology in Context* no. 2 (Autumn 2020): 34-56, online https://www.jbtc.org.uk/wp-content/uploads/2020/11/Journal-of-Baptist-Theology-Issue-2.pdf (accessed November 29, 2020). It has been adapted for publication in this book with permission from the *Journal of Baptist Theology in Context*.
7. My panel response was published as Steven R. Harmon, "A Eucharistically-Malnourished Baptist's Desire for Intercommunion," *Horizons: The Journal of the College Theology Society* 45, no. 2 (December 2018): 399-402. It is adapted for this book with the permission of *Horizons*.
8. This response was published as Steven R. Harmon, "Baptist World Alliance Commission on Baptist Doctrine and Christian Unity," chapter in *Churches Respond to The Church: Towards a Common Vision*, ed. Ellen

Wondra, Stephanie Dietrich, and Ani Ghazaryan Drissi (Faith and Order Paper No. 232; Geneva: World Council of Churches Publications, 2021), vol. 2, 279-95. It has been published in the form of the appendix in the present book with the permission of the Baptist World Alliance Commission on Baptist Doctrine and Christian Unity.

9. A revision of this presentation was published as Steven R. Harmon, "Baptist Moral Discernment: Congregational Hearing and Weighing," in *Churches and Moral Discernment, Volume 1: Learning from Traditions*, ed. Myriam Wijlens and Vladimir Shmaliy (Faith and Order Paper no. 228; Geneva: WCC Publications, 2021), 99-114. It has been published in the form of the appendix in the present book with the permission of the WCC Commission on Faith and Order.

10. W. Barry Garrett, "Council Adjourns with Unfinished Business," *Baptist Press* (November 25, 1964), online http://media.sbhla.org.s3.amazonaws.com/1981,25-Nov-1964.pdf (accessed September 28, 2020).

11. "The Dallas Connection: Albert Outler, Dean of Observers," *The Texas Catholic: The Official Newspaper of the Diocese of Dallas* (January 30, 2013), online http://www.texascatholic.com/2013/01/30/the-dallas-connection-albert-outler-dean-of-observers/ (accessed November 29, 2020). According to the article, Outler, an observer delegated by the World Methodist Conference, recounted in a 1980 television documentary: "'We had the best seats in the house,' he recalled. 'They placed us in the Tribunal of Saint Longinus, only the council presidents had better seats. We soon styled ourselves as the Brotherhood of Saint Longinus.' The 'Brotherhood' grew during the council from about 50 to nearly 100, allowing for substitutes from time to time; it is estimated that nearly 200 representatives of Protestant and Orthodox denominations joined the brotherhood. Observers could not participate in the council's debates, but they were invited to smaller group meetings where they could speak but not vote. 'Our views were sought particularly in the discussions on the Decree on Ecumenism and the Declaration on Religious Liberty,' he said. 'Of course there were a lot of informal discussions during breaks at the Bar Jonah, which is where coffee and refreshments were served.'"

12. For elaboration of this observation, see Harmon, *Baptist Identity and the Ecumenical Future*, 244-45, n. 4.

13. Giuseppe Alberigo and Joseph A. Komonchak, eds., *History of Vatican II*, 5 vols., trans. Matthew J. O'Connell (Maryknoll, NY: Orbis, 1995-2006), 2:178-79.

14. Yves Congar, *My Journal of the Council*, trans. Mary John Ronayne and Mary Cecily Boulding, ed. Denis Minns (Collegeville, MN: Liturgical Press, 2012).

15. John R. H. Moorman, "Observers and Guests at the Council," in *Vatican II: By Those Who Were There*, ed. Alberic Stacpoole (London: G. Chapman, 1986), 166 (155-69).
16. Donald W. Norwood, "The Impact of Non-Roman Catholic Observers at Vatican II," *Ecclesiology* 10 (2014): 293 (293-312).
17. Norwood, "The Impact of Non-Roman Catholic Observers at Vatican II," 311. In support of this last assertion, Norwood cites John A. Coleman, "Vatican II as a Social Movement," in *The Belgian Contribution to the Second Vatican Council: International Research Conference at Mechelen, Leuven and Louvain-la-Neuve (September 12-16, 2005)*, ed. Doris Donnelly (Bibliotheca Ephemeridum theologicarum Lovaniensium, no. 216; Leuven and Dudley, MA: Peeters, 2008), 9 (5-28), and Melissa J. Wilde, *Vatican II: A Sociological Analysis of Religious Change* (Princeton, NJ: Princeton University Press, 2007).
18. Jackson documented his experiences at the Council as a guest of the Secretariat for Promoting Christian Unity in J. H. Jackson, *Many but One: The Ecumenics of Charity* (New York: Sheed and Ward, 1964).
19. Richard L. Young and J. Kenneth Sanford, *Fifty Favored Years: A History of St. John's Baptist Church* (Charlotte, NC: St. John's Baptist Church, 1972), 20-21; Claude U. Broach, *Before It Slips My Mind* (Charlotte, NC: Delmar Printing Co., 1974), 88.
20. Vatican II, Decree on Ecumenism *Unitatis Redintegratio* (21 November 1964), § 1, online http://www.vatican.va/archive/hist_councils/ii_vatican_council/documents/vat-ii_decree_19641121_unitatis-redintegratio_en.html (accessed September 28, 2020).
21. See Nelson H. Minnich, "'Wie in dem basilischen concilio den Behemen gescheen'? The Status of the Protestants at the Council of Trent," in *The Contentious Triangle: Church, State, and University. A Festschrift in Honor of Professor George Hunston Williams*, ed. Rodney L. Peterson and Calvin Augustine Pater (Sixteenth Century Essays & Studies, vol. 51; Kirksville, MO: Truman State University Press, 1999), 217-18 (201-19).
22. Minnich, "The Status of the Protestants at the Council of Trent," 218.
23. Walter Cardinal Kasper, "The Week of Prayer for Christian Unity: Origin and Continuing Inspiration of the Ecumenical Movement," in *A Century of Prayer for Christian Unity*, ed. Catherine E. Clifford (Grand Rapids, MI: William B. Eerdmans, 2009), 27 (25-40).
24. See Charles Lindley Wood Halifax, *The Conversations at Malines, 1921-1925: Original Documents* (London: Philip Allan, 1930); John A. Dick, *The Malines Conversations Revisited* (Bibliotheca Ephemeridum theologicarum Lovaniensium, no. 85; Leuven: Leuven University Press, 1989).

25. Yves Congar, *Chrétiens désunis: principes d'un "oecuménisme" catholique* (Unum Sanctam, no. 1; Paris: Éditions du Cerf, 1937); English translation, *Divided Christendom: A Catholic Study of the Problem of Reunion*, trans. M. A. Bousfield (London: Geoffrey Bles/Centenary Press, 1939).
26. See Walter Cardinal Kasper, "The Decree on Ecumenism—Read Anew After Forty Years," in *Searching for Christian Unity*, ed. Walter Cardinal Kasper (Hyde Park, NY: New City Press, 2007), 18-36.
27. See Robert Nugent, *Silence Speaks: Teilhard de Chardin, Yves Congar, John Courtney Murray, and Thomas Merton* (New York: Paulist Press, 2010), 33-48.
28. Kasper, "The Week of Prayer for Christian Unity," 27.
29. For example, by claiming that the Catholic Church did not regard members of other churches as Christians until Vatican II.
30. Congregation for the Doctrine of the Faith, "Declaration '*Dominus Iesus*' On the Unicity and Salvific Universality of Jesus Christ and the Church," online http://www.vatican.va/roman_curia/congregations/cfaith/documents/rc_con_cfaith_doc_20000806_dominus-iesus_en.html (accessed November 29, 2020); idem, "Responses to Some Questions Regarding Certain Aspects of the Doctrine of the Church," online http://www.vatican.va/roman_curia/congregations/cfaith/documents/rc_con_cfaith_doc_20070629_responsa-quaestiones_en.html (accessed November 29, 2020).
31. On the relationship between *aggiornamento* and *ressourcement* in the theological underpinnings of the Second Vatican Council, see Marecellino D'Ambrosio, "Ressourcement Theology, Aggiornamento, and the Hermeneutics of Tradition," *Communio* 18 (Winter 1991): 530-55; and John F. Kobler, "On D'Ambrosio and Ressourcement Theology," *Communio* 19 (Summer 1992): 321-25.
32. Congregation for the Doctrine of the Faith, *Dominus Iesus*, § 17; idem, "Responses to Some Questions," question 5.
33. For the official Latin texts of these documents, see Congregation for the Doctrine of the Faith, "Declaratio *Dominus Iesus* de Iesu Christi atque Ecclesiae Unicitate et Universalitate Salvifica," online http://www.vatican.va/roman_curia/congregations/cfaith/documents/rc_con_cfaith_doc_20000806_dominus-iesus_lt.html (accessed November 29, 2020); idem, "Responsa ad Quaestiones de Aliquibus Sententiis ad Doctrinam de Ecclesia Pertinentibus," online http://www.vatican.va/roman_curia/congregations/cfaith/documents/rc_con_cfaith_doc_20070629_responsa-quaestiones_lt.html#_ftnref20 (accessed November 29, 2020).
34. See Charlton T. Lewis and Charles Short, eds. *A Latin Dictionary*, rev. ed. (Oxford: Clarendon Press, 1955), s.v. "proprius, -a, -um," I.A-B.

35. Vatican II, Dogmatic Constitution on the Church *Lumen Gentium* (21 November 1964), online http://www.vatican.va/archive/hist_councils/ii_vatican_council/documents/vat-ii_const_19641121_lumen-gentium_en.html (accessed November 29, 2020).
36. Vatican II, Decree on the Catholic Churches of the Eastern Rite *Orientalium Ecclesiarum* (21 November 1964), online http://www.vatican.va/archive/hist_councils/ii_vatican_council/documents/vat-ii_decree_19641121_orientalium-ecclesiarum_en.html (accessed November 29, 2020).
37. Vatican II, *Unitatis Redintegratio*, § 1.
38. Vatican II, *Unitatis Redintegratio*, § 3.
39. Vatican II, *Unitatis Redintegratio*, § 4.
40. Vatican II, *Lumen Gentium*, § 8.
41. For the official Latin texts of the documents in which these constructions appear, see Vatican II, "Constitutio Dogmatica de Ecclesia *Lumen Gentium*" (21 November 1964), online http://www.vatican.va/archive/hist_councils/ii_vatican_council/documents/vat-ii_const_19641121_lumen-gentium_lt.html (accessed November 29, 2020); idem, "Decretum de Oecumenismo *Unitatis Redintegratio*" (21 November 1964), online http://www.vatican.va/archive/hist_councils/ii_vatican_council/documents/vat-ii_decree_19641121_unitatis-redintegratio_lt.html (accessed November 29, 2020).
42. Congar (*My Journal of the Council*, entry for 30 November 1962) lamented, with capitalized emphasis, an intervention by Archbishop Heenan of Liverpool during discussion in St. Peter's Basilica of the schema *De Unitate*: "HE SPOKE IN TERMS OF A RETURN."
43. I have explored the history of the Wake Forest University/Belmont Abbey College Ecumenical Institute in the unpublished paper "From Revolution to Retrenchment: The History of the Wake Forest University/Belmont Abbey College Ecumenical Institute, 1968-2018," presented to the annual joint meeting of the College Theology Society and the NABPR Region-at-Large, Saint Catherine University, St. Paul, Minnesota, May 31-June 3, 2018.
44. On the ecumenical work of Claude Broach, see Steven R. Harmon, "A Word About…Claude Broach, Pastoral Ecumenical Activist," *Review and Expositor* 118, no. 1 (February 2021): 11-17.
45. American Baptist Churches, USA and United States Conference of Catholic Bishops, "Growing in Understanding: A Progress Report on American Baptist-Roman Catholic Dialogue," in *Building Unity: Ecumenical Dialogues with Roman Catholic Participation in the US*, ed.

Joseph Burgess and Jeffrey Gros (Mahwah, NJ: Paulist Press, 1989), 39-44; Department of Interfaith Witness of the Home Mission Board of the Southern Baptist Convention and United States Conference of Catholic Bishops, "Summary Statement of the Second Triennium in the Dialogue between Southern Baptist and Roman Catholic Scholars (1982-1984)," in *Building Unity*, ed. Burgess and Gros, 45-51; idem, "How We Agree/How We Differ: Roman Catholic-Southern Baptist Scholars' Dialogue (1986-88)," in *Growing Consensus: Church Dialogues in the United States, 1962-1991*, ed. Joseph A. Burgess and Jeffrey Gros, (Ecumenical Documents, no. 5; New York: Paulist Press, 1995), 557-65; idem, "Report on Sacred Scripture: Southern Baptist-Roman Catholic Conversation, 1999," in *Growing Consensus II: Church Dialogues in the United States, 1992-2004*, ed. Lydia Veliko and Jeffrey Gros (Washington, DC: Bishops' Committee for Ecumenical and Interreligious Affairs, United States Conference of Catholic Bishops, 2005), 334-38.

46. Comité mixte baptiste-catholique en France, *Rendre témoinage au Christ* (Documents d'Église; Paris: Les Éditions du Cerf, 1992); Comité mixte baptiste-catholique en France, *Du Baptême à l'Eglise: Accords et divergences actuels* (Documents d'Église; Paris: Les Éditions du Cerf, 2006); Comité mixte baptiste-catholique en France, *Marie* (Documents episcopat, no. 10; Paris: Le secretariat général de la conférence des évêques de France, 2009).

47. Klaus Rösler, "Italy: When Baptists Marry Catholics," *European Baptist Federation News* (July 7, 2009), online http://ebf.org/italy-when-baptists-marry-catholics (accessed November 27, 2020).

48. Baptist World Alliance and Catholic Church, "Summons to Witness to Christ in Today's World: A Report on Conversations 1984-1988," in *Growth in Agreement II: Reports and Agreed Statements of Ecumenical Conversations on a World Level, 1982-1998*, ed. Jeffrey Gros, Harding Meyer, and William G. Rusch (Geneva: WCC Publications and Grand Rapids, MI: William B. Eerdmans, 2000), 373-85.

49. Baptist World Alliance and Catholic Church, "Summons to Witness to Christ in Today's World," §§ 45-57.

50. Baptist World Alliance and Catholic Church, "The Word of God in the Life of the Church: A Report of International Conversations between the Catholic Church and the Baptist World Alliance 2006-2010," *American Baptist Quarterly* 31, no. 1 (Spring 2012): 28-122. The report from the 2006-2010 conversations is also published in *Pontifical Council for Promoting Christian Unity Information Service* 142 (2013): 20-65 and on the Vatican website: http://www.christianunity.va/content/unitacristiani/en/dialoghi/sezione-occidentale/alleanza-battista-

mondiale/dialogo-internazionale-tra-la-chiesa-cattolica-e-l-alleanza-batt/documenti-di-dialogo/2010-la-parola-di-dio-nella-vita-della-chiesa/testo-del-documento-in-inglese.html (accessed October 27, 2020).

51. Baptist World Alliance and Catholic Church, *The Word of God in the Life of the Church*, § 37.
52. Baptist World Alliance and Catholic Church, *The Word of God in the Life of the Church*, § 58.
53. Baptist World Alliance and Catholic Church, *The Word of God in the Life of the Church*, §§ 101-06. See also Baptist World Alliance and Anglican Consultative Council, *Conversations Around the World 2000-2005: The Report of the International Conversations between the Anglican Communion and the Baptist World Alliance* (London: Anglican Communion Office, 2005), 44-51; and Baptist Union of Great Britain and Church of England, *Pushing at the Boundaries of Unity: Anglicans and Baptists in Conversation* (London: Church House Publishing, 2005), 31-57.
54. Baptist World Alliance and Catholic Church, *The Word of God in the Life of the Church*, §§ 150 and 156. On the possibility of praying with Mary in the communion of saints in Baptist perspective, see Paul S. Fiddes, Brian Haymes, and Richard Kidd, *Baptists and the Communion of Saints: A Theology of Covenanted Disciples* (Waco, TX: Baylor University Press, 2014), 73-101.
55. Baptist World Alliance and Catholic Church, *The Word of God in the Life of the Church*, §§ 173 and 182.
56. Vatican II, *Unitatis Redintegratio*, § 2.
57. World Council of Churches, *Baptism, Eucharist and Ministry* (Faith and Order Paper no. 111; Geneva: World Council of Churches, 1982); idem, *The Church: Towards a Common Vision* (Faith and Order Paper no. 214; Geneva: World Council of Churches, 2013).
58. World Council of Churches, *The Church*, §§ 11-32 (pp. 9-19).
59. World Council of Churches, *The Church*, §§ 1-10 (pp. 5-8).
60. World Council of Churches, *The Church*, § 13 (p. 10).
61. Vatican II, *Unitatis Redintegratio*, § 2.
62. World Council of Churches, *The Church*, §§ 33, 35, 37 (pp. 21-22).
63. Vatican II, *Unitatis Redintegratio*, § 2. Cf. the use of the "pilgrim church" motif in idem, *Lumen Gentium*, §§ 7 and 48.
64. John Paul II, "On Commitment to Ecumenism (*Ut Unum Sint*)" (May 25, 1995), § 8, online http://www.vatican.va/holy_father/john_paul_ii/encyclicals/documents/hf_jp-ii_enc_25051995_ut-unum-sint_en.html (downloaded September 29, 2020).

65. "Receptive ecumenism" is an approach to ecumenical dialogue according to which the communions in conversation with one another seek to identify the distinctive gifts that each tradition has to offer the other and which each could receive from the other with integrity. See Paul D. Murray, ed., *Receptive Ecumenism and the Call to Catholic Learning: Exploring a Way for Contemporary Ecumenism* (Oxford: Oxford University Press, 2008). While the nomenclature is more recent in origin, "receptive ecumenism" names a paradigm for ecumenical convergence already long practiced among the churches and articulated by *Ut Unum Sint*, § 28: "Dialogue is not simply an exchange of ideas. In some ways it is always an 'exchange of gifts'." (Chapter 3 of this book will apply the paradigm of receptive ecumenism to the Baptist encounter with Catholic (and catholic) Christianity.
66. Vatican II, *Unitatis Redintegratio*, §§ 4-5.
67. John Paul II, *Ut Unum Sint*, § 3.
68. This manner of distinguishing between the interrelated "quantitative" and "qualitative" dimensions of the catholicity of the church in this article, now commonplace in ecumenical theology, has origins in Congar's early ecclesiological work. See Congar, *Chrétiens désunis*, 115-17; idem, *Divided Christendom*, 93-94: "The Catholicity of the Church has long been interpreted in an exclusively geographical or, at any rate, quantitative sense, as the temporal and especially the local extension of the Church among all men and throughout the who world. . . . But in the Fathers, except perhaps St. Augustine, and in the early theologians, this quantitative aspect is never affirmed in isolation, it is enumerated among other elements. . . . On thinking it over one is very quickly led to see that there cannot be quantitative Catholicity without qualitative, this being the necessary cause of the former."
69. See C. Douglas Weaver, *In Search of the New Testament Church: The Baptist Story* (Macon, GA: Mercer University Press, 2008).
70. Here I am echoing language from Alasdair MacIntyre's characterization of "a living tradition" as "an historically extended, socially embodied argument, and an argument precisely in part about the goods which constitute that tradition" (Alasdair MacIntyre, *After Virtue: A Study in Moral Theory*, 2nd ed. [Notre Dame, IN: University of Notre Dame Press, 1984], 222).
71. I develop this assertion at length in Harmon, *Baptist Identity and the Ecumenical Future*. It is rooted in the historic Baptist quest for a church that is fully under the rule of Christ, for which Baptists locate the ideal exemplar not in any past or present instantiation of church but rather in the eschatological future.

72. Here I am alluding to the statement in the introduction of *Dei Verbum* regarding the relationship of the constitution to the teaching of previous councils: "This council aims, then, following in the steps of the councils of Trent and Vatican I (*conciliorum Tridentini et Vaticani I inhaerens vestigiis*), to set forth authentic teaching on God's revelation and how it is communicated. . ." (Vatican II, *Dogmatic Constitution on Divine Revelation Dei Verbum* [18 November 1965], trans. Robert Murray, in *Decrees of the Ecumenical Councils*, ed. Norman P. Tanner, vol. 2, *Trent to Vatican II* [London: Sheed & Ward and Washington, DC: Georgetown University Press, 1990], proem., 971-72). In doing so, I have opted for Karl Barth's suggested translation of *inhaerens vestigiis*. Barth's rather positive assessment of *Dei Verbum* was rooted in his aversion to one possible translation, "in the succession of the Councils of Trent and First Vatican," which suggested to Barth that "following in their tracks, it intended to say the same thing they said," and his preference for understanding the expression instead in the sense of "moving forward from the footsteps of those councils" (Karl Barth, "'Conciliorum Tridentini et Vaticani I Inhaerens Vestigiis'," in *Ad Limina Apostolorum: An Appraisal of Vatican II*, trans. Keith B. Crim [Richmond, VA: John Knox Press, 1968], 43-45). Joseph Ratzinger concurred that "we can entirely agree with Karl Barth's suggested translation of this formula," which meant for Ratzinger that between these previous councils and Vatican II there is "a continuity that is not a rigid external identification with what has gone before, but a preservation of the old, established in the midst of progress," so "that we might perhaps see the relation of this text to its predecessors as a perfect example of doctrinal development. . ." (Ratzinger, "Dogmatic Constitution on Divine Revelation: Preface," trans. William Glen-Doepel, in *Commentary on the Documents of Vatican II*, ed. Herbert Vorgrimler [New York: Herder and Herder, 1967-69], vol. 3, 168-69).

73. The reports and agreed statements from these dialogues between the Catholic Church and other communions, along with the documents of the dialogues among non-Catholic churches that were inspired by the dialogue initiatives of the Catholic Church that followed Vatican II, are gathered in the *Growth in Agreement* series published by the World Council of Churches Commission on Faith and Order: Harding Meyer and Lukas Vischer, eds., *Growth in Agreement: Reports and Agreed Statements of Ecumenical Conversations on a World Level* (Faith and Order Paper no. 108; New York: Paulist Press and Geneva: World Council of Churches, 1984); Jeffrey Gros, Harding Meyer, and William G. Rusch, eds., *Growth in Agreement II: Reports and Agreed Statements of Ecumenical Conversations on a World Level, 1982-1998* (Faith and Order Paper no.

187; Geneva: WCC Publications and Grand Rapids, MI: William B. Eerdmans, 2000); Jeffrey Gros, Thomas F. Best, and Lorelei F. Fuchs, eds., *Growth in Agreement III: International Dialogue Texts and Agreed Statements, 1998-2005* (Faith and Order Paper no. 204; Geneva: WCC Publications and Grand Rapids, MI: William B. Eerdmans, 2007); Thomas F. Best, Lorelei F. Fuchs, John Gibaut, Jeffrey Gros, and Despina Prassas, eds., *Growth in Agreement IV: International Dialogue Texts and Agreed Statements, 2004-2014, Books 1 and 2*, 2 vols. (Faith and Order Paper no. 219; Geneva: WCC Publications, 2017). Most of these documents from international dialogues with Catholic participation are also available online on the Pontifical Council for Promoting Christian Unity site's "Ecumenical Relations" page at http://www.christianunity.va/content/unitacristiani/en/dialoghi.html (accessed October 27, 2020).

74. Baptist World Alliance and Catholic Church, "Summons to Witness to Christ in Today's World: A Report on Conversations 1984-1988," *The Pontifical Council for Promoting Christian Unity Information Service* 72 (1990): 5-13; also published in *Deepening Communion: International Ecumenical Documents with Roman Catholic Participation*, ed. William G. Rusch and Jeffrey Gros (Washington, DC: United States Catholic Conference, 1998), 343-60; *Growth in Agreement II: Reports and Agreed Statements of Ecumenical Conversations on a World Level, 1982-1998*, ed. Jeffrey Gros, Harding Meyer, and William G. Rusch (Geneva: WCC Publications and Grand Rapids, MI: William B. Eerdmans, 2000), 373-85; and online at http://www.christianunity.va/content/unitacristiani/en/dialoghi/sezione-occidentale/alleanza-battista-mondiale/dialogo-internazionale-tra-la-chiesa-cattolica-e-l-alleanza-batt/documenti-di-dialogo/1988-chiamati-ad-essere-testimoni-di-cristo-nel-mondo-di-oggi-/testo-del-documento-in-inglese.html (accessed October 27, 2020).

75. Baptist World Alliance and Catholic Church, *The Word of God in the Life of the Church*, § 1.

76. Joseph Ratzinger, "Dogmatic Constitution on Divine Revelation: Chapter II, The Transmission of Divine Revelation," trans. William Glen-Doepel, in *Commentary on the Documents of Vatican II*, ed. Herbert Vorgrimler, vol. 3 (New York: Herder and Herder, 1967-69), 181-98.

77. See the discussion of meaning of and significance for non-Catholic Christians of the Congregation for the Doctrine of the Faith's "Declaration '*Dominus Iesus*' On the Unicity and Salvific Universality of Jesus Christ and the Church" in chapter 1 of this book.

78. Baptist World Alliance and Catholic Church, "The Word of God in the Life of the Church: A Report of International Conversations between the

Catholic Church and the Baptist World Alliance 2006-2010," *American Baptist Quarterly* 31, no. 1 (Spring 2012): 28-122; online, http://www.christianunity.va/content/unitacristiani/en/dialoghi/sezione-occidentale/alleanza-battista-mondiale/dialogo-internazionale-tra-la-chiesa-cattolica-e-l-alleanza-batt/documenti-di-dialogo/2010-la-parola-di-dio-nella-vita-della-chiesa/testo-del-documento-in-inglese.html (accessed October 27, 2020).

79. Lutheran World Federation and Catholic Church, *Joint Declaration on the Doctrine of Justification* (Grand Rapids, MI: William B. Eerdmans, 2000), §§ 5, 14, and 40 (pp. 10-11, 15, 25-26). While the *Joint Declaration* itself does not use the precise expression "differentiated consensus" to describe the agreement reached between the Lutheran World Federation and the Roman Catholic Church, the concept is certainly present in the language "consensus on basic truths" with "remaining differences" or "differing explications," and in the reception of the *Joint Declaration* the language "differentiated consensus" has become identified with the *Joint Declaration*. See Harding Meyer, "Die Prägung einer Formel: Ursprung und Intention," in *Einheit—Aber Wie? Zur Tragfähigkeit der ökumenischen Formel vom "Differenzierten Konsens"*, ed. Harald Wagner (Quaestiones Disputatae, ed. Peter Hünermann and Thomas Söding, vol. 184; Freiburg: Herder, 2000), 36-58.

80. Steven R. Harmon, *Ecumenism Means You, Too: Ordinary Christians and the Quest for Christian Unity* (Eugene, OR: Cascade Books, 2010), 116.

81. Paul S. Fiddes, the Baptist co-chair of the Baptist-Catholic joint commission for Phase II of the dialogue, has been a noteworthy contributor to this renewal of Trinitarian theology with his book *Participating in God: A Pastoral Doctrine of the Trinity* (Louisville, KY: Westminster John Knox Press, 2000). While Fiddes's own perspectives on Trinitarian theology were influential for this emphasis of the Baptist-Catholic Phase II dialogue, they found broad resonance with both Baptist and Catholic members of the joint commission.

82. During our 2007 meeting in Rome, we presented and discussed two papers offering a Baptist and a Catholic perspective on *Dei Verbum* § 9, in which the Catholic understanding of the relationship between Scripture and tradition is elaborated. A revision of my own contribution to that aspect of our work was published as Steven R. Harmon, "*Dei Verbum* § 9 in Baptist Perspective," *Ecclesiology* 5, no. 3 (September 2009): 299-321; a further adaptation appears in Harmon, *Baptist Identity and the Ecumenical Future*, 91-112.

83. Another of my contributions to our dialogue on Scripture and tradition was a paper I presented during our 2006 meeting in Birmingham,

Alabama, published as Steven R. Harmon, "Scripture in the Life of the Baptist Churches: Openings for a Differentiated Catholic-Baptist Consensus on Sacred Scripture," *Pro Ecclesia* 18, no. 2 (Spring 2009): 187-215; the material was also published in adapted form in Harmon, *Baptist Identity and the Ecumenical Future*, 55-89.

84. Harmon, *Ecumenism Means You, Too*, 116.
85. I develop these proposals about facilitating the reception of reports from ecumenical dialogues more fully in Harmon, *Baptist Identity and the Ecumenical Future*, 262-66.
86. On local ecumenical covenants as a practice of grassroots ecumenical engagement, see Michael Kinnamon, *Can a Renewal Movement Be Renewed? Questions for the Future of Ecumenism* (Grand Rapids, MI: William B. Eerdmans, 2014), 15-16, 83-84.
87. James Robert Coggins, *John Smyth's Congregation: English Separatism, Mennonite Influence, and the Elect Nation* (Studies in Anabaptist and Mennonite History, no. 32; Waterloo, Ontario: Herald Press, 1991), 61-65. Smyth set forth the theological rationale for his rejection of the baptisms of other churches as "anti-Christian" in his 1609 treatise *The Character of the Beast of the False Constitution of the Church* (W. T. Whitley, ed., *The Works of John Smyth, Fellow of Christ's College, 1594-8* [Cambridge: Cambridge University Press, 1915], 2 vols.).
88. World Council of Churches, *Baptism, Eucharist and Ministry*, Faith and Order Paper No. 111 (Geneva: World Council of Churches, 1982).
89. Reported in Anglican Consultative Council and Baptist World Alliance, *Conversations Around the World 2000-2005: The Report of the International Conversations between the Anglican Communion and the Baptist World Alliance* (London: The Anglican Communion Office, 2005), 50-51.
90. Coggins, *John Smyth's Congregation*, 77-81.
91. Timothy F. George, *Faithful Witness: The Life and Mission of William Carey* (Birmingham, AL: New Hope, 1991), 162.
92. By-laws of the Faith and Order Commission of the World Council of Churches, quoted in *Faith and Order: Toward a North American Conference. Study Guide*, ed. Norman A. Hjelm (Grand Rapids, MI: William B. Eerdmans, 2005), vii.
93. William R. Estep, *Baptists and Christian Unity* (Nashville: Broadman Press, 1966), 168-88.
94. See Paul D. Murray, ed., *Receptive Ecumenism and the Call to Catholic Learning: Exploring a Way for Contemporary Ecumenism* (Oxford: Oxford University Press, 2008).
95. John Paul II, *Ut Unum Sint*, § 8.

96. Catholic Church and World Methodist Council, *The Grace Given You in Christ: Catholics and Methodists Reflect Further on the Church* (Lake Junaluska, NC: World Methodist Council, 2006).
97. Quotation from a briefing document distributed to conference participants in Walter Cardinal Kasper's "Foreword" to *Receptive Ecumenism and the Call to Catholic Learning*, ed. Murray, vii.
98. *Second London Confession* 26.1, in *Baptist Confessions of Faith*, rev. ed., ed. William L. Lumpkin (Valley Forge, PA: Judson Press, 1969), 285; *Orthodox Creed* 29, in Lumpkin, *Baptist Confessions of Faith*, 318.
99. *Orthodox Creed* 38, in Lumpkin, *Baptist Confessions of Faith*, 326.
100. *Second London Confession* 26.1, in Lumpkin, *Baptist Confessions of Faith*, 285; *Orthodox Creed* 29, in Lumpkin, *Baptist Confessions of Faith*, 318.
101. *Second London Confession* 2.3 and 8.1-7, in Lumpkin, *Baptist Confessions of Faith*, 253 and 260-62; *Orthodox Creed* 3-7, in Lumpkin, *Baptist Confessions of Faith*, 299-301.
102. Justin Martyr *1 Apology* 67 (English translation in *Ante-Nicene Fathers*, ed. Alexander Roberts and James Donaldson [New York: Christian Literature Publishing Co., 1885], 1:185-86).
103. Ernest Payne, *The Fellowship of Believers: Baptist Thought and Practice Yesterday and Today* (London: Carey Kingsgate Press, 1952), 96.
104. Christopher J. Ellis, *Gathering: A Theology and Spirituality of Worship in Free Church Tradition* (London: SCM Press, 2004), 152.
105. John Rippon, *A Selection of Hymns from the Best Authors, intended to be an appendix to Dr. Watts's Psalms and Hymns* (London: 1787), preface; quoted in Ellis, *Gathering for Worship*, 152.
106. Wesley L. Forbis, ed., *The Baptist Hymnal* (Nashville: Convention Press, 1991).
107. Mike Harland, ed., *Baptist Hymnal* (Nashville: Lifeway Worship, 2008).
108. Tom McAfee, John Simons, David Music, Milburn Price, Stanley Roberts, and Mark Edwards, eds., *Celebrating Grace Hymnal* (Macon, GA: Celebrating Grace, Inc., 2010).
109. Dayspring Baptist Church, online http://ourdayspring.org (accessed November 27, 2020).
110. Dayspring Baptist Church, "Who We Are," online http://ourdayspring.org/about-us/who-we-are/ (accessed November 27, 2020).
111. Dayspring Baptist Church, "Liturgical Seasons," http://ourdayspring.org/about-us/who-we-are/#tab-section-402318 (accessed November 27, 2020).
112. Dayspring Baptist Church, "The Worship of God: Trinity Sunday, June 7, 2020," online https://4e3aeac139a83f50ab54-c01dfbb6de6c-

382355cbbb12ce96d6b9.ssl.cf2.rackcdn.com/uploaded/6/
0e10509356_1591382105_6-7-20-trinity.pdf (accessed November 27,
2020).
113. Dayspring Baptist Church, "Practicing Silence," online http://ourdayspring.org/about-us/who-we-are/#tab-section-402318 (accessed November 27, 2020).
114. Daniel Buttry, "Baptists Amid Georgian Revolutions," *Baptists Today* 23, no. 8 (August 2005), 9.
115. W. Benjamin Boswell, "Liturgy and Revolution Part 1: Georgian Baptists and the Non-violent Struggle for Democracy," *Religion in Eastern Europe* 27, no. 2 (May 2007), 59.
116. Evangelical Baptist Church of Georgia, online: http://www.ebcgeorgia.org/Neue_Dateien/start.html (accessed November 27, 2020); Malkhaz Songulashvili, *Evangelical Christian Baptists of Georgia: The History and Transformation of a Free Church Tradition* (Studies in World Christianity; Waco, TX: Baylor University Press, 2015).
117. Archbishop Malkhaz Songulashvili, interview correspondence quoted in Boswell, "Liturgy and Revolution," 59.
118. Paul S. Fiddes, "Learning from Others: Baptists and Receptive Ecumenism," *Louvain Studies* 33, nos. 1-2 (2008): 54-73.
119. Baptist World Alliance and Catholic Church, "Summons to Witness to Christ in Today's World: A Report on Conversations 1984-1988," *The Pontifical Council for Promoting Christian Unity Information Service* 72 (1990): 5-13; also published in *Deepening Communion: International Ecumenical Documents with Roman Catholic Participation*, ed. William G. Rusch and Jeffrey Gros (Washington, DC: United States Catholic Conference, 1998), 343-60; *Growth in Agreement II: Reports and Agreed Statements of Ecumenical Conversations on a World Level, 1982-1998*, ed. Jeffrey Gros, Harding Meyer, and William G. Rusch, 373-85 (Geneva: WCC Publications and Grand Rapids, MI: William B. Eerdmans, 2000); and online at http://www.vatican.va/roman_curia/pontifical_councils/chrstuni/Bapstist%20alliance/rc_pc_chrstuni_doc_19880723_baptist-convers_en.html (accessed October 27, 2020).
120. Baptist World Alliance and Catholic Church, *The Word of God in the Life of the Church: A Report of International Conversations between the Catholic Church and the Baptist World Alliance 2006-2010* (2013), published in *American Baptist Quarterly* 31, no. 1 (Spring 2012): 28-122; *Pontifical Council for Promoting Christian Unity Information Service* 142 (2013): 20-65; online http://www.vatican.va/roman_curia/pontifical_councils/chrstuni/Bapstist%20alliance/rc_pc_chrstuni_doc_20101213_report-2006-2010_en.html (accessed November 29, 2020). The boldface

paragraph is a common affirmation by both delegations to the joint commission, and the following paragraph in regular type is "a further elaboration of our convergence" (§ 6).

121. Lutheran World Federation and Mennonite World Conference, *Healing Memories: Reconciling in Christ. Report of the Lutheran-Mennonite International Study Commission* (Geneva and Strasbourg: Lutheran World Federation and Mennonite World Conference, 2010); online https://www.lutheranworld.org/sites/default/files/OEA-Lutheran-Mennonites-EN-full.pdf (accessed November 29, 2020).

122. See Undine Kayser, "Creating a Space for Encounter and Remembrance: The Healing of Memories Process," Research Report Written for the Centre for the Study of Violence and Reconciliation and the Institute for Healing of Memories (January 2000), online http://www.csvr.org.za/docs/reconciliation/creatingaspace.pdf (accessed November 30, 2020).

123. Catholic Church and Mennonite World Conference, *Called Together to Be Peacemakers: Report of the International Dialogue between the Catholic Church and Mennonite World Conference 1998-2003* (August 2003); online http://www.vatican.va/roman_curia/pontifical_councils/chrstuni/mennonite-conference-docs/rc_pc_chrstuni_doc_20110324_mennonite_en.html#_ftn170 (accessed November 30, 2020).

124. Lutheran World Federation and Mennonite World Conference, *Healing Memories*, 11.

125. "The Augsburg Confession," in *The Book of Concord: The Confessions of the Evangelical Lutheran Church*, ed. Robert Kolb and Timothy J. Wengert, trans. Charles P. Arand et al. (Minneapolis: Augsburg Fortress, 2000), 40. (Note: these quotations are from the translation of the German text of the Augsburg Confession; this edition also includes a translation of the Latin text of the confession.)

126. "Augsburg Confession," in *Book of Concord*, ed. Kolb and Wengert, trans. Arand et al., 42.

127. "Augsburg Confession," in *Book of Concord*, ed. Kolb and Wengert, trans. Arand et al., 42.

128. "Augsburg Confession," in *Book of Concord*, ed. Kolb and Wengert, trans. Arand et al., 44.

129. "Augsburg Confession," in *Book of Concord*, ed. Kolb and Wengert, trans. Arand et al., 49.

130. "Augsburg Confession," in *Book of Concord*, ed. Kolb and Wengert, trans. Arand et al., 50.

131. "Augsburg Confession," in *Book of Concord*, ed. Kolb and Wengert, trans. Arand et al., 90.

132. Lutheran World Federation and Mennonite World Conference, *Healing Memories*, 12-13.
133. Lutheran World Federation and Mennonite World Conference, *Healing Memories*, 20-72.
134. Lutheran World Federation and Mennonite World Conference, *Healing Memories*, 56.
135. Lutheran World Federation and Mennonite World Conference, *Healing Memories*, 56.
136. Lutheran World Federation and Mennonite World Conference, *Healing Memories*, 71.
137. Lutheran World Federation and Mennonite World Conference, *Healing Memories*, 72.
138. Lutheran World Federation and Mennonite World Conference, *Healing Memories*, 75-77.
139. Lutheran World Federation and Mennonite World Conference, *Healing Memories*, 84-90.
140. Lutheran World Federation and Mennonite World Conference, *Healing Memories*, 78-84.
141. Catholic Church, Lutheran World Federation, and Mennonite World Conference, "Communiqué: Lutheran, Mennonite, Catholic Trilateral Dialogue" (Strasbourg, France, 15-19 September 2017); online http://www.christianunity.va/content/unitacristiani/en/dialoghi/sezione-occidentale/dialoghi-multilaterali/dialogo-trilaterale-cattolico-mennonita-luterano/comunicati-stampa/2017-strasbourg/en.html (accessed November 30, 2020).
142. Lutheran World Federation and Mennonite World Conference, *Healing Memories*, 91-110.
143. Lutheran World Federation and Mennonite World Conference, *Healing Memories*, 108-09.
144. Lutheran World Federation and Mennonite World Conference, *Healing Memories*, 108.
145. Byron Rempel-Burkholder, "Lutherans and Anabaptists Reconcile in Service of Repentance and Forgiveness," *MWC News Service* (July 27, 2010); online http://joomla.mwc-cmm.org/index.php/news-releases/76-lutherans-and-anabaptists-reconcile-in-service-of-repentance-and-forgiveness (accessed November 30, 2020).
146. For a critical examination of the historical sources for this emergence of the Baptists and the relationship of the Smyth congregation to the Mennonites, see James Robert Coggins, *John Smyth's Congregation: English Separatism, Mennonite Influence, and the Elect Nation* (Studies in

Anabaptist and Mennonite History, no. 32; Waterloo, Ontario: Herald Press, 1991), 61-65.
147. Designation employed, e.g., by Franklin H. Littell, *The Anabaptist View of the Church* (Boston: Starr King, 1952) and Gunnar Westin, *The Free Church through the Ages*, trans. Virgil Olson (Nashville: Broadman Press, 1954).
148. Designation employed, e.g., by Donald F. Durnbaugh, *The Believer's Church: The History and Character of Radical Protestantism* (New York: Macmillan, 1968), and in contributions to James Leo Garrett, Jr., ed., *The Concept of the Believers' Church: Addresses from the 1967 Louisville Conference* (Scottdale, PA: Herald Press, 1969).
149. James Wm. McClendon, Jr., *Systematic Theology*, vol. 1, *Ethics*, rev. ed. (Waco, TX: Baylor University Press, 2012), 17-20.
150. Tarmo Toom, "Baptists on Justification: Can We Join the Joint Declaration on the Doctrine of Justification?" *Pro Ecclesia* 13, no. 3 (Summer 2004): 305 (289-306); Baptist World Alliance and Lutheran World Federation, "A Message to Our Churches," § 1, in *Growth in Agreement II: Reports and Agreed Statements of Ecumenical Conversations on a World Level, 1982-1998*, ed. Jeffrey Gros, Harding Meyer, and William G. Rusch (Faith and Order Paper no. 187; Geneva: WCC Publications and Grand Rapids, MI: William B. Eerdmans, 2000), 155-75.
151. Baptist World Alliance and Catholic Church, *Summons to Witness to Christ in Today's World*, § 43: "In certain traditionally Roman Catholic countries civil constitutions and laws enacted prior to the Second Vatican Council have not been changed to reflect the teaching of the Council. In some settings with a dominant Baptist majority the traditional Baptist stress on separation of church and state as a means to assure religious freedom has been weakened. Both groups need to exercise greater vigilance to ensure respect for religious liberty"; idem, *The Word of God in the Life of the Church*, § 200: "The historical failures of the past among both Baptists and Catholics must be addressed, with due repentance and appropriate action in the present"; § 201, "The new situation created by the spirit of ecumenism invites all brothers and sisters in Christ to re-examine the past and, if appropriate, to revise some of the earlier stances taken by members of our communities. Many within both Christian communions wish to distance themselves from the negative judgments made of each other in the past. Historical failures have been acknowledged from the Catholic side, for instance by John Paul II in his encyclical on ecumenism *Ut unum sint* ('That they may be one') and on occasions such as the liturgy of reconciliation on the First Sunday of Lent during the Jubilee Year 2000. For their part, most contemporary Baptists wish to disassociate

themselves from harsh names applied to the papacy by their ancestors in very different circumstances."
152. Bob Allen, "Catholics in Nagaland Claiming Persecution at Hands of Baptists," *Baptist News Global* (July 27, 2010); online https://baptistnews.com/article/catholics-in-nagaland-claiming-persecution-at-hands-of-baptists/#.Xe6N1qeZNQI (accessed November 30, 2020).
153. Congregation for the Doctrine of the Faith, "Declaration '*Dominus Iesus*' (August 6, 2000), online https://www.vatican.va/roman_curia/congregations/cfaith/documents/rc_con_cfaith_doc_20000806_dominus-iesus_en.html (accessed November 29, 2020); Francis A. Sullivan, "The Impact of *Dominus Iesus* on Ecumenism," *America* (October 28, 2000), online https://www.americamagazine.org/issue/386/article/impact-dominus-iesus-ecumenism (accessed November 30, 2020); Congregation for the Doctrine of the Faith, "Responses to Some Questions Regarding Certain Aspects of the Doctrine of the Church" (June 29, 2007), online https://www.vatican.va/roman_curia/congregations/cfaith/documents/rc_con_cfaith_doc_20070629_responsa-quaestiones_en.html (accessed November 29, 2020).
154. Baptist World Alliance and Catholic Church, *Summons to Witness to Christ in Today's World*.
155. I have explored the history of this Baptist-Catholic ecumenical academic collaboration in Steven R. Harmon, "The Traditioned Word in the Life of the Church: The Influence of the NABPR Region-at-Large/CTS Partnership on the Second Baptist–Catholic International Dialogue (2006–2010)," in *American Catholicism in the 21st Century: Crossroads, Crisis, or Renewal?*, ed. Benjamin Peters and Nicholas Rademacher (Maryknoll, NY: Orbis Books, 2018), 177-88.
156. John Paul II, "On Commitment to Ecumenism (*Ut Unum Sint*)," May 25, 1995, § 96, online http://www.vatican.va/holy_father/john_paul_ii/encyclicals/documents/hf_jp-ii_enc_25051995_ut-unum-sint_en.html (downloaded September 29, 2020).
157. The panel presentations were published as a Theological Roundtable on "Shared Communion" in *Horizons: The Journal of the College Theology Society* 45, no. 2 (December 2018): 375-411.
158. Curtis W. Freeman, "Can Catholics and Baptists Share Communion without Breaking the Rules?" *Horizons: The Journal of the College Theology Society* 45, no. 2 (December 2018): 376 (375-94).
159. Ludwig Wittgenstein, *Philosophical Investigations*, rev. 4th ed., trans. G. E. M. Anscombe, P. M. S. Hacker, and Joachim Schulte (Chichester, UK: Wiley-Blackwell, 2009).

160. Freeman, "Can Catholics and Baptists Share Communion without Breaking the Rules?" 383.
161. Freeman, "Can Catholics and Baptists Share Communion without Breaking the Rules?" 392.
162. Timothy Brunk, "Serious Spiritual Need?" *Horizons: The Journal of the College Theology Society* 45, no. 2 (December 2018): 396 (394-99).
163. Brunk, "Serious Spiritual Need?" 398.
164. Philip E. Thompson, "Being Made a Patient People," *Horizons: The Journal of the College Theology Society* 45, no. 2 (December 2018): 403 (402-06).
165. Thompson, "Being Made a Patient People," 405.
166. Sandra Yocum, "Fulfilling the Rules," *Horizons: The Journal of the College Theology Society* 45, no. 2 (December 2018): 408 (406-09).
167. Derek Hatch, "Discerning the Questions," *Horizons: The Journal of the College Theology Society* 45, no. 2 (December 2018): 409-11.
168. Steven R. Harmon, "A Eucharistically-Malnourished Baptist's Desire for Intercommunion," *Horizons: The Journal of the College Theology Society* 45, no. 2 (December 2018): 399-402.
169. Outlined in Avery Dulles, "Eucharistic Sharing as an Ecumenical Problem," chapter in *The Resilient Church* (Garden City, NY: Doubleday, 1977), 153-71.
170. I have commended to Baptists the practice of reciting the ancient creeds as an act of worship, offering a Baptist ecclesiological rationale for the practice and citing precedents within the Baptist tradition for doing so, in Steven R. Harmon, *Towards Baptist Catholicity: Essays on Tradition and the Baptist Vision* (Studies in Baptist History and Thought, vol. 27; Milton Keynes, UK: Paternoster, 2006), 163-65.
171. On hymnody as a locus for Baptist practices of receptive ecumenism, see Steven R. Harmon, *Baptist Identity and the Ecumenical Future: Story, Tradition, and the Recovery of Community* (Waco, TX: Baylor University Press, 2016), 153-56.
172. I treat various worship practices with roots in ancient Christian liturgy as means by which Baptists may re-appropriate catholicity liturgically in Harmon, *Towards Baptist Catholicity*, 151-77.
173. Catherine E. Clifford and James F. Puglisi, eds., *A Century of Prayer for Christian Unity* (Grand Rapids, MI: William B. Eerdmans, 2009); Thomas Orians, "Brief History of the Week of Prayer for Christian Unity," online https://geii.org/week_of_prayer_for_christian_unity/week_of_prayer_history.html (accessed December 7, 2020).

174. Steven R. Harmon, *Ecumenism Means You, Too: Ordinary Christians and the Quest for Christian Unity* (Eugene, OR: Cascade Books, 2010).
175. World Council of Churches, "Week of Prayer for Christian Unity Asks What Victory Means for Unity," online https://www.oikoumene.org/news/week-of-prayer-2012-asks-what-victory-means-for-unity (accessed December 7, 2020); Graymoor Ecumenical & Interreligious Institute, "2012 Week of Prayer Materials," online https://geii.org/week_of_prayer_for_christian_unity/week_of_prayer_materials.html (accessed December 7, 2020).
176. World Council of Churches, "Report of the Section on Unity," in *The New Delhi Report: The Third Assembly of the World Council of Churches, 1961* (New York: Association Press, 1962), 116 (116-35).
177. Drafted by Steven R. Harmon (Professor Historical Theology, Gardner-Webb University School of Divinity, Boiling Springs, North Carolina, USA); revised in light of input from the membership of the BWA Commission on Baptist Doctrine and Christian Unity meeting in Nassau, The Bahamas, 8-12 July 2019.
178. These statistics for the total number of local congregations and individual church members affiliated with the BWA were current as of December 31, 2017; the number of 240 member unions reflects the reception of one additional member union by the BWA during its 2019 General Council meeting (Baptist World Alliance, "Statistics," online https://www.bwanet.org/about-us2/stats [downloaded July 1, 2019]). Since Baptist churches do not include in their membership statistics children whose families participate in the life of the congregation but who have not yet been baptized, the actual number of persons affiliated with churches included in the global fellowship of the BWA is significantly larger than 47,500,324 members.
179. Baptist World Alliance, "Constitution of the BWA," online https://secureservercdn.net/166.62.112.219/o7e.4a3.myftpupload.com/wp-content/uploads/2020/08/BWA-Constitution-and-Bylaws-2020.pdf (downloaded March 3, 2021), "Preamble" and "II. Objectives." While the largest national union of Baptists in the world, the Southern Baptist Convention—which was instrumental in the founding of the BWA in 1905—ceased to be a member union of the BWA in 2004, Southern Baptists nevertheless continue to participate individually in the commissions and gatherings of the BWA.
180. Baptist World Alliance, "Commissions of Mission and Evangelism," online https://www.bwanet.org/images/MissionEvangelism.pdf (downloaded July 1, 2019).

181. Ernest A. Payne, "Baptists and the Ecumenical Movement," *Baptist Quarterly* 8: 263 (258-67).
182. World Council of Churches, "Church Families: Baptist Churches," online https://www.oikoumene.org/en/church-families/baptist-churches (downloaded July 1, 2019).
183. World Council of Churches, *The Church: Towards a Common Vision* (Faith and Order Paper No. 214; Geneva: WCC Publications, 2013), 1.
184. World Council of Churches, *The Church*, viii-ix.
185. These Baptist ecclesial responses are published in *Churches Respond to Baptism, Eucharist and Ministry*, 6 vols., ed. Max Thurian (Geneva: World Council of Churches, 1986-88). They include the Baptist Union of Great Britain and Ireland (1:70-77), All-Union Council of Evangelical Christians-Baptists in the USSR (3:227-29), Baptist Union of Scotland (3:230-45), Baptist Union of Denmark (3:246-53), Covenanted Baptist Churches in Wales (3:254-56), American Baptist Churches, USA (3:257-63), Burma Baptist Convention (4:184-90), Union of the Evangelical Free Churches in the GDR (Baptists) (4:191-99), and Baptist Union of Sweden (4:200-13).
186. R. J. Kerstan and R. J. Burke, eds., *Out of Darkness into the Light of Christ: Official Report of the Fifteenth Baptist World Congress, Los Angeles, California, USA July 2-7, 1985* (McLean, VA: Baptist World Alliance, 1985), 146-55; William R. Estep, "A Response to *Baptism, Eucharist and Ministry*: Faith and Order Paper No. 111," in *Faith, Life and Witness: The Papers of the Study and Research Division of the Baptist World Alliance 1986-1990*, ed. William H. Brackney and R. J. Burke (Birmingham, AL: Samford University Press, 1990), 2-16. The earlier version prepared by George Beasley Murray, Morris West, and Robert Thompson is noted by Ken Manley, "A Survey of Baptist World Alliance Conversations with Other Churches and Some Implications for Baptist Identity," paper presented to the joint meeting of the BWA Baptist Heritage and Identity Commission and Doctrine and Interchurch Cooperation Commission, Seville, Spain, July 11, 2002, online http://bwa-baptist-heritage.org/wp-content/uploads/2016/07/Survey-of-Conversations-with-Other-Churches.pdf (downloaded July 1, 2019).
187. While Estep's expanded response was presented to the BWA Commission on Baptist Doctrine and Interchurch Cooperation and published in the collected papers of the Study and Research Division for 1986-1990, it was not published in the six volumes of responses to *BEM* (*Churches Respond to Baptism, Eucharist and Ministry*, 6 vols., ed. Thurian).

188. World Council of Churches, *The Nature and Mission of the Church: A Stage on the Way to a Common Statement* (Faith and Order Paper No. 198; Geneva: WCC Publications, 2005).
189. Curtis W. Freeman, "'The Church of the Triune God': A Baptist Response to *The Nature and Mission of the Church: A Stage on the Way to a Common Statement* (Faith and Order Paper 198)," in *Baptist Faith & Witness, Book 5: Papers of the Commission on Mission, Evangelism and Theological Reflection of the Baptist World Alliance 2010-2015*, ed. Eron Henry (Falls Church, VA: Baptist World Alliance, 2015), 7-24; Elizabeth Newman, "'The Church: Growing in Communion': Response to Chapter III of *The Church: Towards a Common Vision* (Faith and Order Paper 214)," in *Baptist Faith & Witness, Book 5*, 25-36; Paul S. Fiddes, "'*Koinonia*: The Church in and for the World': Comment on the Final Part of *The Church: Towards a Common Vision* (Faith and Order Paper 214)," in *Baptist Faith & Witness, Book 5*, 37-47 [note: while the subtitle of the volume in which these responses appear refers to a "Commission" on Mission, Evangelism and Theological Reflection, its proper designation during this period was the "Division of Mission, Evangelism, and Theological Reflection," a division which included multiple study commissions of the BWA, among them the Commission on Baptist Doctrine and Christian Unity].
190. Derek C. Hatch, "*Koinonia* as Ecumenical Opening for Baptists," *The Ecumenical Review* 71, nos. 1-2 (January-April 2019): 175-88; Joshua T. Searle, "Moving towards an Ecumenism of *Koinonia*: A Critical Response to 'The Church: Towards a Common Vision' from a Baptistic Perspective," *Journal of European Baptist Studies* 15, no. 2 (January 2015): 17-27; Alexander Abramov, Alexander Geichenko, and Mary Raber, "The Importance, Relevance, and Challenge of 'The Church: Towards a Common Vision,'" *Journal of European Baptist Studies* 15, no. 2 (January 2015): 28-33; Octavian D. Baban, "Four Views and a Response on WCC Church Vision," *Journal of European Baptist Studies* 15, no. 2 (January 2015): 34-45; Teun van der Leer, "*The Church: Towards a Common Vision*: A Believers Church Response," *Journal of European Baptist Studies* 15, no. 3 (May 2015): 21-31; Steven R. Harmon, "How Might We Envision the Unity We Have? Engaging *The Church: Towards a Common Vision*, Part 1" (online http://www.lainterchurch.org/documents/Speaker-Harmon-SessionOne-3-3-15.pdf) and idem, "What Can We Do About the Unity We Envision? Engaging *The Church: Towards a Common Vision*, Part 2" (online http://www.lainterchurch.org/documents/Speaker-Harmon-SessionTwo-3-3-15.pdf), addresses presented

to the annual assembly of the Louisiana Interchurch Conference, The Wesley Center, Woodworth, Louisiana, March 2-3, 2015 (downloaded July 1, 2019).
191. World Council of Churches, *The Church*, viii-ix.
192. Baptist World Alliance, "Commissions of Mission and Evangelism."
193. Baptist World Alliance and Catholic Church, *The Word of God in the Life of the Church: A Report of International Conversations between the Catholic Church and the Baptist World Alliance 2006-2010* (2013), published in *American Baptist Quarterly* 31, no. 1 (Spring 2012): 28-122; *Pontifical Council for Promoting Christian Unity Information Service* 142 (2013): 20-65; also published online by the BWA at https://www.bwanet.org/images/pdf/baptist-catholic-dialogue.pdf and the Catholic Church at http://www.vatican.va/roman_curia/pontifical_councils/chrstuni/Bapstist%20alliance/rc_pc_chrstuni_doc_20101213_report-2006-2010_en.html (downloaded July 1, 2019).
194. World Council of Churches, *The Church*, 3.
195. Baptist theologian Paul Fiddes has explained the embodied "Baptist experience" that informs Baptist efforts to bring their faith and practice under the rule of Christ in this way: "The liberty of local churches to make decisions about their own life and ministry is not based in a human view of autonomy or independence, or in selfish individualism, but in a sense of being under the direct rule of Christ who relativizes other rules. This liberating rule of Christ is what makes for the distinctive 'feel' of Baptist congregational life, which allows for spiritual oversight (*episkopē*) both by the *whole* congregation gathered together in church meeting, and by the minister(s) called to lead the congregation.... Since the same rule of Christ can be experienced in assemblies of churches together, there is also the basis here for Baptist associational life, and indeed for participating in ecumenical clusters" (Paul S. Fiddes, *Tracks and Traces: Baptist Identity in Church and Theology* [Studies in Baptist History and Thought, vol. 13; Milton Keynes, UK: Paternoster, 2003], 6). Elsewhere Fiddes elaborates what it means for the whole congregation to seek together the mind of Christ in what British Baptists call "church meeting": "Upon the whole people in covenant there lies the responsibility of finding a common mind, of coming to an agreement about the way of Christ for them in life, worship and mission. But they cannot do so unless they use the resources that God has given them, and among those resources are the pastor, the deacons and (if they have them) the elders. The church meeting is not 'people power' in the sense of simply counting votes and canvassing a majority.... The aim is to search for consent about the

mind of Christ, and so people should be sensitive to the voices behind the votes, listening to them according to the weight of their experience and insight. As B[arrington] White puts it, 'One vote is not as good as another in church meeting,' even though it has the same strictly numerical value" (Fiddes, *Tracks and Traces*, 86). Cf. also Mikael Broadway, Curtis W. Freeman, Barry Harvey, James Wm. McClendon, Jr., Elizabeth Newman, and Philip E. Thompson, "Re-envisioning Baptist Identity: A Manifesto for Baptist Communities in North America," § 1: "*We affirm Bible Study in reading communities* rather than relying on private interpretation or supposed 'scientific' objectivity.... We thus affirm an open and orderly process whereby faithful communities deliberate together over the Scriptures with sisters and brothers of the faith, excluding no light from any source. When all exercise their gifts and callings, when every voice is heard and weighed, when no one is silenced or privileged, the Spirit leads communities to read wisely and to practice faithfully the direction of the gospel" (published in *Baptists Today* [June 1997], 8-10; *Perspectives in Religious Studies* 24, no. 3 [Fall 1997]: 303-10; also available online, http://divinity.duke.edu/sites/divinity.duke.edu/files/documents/faculty-freeman/reenvisioning-baptist-identity.pdf). For an exploration of the theological practice by local churches of discernment through inter-contextual listening to a wide range of voices beyond the local church, see Amy L. Chilton and Steven R. Harmon, eds., *Sources of Light: Resources for Baptist Churches Practicing Theology* (Perspectives on Baptist Identities, no. 3; Macon, GA: Mercer University Press, 2020).

196. World Council of Churches, *The Nature and Purpose of the Church: A Stage on the Way to a Common Statement* (Faith and Order Paper No. 181; Geneva: WCC Publications, 1998); idem, *The Nature and Mission of the Church: A Stage on the Way to a Common Statement* (Faith and Order Paper No. 198; Geneva: WCC Publications, 2005).

197. Martin Luther King, Jr., "Letter from Birmingham Jail" (April 16, 1963), p. 2, online http://okra.stanford.edu/transcription/document_images/undecided/630416-019.pdf (downloaded July 1, 2019).

198. During years in which the quinquennial Baptist World Congress is held, the award is designated as the BWA Congress Quinquennial Human Rights Award; in non-Baptist World Congress years, the prize is awarded as the Denton and Janice Lotz Human Rights Award, named after a former General Secretary of the BWA and his wife.

199. Syrian Orthodox Metropolitan Geevarghese Mar Coorilos of India called the dispossessed and disempowered "the actual church amongst communities of people in their struggle for the fullness of life," going on to say, "In India, for the ["untouchable" members of the Dalit caste] who

form the majority of the Indian church, the body of Christ is a Dalit body, a 'broken body' (the word Dalit literally means 'broken' and 'torn asunder'). Jesus Christ became a Dalit because he was torn-asunder and mutilated on the cross. The Church as 'body of Christ,' in the Indian context, therefore, has profound theological and sociological implications for a Dalit ecclesiology. . . . [*The Nature and Mission of the Church*], however, fails to strike chords and resonate with such contextual theological challenges. . . . In other words, the text fails to encounter the real *ecclesia* among communities of people in pain and suffering" (Geevarghese Mar Coorilos, "The Nature and Mission of the Church: An Indian Perspective," in *Called to Be the One Church: Faith and Order at Crete*, ed. John Gibaut [Faith and Order Paper No. 212; Geneva: WCC Publications, 2012], 188-92). Also at the meeting of the Plenary Commission on Faith and Order in Crete, members of the Plenary Commission recommended that those responsible for drafting "shorten the text and . . . make it more contextual, more reflective of the lives of the churches throughout the world, and more accessible to a wider readership" (World Council of Churches, *The Church*, 45).

200. E. Glenn Hinson, "William Carey and Ecumenical Pragmatism," *Journal of Ecumenical Studies* 17, no. 2 (Spring 1980): 76-77 (73-83).

201. Hans Luckey, *Johann Gerhard Oncken und die Anfänge des deutschen Baptismus*, 3rd ed. (Kassel: Oncken Verlag, 1958).

202. For example, Lorelei Fuchs, *Koinonia and the Quest for an Ecumenical Ecclesiology: From Foundations through Dialogue to Symbolic Competence for Communionality* (Grand Rapids, MI: William B. Eerdmans, 2008).

203. Vatican II, *Decree on Ecumenism (Unitatis Redintegratio)*, 21 November 1964, § 2, in *Decrees of the Ecumenical Councils*, ed. Norman Tanner, vol. 2, *Trent to Vatican II*, 908-20 (London: Sheed & Ward and Washington, DC: Georgetown University Press, 1990).

204. Baptist World Alliance and Catholic Church, *The Word of God in the Life of the Church*, § 8: "In recent years this [the *koinonia* of the Triune God as the foundation for the communion of the church] has become our common language, whether Catholic or Protestant, or specifically Baptist."

205. This thoroughly eschatological pilgrim church motif had already been expressed in the Vatican II Decree on Ecumenism, which said that the church "makes its pilgrim way in hope toward the goal of the fatherland above," with that goal defined in the next sentence as "the sacred mystery of the unity of the Church" (Vatican II *Decree on Ecumenism* [*Unitatis Redintegratio*], November 21, 1964, in *Vatican Council II: The Conciliar*

and *Post Conciliar Documents*, rev. ed., ed. Austin Flannery [Vatican Collection, vol. 1; Northport, NY: Costello Publishing Co., 1992] § 2). This pilgrim church conception of ecclesial identity, however, belongs broadly to the modern ecumenical movement and all churches that participate in it. The concept was clearly expressed in reports and documents issued in connection with assemblies of the WCC that preceded and followed the Second Vatican Council—Evanston in 1954 and New Delhi in 1961, as well as Uppsala in 1968. The New Delhi assembly issued a Report on Witness that urged "a reappraisal of the patterns of church organization and institutions inherited by the younger churches" so that "outdated forms . . . may be replaced by strong and relevant ways of evangelism." It offered this as an example of "How the Church may become the Pilgrim Church, which goes forth boldly as Abraham did into the unknown future, not afraid to leave behind the securities of its conventional structure, glad to dwell in the tent of perpetual adaptation, looking to the city whose builder and maker is God." The New Delhi assembly also proposed a vision of the ecumenical future toward which the pilgrim church journeys in its definition of the unity sought by the modern ecumenical movement: "We believe that the unity which is both God's will and [God's] gift to [God's] Church is being made visible as all in each place who are baptized into Jesus Christ and confess him as Lord and Savior are brought by the Holy Spirit into one fully-committed fellowship, holding the one apostolic faith, preaching the one Gospel, breaking the one bread, joining in common prayer, and having a corporate life reaching out in witness and service to all and who at the same time are united with the whole Christian fellowship in all places and all ages, in such wise that ministry and members are accepted by all, and that all can act and speak together as occasion requires for the tasks to which God calls [God's] people" (World Council of Churches, "Report of the Section on Unity," in *The New Delhi Report: The Third Assembly of the World Council of Churches, 1961* [New York: Association Press, 1962], 116).

206. See Steven R. Harmon, *Baptist Identity and the Ecumenical Future: Story, Tradition, and the Recovery of Community* (Waco, TX: Baylor University Press, 2016), chap. 9, "The Theology of a Pilgrim Church," 213-42.

207. On the distinction between "quantitative" and "qualitative" catholicity, see Yves Congar, *Chrétiens désunis: principes d'un "oecuménisme" catholique* (Unum Sanctam, no. 1; Paris: Éditions du Cerf, 1937), 115-17; idem, *Divided Christendom: A Catholic Study of the Problem of Reunion*, trans. M. A. Bousfield (London: Geoffrey Bles/Centenary Press, 1939), 93-94.

208. World Council of Churches, "Report of the Section on Unity," 116 (emphasis added).
209. The BWA has previously embraced this conception of the interdependency of the local church and expressions of church beyond the local church. In conjunction with the German Union of Free Evangelical (Baptist) Churches, the BWA sponsored a Symposium on Baptist Identity and Ecclesiology in Elstal, Germany, March 21-24, 2007, that addressed the question "Are Baptist Churches Autonomous?" Among the five affirmations agreed upon by the sixty-plus conference participants were these two: "That for Baptists, the local church is wholly church but not the whole church," and "That our local churches and Conventions/Unions are participants in the one church that God has called into being as we anticipate the full revelation of the children of God." This language derives from Jean-Jacques von Allmen, "L'Église locale parmi les autres Eglises locales," *Irénikon* 43 (1970): 512 (512-37), who as a Reformed ecumenist insisted that the local church is "wholly the church, but not the whole church," language closely echoed in the Elstal affirmation. (The statement from the Elstal symposium and the press release reporting on its proceedings are no longer available online at the BWA website, but the affirmation referenced here is quoted and engaged by Elizabeth Newman, "Are Local Baptist Churches Wholly Autonomous?" *Baptist News Global* [June 12, 2007], accessed July 1, 2019, http://baptistnews.com/archives/item/2582-opinion-are-local-baptist-churches-wholly-autonomous. This statement by the BWA, along with the papers from this symposium, are published in a thematic issue on "Congregational Independence—Associational Interdependence" in *American Baptist Quarterly* 38, no. 1 [Spring 2019]; see "Statement from the Baptist World Alliance Symposium on Baptist Identity and Ecclesiology (Are Baptist Churches Autonomous?)," the editorial introduction by Curtis W. Freeman "Wholly Church but not the Whole Church," and the articles "Words Are Inadequate to Express Our Convictions: The Problem of the Autonomy of the Local Church" by William H. Brackney and "Are Baptist Churches Autonomous?" by Nigel G. Wright.)
210. Receptive ecumenism is a more recent approach to ecumenical dialogue according to which the communions in conversation with one another seek to identify the distinctive gifts that each tradition has to offer the other and which each could receive from the other with integrity, but in which "the primary emphasis is on learning rather than teaching. . . . [E]ach tradition takes responsibility for its own potential learning from others and is, in turn, willing to facilitate the learning of others as re-

quested but without dictating terms and without making others' learning a precondition to attending to ones' own" (quotation is from a briefing document distributed to participants in an international conference on receptive ecumenism held at Durham University [UK] in 2006 and included in Walter Cardinal Kasper's "Foreword" to Paul D. Murray, ed., *Receptive Ecumenism and the Call to Catholic Learning: Exploring a Way for Contemporary Ecumenism* [Oxford: Oxford University Press, 2008], vii).

211. World Council of Churches, *The Third World Conference on Faith and Order, Lund 1952*, ed. Oliver S. Tomkins (London: SCM Press, 1953), 15-16.

212. Baptist World Alliance and World Methodist Council, *Faith Working through Love: Report of the International Dialogue between the Baptist World Alliance and the World Methodist Council* (2018), online https://www.bwanet.org/images/MEJ/Final-Report-of-the-International-Dialogue-between-BWA-and-WMC.pdf (downloaded July 1, 2019).

213. Steven R. Harmon, "'One Baptism': A Study Text for Baptists," *Baptist World: A Magazine of the Baptist World Alliance* 58, no. 1 (January/March 2011): 9-10.

214. *Conversations Around the World 2000-2005: The Report of the International Conversations between the Anglican Communion and the Baptist World Alliance* (London: Anglican Communion Office, 2005), §§ 40-52 (pp. 44-51); Baptist World Alliance and Catholic Church, *The Word of God in the Life of the Church*, §§ 101-06; Baptist World Alliance and World Methodist Council, *Faith Working through Love*, §§ 70-80.

215. Fiddes, "'*Koinonia*: The Church in and for the World'," 43-44.

216. World Council of Churches, *Moral Discernment in the Churches: A Study Document* (Faith and Order Paper No. 215; Geneva: WCC Publications, 2013).

217. Fiddes, "'*Koinonia*: The Church in and for the World'," 46.

218. For the published report of the dialogue, see Anglican Consultative Council and Baptist World Alliance, *Conversations Around the World: The Report of the International Conversations between the Anglican Communion and the Baptist World Alliance 2000-2005* (London: Anglican Communion Office, 2005).

219. Steven R. Harmon, "Baptist Understandings of Authority, with Special Reference to Baptists in North America," paper presented to the Anglican-Baptist International Commission—North American Phase, Acadia University, Wolfville, Nova Scotia, September 10-13, 2003; subsequently published as idem, "Baptist Understandings of Theological Authority: A North American Perspective," *International Journal for the Study of the Christian Church* 4, no. 1 (2004): 50-63. A further revision appeared as

a chapter in idem, *Towards Baptist Catholicity: Essays on Tradition and the Baptist Vision* (Studies in Baptist History and Thought, vol. 27; Milton Keynes, UK: Paternoster, 2006), 23-38.
220. Ronald C. Stevenson, "An Anglican Understanding of Authority," paper presented to the Anglican-Baptist International Commission—North American Phase, Acadia University, Wolfville, Nova Scotia, September 10-13, 2003.
221. Sarah Moses, "The Ethics of 'Recognition': Rowan Williams's Approach to Moral Discernment in the Christian Community," *Journal of the Society of Christian Ethics* 35, no. 1 (2015): 148 (147-65); quotation is from Rowan Williams, "The Challenge and Hope of Being an Anglican Today: A Reflection for the Bishops, Clergy, and Faithful of the Anglican Communion," June 27, 2006, http://rowanwilliams.archbishopofcanterbury.org/articles.php/1478/the-challenge-and-hope-of-being-an-anglican-today-a-reflection-for-the-bishops-clergy-and-faithful-o.
222. Neville Callam, "When the Churches Present Inconsistent Moral Teachings," *Baptist World Alliance General Secretary's Blog*, March 1, 2016, http://www.bwanet.org/dialogue/entry/when-the-churches-present-inconsistent-moral-teachings. Callam's reflections were occasioned by concerns expressed by thirteen cardinals of the Catholic Church in the aftermath of the Ordinary General Assembly of the Synod of Bishops of the Roman Catholic Church that met October 4-25, 2015 regarding what the cardinals perceived as a trend toward moral relativism in "liberal Protestant churches," which they hoped would not be mirrored in the ongoing process of moral discernment by the Synod of Bishops. Callam wrote, "Whatever we make of the cardinals' claims, it seems to me that the church needs to hear a stark warning in what they voice." After the sentence quoted in the body text above ("Yet, we should not fail to recognize the complexity of the process by which we can hear the voice of God as we seek to relate the teaching of Scripture to the vexed issues of contemporary life"), Callam continued:

> First, we should note that discerning the mind of Christ is not simply about a Christian taking the counsel that is given in the Bible and applying it directly to a particular issue of concern. One reason for this is that, in this individualistic world, discernment of the voice of Christ is best done in community with other Christians. God can speak to each of us in the privacy of our place of prayer. But we must test what we believe we are hearing against the wider sense of the believing community. Of course, this is a principle that was firmly advocated by the earliest Baptists and it has been affirmed in several other Christian World Communions. Relating the Scripture

to contemporary issues requires corporate, and not simply private, activity. We should not simply rest on the conclusions that we each draw from our reading of Scripture.

Another reason why discerning God's mind is a complex process is that we do not come to the process of applying biblical teaching to issues of the day with a tabula rasa. Instead, we come to the issues with our minds flooded with all sorts of ideas. Serious Christians who apply biblical insights in the process of decision making may wish to admit that among the things they bring to the process of decision-making are the values formed in them in their early development at home, school and church. They also bring the traditions of biblical interpretation and the body of social teaching that they have learned in their church.

Yet, another reason why the interpretive task is a complex affair is that, in God's freedom, believers may receive "more light and truth" issuing from God's Word than they earlier experienced. Of course, every text of Scripture needs to be read in its context. Furthermore, each text of Scripture needs to be read in the light of the whole of Scripture. Moreover, because God has witnesses in every place and every culture, God may choose to speak to us through human culture and history as well. Still, there are times when the values of culture are antithetical to what our faith teaches. In this complex situation, there is simply no easy way to speak with confidence and sincerity about the will of God.

Thankfully, about one thing Baptists have made consistent affirmation: once the church has discerned the normative teaching of Scripture, whatever is inconsistent with this is an unacceptable foundation for Christian praxis.

223. World Council of Churches, *Moral Discernment in the Churches: A Study Document* (Faith and Order Paper no. 215; Geneva: WCC Publications, 2013), 23-32.

224. Some material in this subsection has been abridged and adapted from Steven R. Harmon, *Baptist Identity and the Ecumenical Future: Story, Tradition, and the Recovery of Community* (Waco, TX: Baylor University Press, 2016), 70-78.

225. Harmon, *Towards Baptist Catholicity*, 71-87; idem, "Baptist Confessions of Faith and the Patristic Tradition," *Perspectives in Religious Studies* 29, no. 4 (Winter 2002): 349-58.

226. Baptists share this conviction with the whole church, expressed as a matter of fundamental consensus in World Council of Churches, *Moral Discernment in the Churches*, 23-24: "For Christians, moral discernment also

involves a desire to act in agreement with their belief, the centre of which is faith in the Triune God" (§ 30) and "Faith sources are ways through which Christians access the ultimate source of truth and authority, which is God as revealed in Jesus Christ through the Holy Spirit" (§ 31).

227. *Baptist Confessions of Faith*, ed. Lumpkin, rev. Leonard, 378: "We believe [that] the Holy Bible was written by men divinely inspired, and is a perfect treasure of heavenly instruction; that it has God for its author, salvation for its end, and truth, without any mixture of error, for its matter; that it reveals the principles by which God will judge us; and therefore is, and shall remain to the end of the world, the true centre of Christian union, and the supreme standard by which all human conduct, creeds, and opinions should be tried."

228. Whereas the *New Hampshire Confession* called the Bible "the supreme standard by which all human conduct, creeds, and opinions should be tried," the 1925 *Baptist Faith and Message* qualified the "opinions" as "*religious* opinions." This modification subtly limited the scope of biblical authority to matters of faith and practice—in other words, not scientific matters—and enabled both those who allowed for the possibility that evolution was the means by which God created human beings and those who opposed all forms of evolutionary theory to affirm the same statement on the authority of the Bible. It is significant that the convention declined to adopt a proposed anti-evolution amendment to the article on "Man" (*Baptist Confessions of Faith*, ed. Lumpkin, rev. Leonard, 408). The 1963 revision of the *Baptist Faith and Message* added a phrase and a sentence to the article on the Scriptures in the 1925 statement. The first addition asserted that the Bible "is the record of God's revelation of Himself to man," distinguishing between the Bible and the revelation that preceded and resulted in the writing of Scripture and subtly allowing for interpretive approaches that reckoned seriously with the human dimensions of the biblical text. The second addition, "The criterion by which the Bible is to be interpreted is Jesus Christ," was perceived by some as permitting those who saw some moral and theological progression in God's revelation from the earliest layers of the Old Testament to God's definitive revelation in Jesus Christ (e.g., a progression from the divine sanctioning of "holy war" in the Old Testament to the peacemaking ethic of the reign of God taught by Jesus Christ in the New Testament) to affirm the statement in good conscience. The 1963 revision thus seemed to combine an affirmation of the trustworthiness of the Bible with openness to the contributions of contemporary biblical and theological scholarship to its interpretation. Following decades of theological controversy from which more conservative Southern Baptists emerged

in control of denominational agencies, however, a revision of the article on the Scriptures in 2000 moved in a different direction from its 1925 and 1963 predecessors. The article alters the statement that the Bible "is the *record* of God's revelation of Himself to man" to read that the Bible "*is* God's revelation of Himself to man" (emphasis added), thus seeming to equate the Bible, in its entirety, with revelation proper—though, it should be noted, this language does not require such an equation (*Baptist Faith and Message* [2000] § 1, in *Baptist Confessions of Faith*, 2nd rev. ed., ed. Lumpkin, rev. Leonard, 512). The final sentence added in the 1963 revision, "The criterion by which the Bible is to be interpreted is Jesus Christ," is deleted and replaced with "All Scripture is a testimony to Christ, who is Himself the focus of divine revelation." These most recent modifications reflect a shift in North America's largest Baptist group toward an understanding of biblical authority defined in terms of a theory of biblical inerrancy along the lines of the 1978 Chicago Statement on Biblical Inerrancy drafted by a group of North American evangelical theologians (International Council on Biblical Inerrancy, "Chicago Statement on Biblical Inerrancy," *Journal of the Evangelical Theological Society* 21 [December 1978]: 289-96; for various Southern Baptist perspectives on the appropriateness of this conceptualization of the nature of biblical inspiration and authority, alongside representative non-Baptist evangelical perspectives, see Conference on Biblical Inerrancy, *The Proceedings of the Conference on Biblical Inerrancy, 1987* [Nashville: Broadman Press, 1987]).

229. For example, L. Russ Bush and Thomas J. Nettles, *Baptists and the Bible*, rev. ed. (Nashville: Broadman & Holman, 1999).

230. For example, many of the essays in Robison B. James, ed., *The Unfettered Word: Southern Baptists Confront the Authority-Inerrancy Question* (Waco, TX: Word Books, 1987).

231. For example, Mikael Broadway, Curtis W. Freeman, Barry Harvey, James Wm. McClendon, Jr., Elizabeth Newman, and Philip E. Thompson, "Re-envisioning Baptist Identity: A Manifesto for Baptist Communities in North America," published initially in *Baptists Today* (June 1997): 8-10, and *Perspectives in Religious Studies* 24, no. 3 (Fall 1997): 303-10.

232. Garrett, "Sources of Authority in Baptist Thought," *Baptist History and Heritage* 13 (1978): 43 (41-49).

233. James Leo Garrett, Jr., *Systematic Theology: Biblical, Historical, and Evangelical*, vol. 1 (Grand Rapids, MI: William B. Eerdmans, 1990), 181, suggested that "Baptists who emphasize the use of Baptist confessions of faith and who insist on a clearly articulated doctrine of the Trinity, often using terms easily traceable to the patristic age, would do well to

affirm *suprema Scriptura*." Garrett's suggestion of *Suprema Scriptura* as a more accurate descriptor of this functional pattern of authority among Baptists has influenced the text of the reports from the conversations between the Baptist World Alliance and the Anglican Consultative Council and from the second series of conversations between the Baptist World Alliance and the Catholic Church, both of which describe the Baptist perspective as *"suprema Scriptura"* (Anglican Consultative Council and Baptist World Alliance, *Conversations Around the World 2000-2005*, § 26; Baptist World Alliance and Catholic Church, *The Word of God in the Life of the Church*, § 62).

234. See Harmon, *Towards Baptist Catholicity*, 71-87; idem, "Baptist Confessions of Faith and the Patristic Tradition," 349-58.
235. See Harmon, *Towards Baptist Catholicity*, 1-21; idem, "'Catholic Baptists' and the New Horizon of Tradition in Baptist Theology," in *New Horizons in Theology*, ed. Terrence W. Tilley (Maryknoll, NY: Orbis Books, 2005), 117-43; and the literature by "catholic Baptist" theologians cited therein.
236. *An Orthodox Creed (1678)*, § 38, in *Baptist Confessions of Faith*, ed. Lumpkin, rev. Leonard, 337-38.
237. G. Keith Parker, *Baptists in Europe: History & Confessions of Faith* (Nashville: Broadman Press, 1982), 57.
238. Parker, *Baptists in Europe: History & Confessions of Faith*, 111.
239. World Council of Churches, *Moral Discernment in the Churches*, 26: "All churches have some form of teaching authority, which has the responsibility to preserve the faith in moral convictions, determine the binding force of a doctrine, and consequently identify whether, or to what extent, diversity on a given moral issue is possible" (§ 35).
240. For an ecumenical framing of the role of magisterium in ecclesial moral discernment, see Gerard Mannion, "Retrieving a Participatory Teaching 'Office': A Comparative and Ecumenical Analysis of Magisterium in the Service of Moral Discernment," *Journal of the Society of Christian Ethics* 34, no. 2 (2014): 61-86.
241. The relation of the teaching authority exercised by the bishops in council to the coinherence of Scripture and tradition in Catholic understanding is summarized in *Lumen Gentium* § 25 and *Dei Verbum* § 10 from the documents of the Second Vatican Council. Vatican II, *Dogmatic Constitution on the Church (Lumen Gentium)*, § 25, 21 November 1964, in *Vatican Council II: The Conciliar and Post Conciliar Documents*, rev. ed., ed. Austin Flannery (Northport, NY: Costello Publishing, 1992), 380; idem, *Dogmatic Constitution on Divine Revelation (Dei Verbum)*, § 10, 18 November 1965, in *Vatican Council II*, ed. Flannery, 755-56.

242. That Protestants have their own version of magisterium is suggested by George Huntston William's use of the label "Magisterial Reformation" to distinguish the "classical Protestant" traditions that include the Lutheran and Reformed churches from churches of the "Radical Reformation" exemplified by the Anabaptists (George Huntston Williams, *The Radical Reformation* [Philadelphia: Westminster Press, 1962]. The Magisterial Reformation was accomplished with the cooperation of the civil power, the magistrates, but it was also magisterial in the sense that it was accomplished through the influence of the *magister*, the authoritative teacher, in association with the magistrate. In the origins of this paradigm of Protestant magisterium, the authority of the Catholic bishops could be rejected when, according to the Protestant Reformers, the bishops had failed to teach the truth; instead, they could point to other teachers whose authority derived from their faithful teaching of the Gospel and to authoritative confessional documents that definitively expressed this faithful teaching.

243. The quotation is from the definition of the task of Christian doctrine offered by Baptist theologian James Wm. McClendon, Jr., *Systematic Theology*, vol. 2, *Doctrine* (Waco, TX: Baylor University Press, 2012), 23-24.

244. Some material in the remainder of this subsection has been adapted and abridged from Harmon, *Baptist Identity and the Ecumenical Future*, 176-80.

245. See Harmon, *Towards Baptist Catholicity*, 39-69.

246. This construal of ecclesial tradition as "argument" draws on Alasdair MacIntyre's definition of a "living tradition" as "an historically extended, socially embodied argument, and an argument precisely in part about the goods which constitute that tradition" (Alasdair MacIntyre, *After Virtue: A Study in Moral Theory*, 2nd ed. [Notre Dame, IN: University of Notre Dame Press, 1984], 222), with the goods that constitute the tradition defined in terms of the Christian narrative—the biblical story of the Triune God that is told at length and with great particularity in the Scriptures and summarized in the ancient creeds.

247. McClendon, *Doctrine*, 24.

248. See Harmon, *Towards Baptist Catholicity*, 66.

249. *London Confession* (1644) pref., in *Baptist Confessions of Faith*, 2nd rev. ed., ed. Lumpkin, rev. Leonard, 143.

250. Paul S. Fiddes, *Tracks and Traces: Baptist Identity in Church and Theology* (Studies in Baptist History and Thought, vol. 13; Milton Keynes, UK: Paternoster, 2003), 6.

251. Fiddes, *Tracks and Traces: Baptist Identity in Church and Theology*, 86.

252. For this reason, theological educators also have a key form of participation in Free Church magisterium, for they have the opportunity to supply ministers with these God-given resources from beyond the local congregation and to form them in the skills they need for the discerning use of these resources. I have developed this suggestion more fully in Steven R. Harmon, "What Have Baptist Professors of Religion to Do with Magisterium?" *Perspectives in Religious Studies*, 45, no. 1 (Spring 2018): 37-48.
253. Broadway, Freeman, Harvey, McClendon, Newman, and Thompson, "Re-envisioning Baptist Identity: A Manifesto for Baptist Communities in North America," § 1.
254. World Council of Churches, *Moral Discernment in the Churches*, 23-32. In Harmon, *Baptist Identity and the Ecumenical Future*, 180-88, in response to the questions "What then are the potential sources of light that ought not be excluded as Baptist communities determine what it is they must teach to be the church in the time and place they inhabit? What are the voices that should be heard and weighed without being silenced in their Free Church practice of magisterium?" I suggested that these voices ought to include the following nine types of resources: (1) the ancient creeds that stem from the early church's rule of faith; (2) historic Reformation confessions and catechisms, along with more recent confessional statements from various denominations; (3) Baptist confessions of faith; (4) Catholic magisterial teaching; (5) liturgical texts of other traditions; (6) reports and agreed statements of bilateral and multilateral ecumenical dialogues; (7) contextual theologies that emerge from other social locations; (8) ecclesial resolutions on ethical issues adopted by diverse church bodies; and (9) the lived Christian lives of the saints. For a collaborative exploration of what it might mean to bring these inter-contextual sources to bear on congregational discernment by Baptist churches in their specific local contexts, see Amy L. Chilton and Steven R. Harmon, eds., *Sources of Light: Resources for Baptist Churches Practicing Theology* (Perspectives on Baptist Identities, no. 3; Macon, GA: Mercer University Press, 2020).
255. For the purposes of this paper (and now book appendix) and in keeping with its limitations of length, I have chosen to generalize about Baptist ecclesial moral discernment rather than taking up as test cases of these generalizations how specific Baptist communities have addressed particular moral issues. However, a group of theologians and ministers affiliated with the Baptist Union of Great Britain who hold differing perspectives on the issue of same-sex unions issued in 2016 a document commending Baptist ecclesiology as making space for local Baptist

communities to reach differing conclusions in their exercise of ecclesial moral discernment about matters of human sexuality without these differing conclusions becoming ground for division: Beth Allison-Glenny, Andy Goodliff, Ruth Gouldbourne, Steve Holmes, David Kerrigan, Glen Marshall, and Simon Woodman, "The Courage to be Baptist: A Statement on Baptist Ecclesiology and Human Sexuality," online http://www.somethingtodeclare.org.uk/statement.html (downloaded February 18, 2017).

256. See Fiddes, *Tracks and Traces*, 6: "Since the same rule of Christ can be experienced in assemblies of churches together, there is also the basis here for Baptist associational life, and indeed for participating in ecumenical clusters."

Index of Names and Subjects

16th Street Baptist Church, Birmingham, AL, 49
Advent, 79
Aggiornamento, 30-31
American Baptist Churches, USA, 26, 36, 70, 140
Amsterdam, 69-70, 100
Anabaptists, 17, 73, 89-101
Anglican Communion, 52, 158, 163-64
Anglican Consultative Council, 84
Anglicanism, 16, 29, 51-52, 73-74, 82-84, 103, 126
Anglo-Catholicism, 77
Apartheid, 88
Apostles' Creed, 74, 78-79, 168
Apostolic faith, 48, 64, 92-93, 120, 130, 134
Apostolic succession, 83
Aquinas, Thomas, 49
Arminianism, 73
Ash Wednesday, 78
Athanasian Creed, 74, 168
Augsburg Confession, 94
Austria, 168
Baptism, 36, 47, 49, 51, 58-61, 69-71, 79, 82-83, 85, 89, 91, 99, 101, 114, 130-31, 142, 153, 156, 158-59; believers', 71, 85, 114; infant, 69-70, 82-83, 89, 158
Baptism, Eucharist and Ministry, 19, 39-40, 69, 136, 140-42, 146, 148, 150, 158
Baptist Faith and Message, 167
Baptist Press, 23-24
Baptist Union of Great Britain, 70, 140
Baptist Union of New Zealand, 140
Baptist World Alliance, 15, 17--20, 24-26, 36-37, 47-57, 82-83, 101, 134, 137-61; Commission on Baptist Doctrine and Christian Unity, 137-61
Baptist-Catholic international dialogue, 15, 17-18, 20, 24-25, 36-38, 46-68, 82, 86-88, 91, 101-06
Beasley-Murray, George, 141
Believers' Churches, 73
Belmont Abbey College, 35-36
Benedict XV, 29
Benedict XVI, 49-50
Benedictines, 35, 45
Bible. See Scripture

Birmingham, Alabama, 48-49
Blackfriars Hall, 51
Brenz, Johannes, 97
Broach, Claude U., 27, 35-36
Brunk, Timothy, 116
Burma Baptist Missionary Convention, 140
Busan, South Korea, 137
Callam, Neville, 20, 164
Calvin, John, 82
Calvinism, 73, 75
Cape of Good Hope, 70
Carey, William, 70, 147
Catechesis, 109
Catherine of Siena, 79
Catholic University of America, The, 121
Catholicity, 43, 45, 73, 81-82, 132, 151-53, 155
Chalcedonian Definition, 73-74, 168
China Baptist Council, 140
Chotkis, 81
Christ the King, 79
Christian World Communions, 141, 143, 164
Christian year, 78
Christmastide, 79
Christology, 73-74, 102, 168. See also Jesus Christ
Church of England, 51, 69, 77
College Theology Society, 15, 18-19, 107-25

Communion. See Eucharist
Congar, Yves, 25-26, 29-30
Congregation for the Doctrine of the Faith, 30, 50, 66
Constantinianism, 90
Cooperative Baptist Fellowship, 77
Corinth (church in), 129
Covenant (ecclesiology), 85, 101, 149, 153, 159, 172
Covenant (local ecumenical), 67
Creighton University, 16, 23
Crete, 137, 146, 162
Cross (of Christ), 110-12; 119-20, 124-25
Cross, sign of, 80-81, 110, 120
Dayspring Baptist Church, Waco, TX, 78-79
Dei Verbum, 49, 57
Dignitatis Humanae, 41, 90
Diocletian, 111
Directory for the Application of Principles and Norms on Ecumenism, 115
Discipleship, 38, 48, 50-51, 61-62, 66, 91
Dissenters, 75-76, 170
Dominus Iesus, 30
Duke University Divinity School, 50, 113
Dulles, Avery, 117, 120
Easter, 79, 111

Eastern Area Community Ministries (Louisville, Kentucky), 19, 126-27
Eastern Orthodoxy. See Orthodoxy
Ecclesiology, 20, 31, 33, 46, 55, 63-65, 71, 90-91, 148-53, 155, 158-61, 171, 174
Ecumenical councils, 28, 174
Ecumenical Directory, 115
Ecumenical Institute (Wake Forest University/Belmont Abbey College), 35-36
Edinburgh World Missionary Conference (1910), 29, 146-47
Ellis, Christopher, 76
Elstal Symposium on Baptist Identity and Ecclesiology, 160
England, 51, 70, 75-76, 90, 101, 103, 165, 168
English Reformation, 100
Epiphany, 79
Episcopalian Church USA, 126
Episkope, 38, 50-51, 63-65, 87, 172-73
Erfurt, Germany, 20, 163
Eschatology, 40, 128-29, 131-32, 150
Estep, William, 71, 142
Eucharist, 18-19, 31, 36, 43, 49, 51, 54-56, 58-61, 71, 79, 85, 91, 99, 106-08, 111-25, 130, 142, 153
Evangelical Baptist Church of Georgia, 79-80
Faith, 17, 21, 37, 43-44, 47, 55, 57, 60-61, 68, 70-74, 80-83, 85, 92-94, 102, 104-05, 114, 130-31, 156, 159, 165, 173
Fiddes, Paul, 49, 82-83, 171-72
First Baptist Church in America, Providence, Rhode Island, 122
First Vatican Council. See Vatican I
Florence, Council of, 28
Francis of Assisi, 77
Franciscan Friars of the Atonement, 126
Franciscan Sisters of the Atonement, 126
Free Churches, 73, 101, 159, 170, 173
Freedom of conscience, 79, 85
Freeman, Curtis, 112-17, 119-20
Furman University, 36
Garrett, James Leo, Jr., 26-27
Garrett, W. Barry, 23-24, 26
General Baptists, 75
Georgetown College, 118
Georgia, Republic of, 78-80

Germany, 20, 68, 96, 100, 163, 168
Gloria Patri, 77
Graymoor Spiritual Life Center, 128
Great Schism. See Schism of 1054
Greyfriars Hall, 51
Hatch, Derek, 118
Hayford, Jack, 77
Helwys, Thomas, 70, 101
Holy Spirit, 37, 39, 46-47, 106, 108, 112, 127, 130, 133-34, 147, 152, 165
Holy Week, 78-79
Howard Payne University, 118
Hutterites, 97
Hymns, 75-78, 81, 120
Icons, 78, 80
Incense, 80
India, 70, 104, 130, 147
Ireland, 89
Jackson, J. H., 26
Jesuits, 16
Jesus Christ, 16, 21, 37-39, 42, 46-47, 62, 89, 93, 112, 118, 127-34, 139, 149, 152, 155, 166. See also Christology
John of Damascus, 77
John Paul II, 30, 41-42, 71, 87, 109
John XXIII, 29
John, Gospel of, 108-12

Joint Declaration on the Doctrine of Justification, 12, 52, 101
Justice, 145
Justin Martyr, 74
Kasper, Walter, 30, 50
Keach, Benjamin, 75
Kentucky Council of Churches, 126
King, Martin Luther, Jr., 49, 145
Koinonia, 37, 47-49, 51, 53-56, 58, 136, 148-49, 151-53, 155-56, 158-61
Labyrinths, 81
Latin America, 25, 50, 86, 104
Lausanne Conference on Faith and Order (1927), 29
Lectio divina, 81
Lent, 79, 87
Liturgy of St. James, 77
Liturgy. See Worship
London Confession (Second), 73-75
Lord's Supper. See Eucharist
Lourdes College, 17
Lumen Gentium, 31-33
Lund Principle, 156-58, 161
Luther, Martin, 49, 77, 82, 97
Lutheran World Federation, 17, 52, 83, 88, 94, 96-101
Lutheranism, 44
Lyndon Baptist Church, Louisville, KY, 127
Lyons, Council of, 28

Index of Names and Subjects

MacIntyre, Alasdair, 20
Magisterium, 30, 163, 169-70, 173
Malines Conversations, 29
Marcellinus., 108, 111
Marks of the church, 74, 131
Maronites, 121
Martyrdom, 50, 108, 111
Mary (Virgin; Mother of Jesus), 26, 36-38, 47, 50-51, 61-63
Mass, 51, 74, 107-08, 113, 115, 118, 120-23
McClendon, James Wm., Jr., 113-14
Melanchthon, Philip, 97
Mennonite World Conference, 17, 83, 88-89, 94, 96-97, 100
Mepkin Abbey, 36
Methodism, 44, 76-77, 157-58
Methodist World Council, 52
Mission, 25, 29, 37, 39-40, 47, 64, 70, 104, 137, 146-48, 150, 153, 156-57
Missouri Council of Churches, 26
Möhler, Johann Adam, 29
Monastic orders, 80, 117
Moorman, John, 26
Moral Discernment in the Churches, 162, 165, 169, 174
Mount Aloysius College, 17
Münster Gesangbuch, 77

Münster, 90
Myanmar Baptist Convention, 69-70
Nagaland, India, 104
Nassau, The Bahamas, 20, 138
National Association of Baptist Professors of Religion, 15, 18-19, 107-25
National Baptist Convention, USA, 26, 140
Neale, John Mason, 77
New Delhi definition (of unity), 130, 152-53
New Hampshire Confession, 166
Newman, John Henry, 29
Newport, Rhode Island, 18, 108, 119, 122
Nicaeno-Constantinopolitan Creed, 73-74, 168
Nordenhaug, Josef, 24-25
North America, 76, 133, 163, 166-67
Oberlin Conference on Faith and Order, 133
Ocho Rios, Jamaica, 142
Oncken, Johann Gerhard, 148
Orant, 110
Ordinary Time, 79
Orientalium Ecclesiarum, 32
Orthodox Creed, 73-74, 168
Orthodoxy, 28-29, 43, 74, 79-81, 83-84, 137, 162
Oxford University, 49-51

Particular Baptists, 73-75
Passing of the peace, 120
Pastoral care, 81
Patrick, St., 77
Patristics, 76-77, 80-81, 109, 121, 168
Patterson, W. Morgan, 26
Paul, St., 128-29, 134
Payne, Ernest, 75
Peace, 91-92, 94, 106, 146
Peasants' War, 90
Pentecost, 79
Pentecostalism, 74, 77
Peter the Exorcist, 108-09
Peter, St., 33, 108-11
Petrine primacy, 109
Philadelphia Baptist Association, 75
Pius IX, 28
Pius X, 29
Pius XI, 29
Pontifical Council for Promoting Christian Unity, 15, 17-18, 24, 50-51, 82, 115, 126, 134
Porto Alegre, Brazil, 136
Presbyterians, 44, 128
Priesthood of believers, 41-42
Prudentius, 77
Psalms, 75
Puritans, 100
Radical Reformation, 80
Ratzinger, Joseph, 49-50 (see also Benedict XVI)

"Re-envisioning Baptist Identity," 173
Reception (ecumenical), 13, 26-27, 38, 52, 65-68, 84, 103, 138, 142-43, 154, 160-61
Receptive ecumenism, 16, 20, 41, 69-85, 153-54
Regent's Park College, 50-51
Religious liberty, 27, 40-41, 71, 79, 86, 90, 103-04, 106, 145
"Responses to Some Questions Regarding Certain Aspects of the Doctrine of the Church," 30-31, 105
Ressourcement, 30-31
Resurrection, 24, 111, 128, 132
Rippon, John, 76
Rome, 33-34, 45, 48-50, 87, 102, 107, 111, 153
Rosary, 81
Rule of St. Benedict, 117
Rwanda, 89
Salvation, 32, 34, 46-47, 58-60, 142
Salve Regina University, 18, 108, 119
Samford University, 48-49
Sanctification, 132
Schism of 1054, 28
Scripture, 38, 44, 48-49, 51, 56-58, 71, 73-75, 81-82,

106, 120, 162, 164-69, 173
Second Vatican Council. See Vatican II
Separatists, 69, 73
Seventh Day Baptist General Conference, 140
Sioux Falls Seminary, 116
Sisters of Mercy, 17
Sisters of St. Francis, 17
Small, Joseph, 128
Smyth, John, 69, 100-01
South Africa, 88-89
Southern Baptist Convention, 24-27, 36, 77, 166
Southern Baptist Theological Seminary, The, 26-27
Southwark, England, 75
St. Benet's Hall, 51
St. Catherine University, 113
St. John's Baptist Church, Charlotte, NC, 35
St. Paul's Outside the Walls, 29
St. Peter's Basilica, 24
Stockholm Conference on Life and Work (1925), 29
Stuber, Stanley I., 26
Stuttgart, Germany, 100
Swiss Brethren, 97
Switzerland, 20, 137, 168
Systematic theology, 81
Taizé chant, 133
Tate, Nahum, 76
Teresa of Jesus, 77

The Church: Towards a Common Vision, 19-20, 39, 136-61
Theodulph of Orleans, 77
Theological education, 66-67, 80-81, 84, 106, 122, 157, 161
Thirty-Nine Articles, 73
Thompson, Philip E., 116-17
Thompson, Robert, 141
Toom, Tarmo, 101
Toplady, Augustus, 76
Tradition, 31, 38, 49, 51, 56-58, 64, 74, 82, 162, 168-74
Trent, Council of, 28
Trinity Sunday, 79
Trinity, 37, 39-40, 48-49, 51, 53-56, 59, 73-74, 79, 82, 133-34, 136, 138, 147-51, 159-61, 165-66, 168
Union of Baptist Congregations in the Netherlands, 140
Unitatis Redintegratio, 16, 23-45, 46, 115
United States, 78, 96, 101, 107, 166
University of Dayton, 113, 117
Ut Unum Sint, 30, 41-43, 72, 87
Vatican I, 29
Vatican II, 11, 16, 23-45, 46, 57, 84, 86, 90, 104, 114
Villanova University, 116
Wake Forest University, 35-36
Watts, Isaac, 76

Wattson, Paul, 29, 126
Week of Prayer for Christian Unity, 15, 19, 29, 94, 126-28, 133
Wesley, Charles, 76-77
Wesleyan Quadrilateral, 169
West, Morris, 141
Westminster Confession, 73-74
White, Lurana, 126
Willebrands, Johannes, 24-26
Williams, Rowan, 164
Witness, 37-38, 40, 47-48, 86-88, 92, 99, 102-03, 105-06, 130, 139, 147
World Communion of Reformed Churches, 52, 83
World Council of Churches, 15, 19, 70, 126, 130, 136-37, 140-41, 162; Central Committee, 137; Commission on Faith and Order, 15, 19-20, 39, 71, 126, 136-38, 140-41, 145-46, 156, 158-60, 162, 165
Worship, 38, 46, 49, 58, 60, 74-82, 99, 107-08, 120-25, 133-34, 173
Yocum, Sandra, 117
Zürich, 20, 137

New City Press

New City Press is one of more than 20 publishing houses sponsored by the Focolare, a movement founded by Chiara Lubich to help bring about the realization of Jesus' prayer: "That all may be one" (John 17:21). In view of that goal, New City Press publishes books and resources that enrich the lives of people and help all to strive toward the unity of the entire human family. We are a member of the Association of Catholic Publishers.

www.newcitypress.com
202 Comforter Blvd.
Hyde Park, New York

Periodicals
Living City Magazine
www.livingcitymagazine.com

Scan to join our mailing list for discounts and promotions or go to www.newcitypress.com and click on "join our email list."

www.ingramcontent.com/pod-product-compliance
Lightning Source LLC
Chambersburg PA
CBHW031434160426
43195CB00010BB/724